Performing the Self

That the self is 'performed', created through action rather than having a prior existence, has been an important methodological intervention in our understanding of human experience. It has been particularly significant for studies of gender, helping to destabilise models of selfhood where women were usually defined in opposition to a male norm. In this multidisciplinary collection, scholars apply this approach to a wide array of historical sources, from literature to art to letters to museum exhibitions, which survive from the medieval to modern periods. In doing so, they explore the extent that using a model of performativity can open up our understanding of women's lives and sense of self in the past. They highlight the way that this method provides a significant critique of power relationships within society that offers greater agency to women as historical actors and offers a challenge to traditional readings of women's place in society. An innovative and wide-ranging compilation, this book provides a template for those wishing to apply performativity to women's lives in historical context.

This book was originally published as a special issue of *Women's History Review*.

Katie Barclay is a Research Fellow in the ARC Centre of Excellence for the History of Emotions, University of Adelaide, Australia. She is the author of the double-awarding winning *Love, Intimacy and Power: Marriage and Patriarchy in Scotland, 1650–1850*, and numerous articles on emotions and family life.

Sarah Richardson is an Associate Professor at the University of Warwick, UK. Her latest monograph is *The Political Worlds of Women: Gender and Political Culture in Nineteenth-Century Britain* published by Routledge in 2013.

Performing the Self
Women's Lives in Historical Perspective

Edited by
Katie Barclay and Sarah Richardson

LONDON AND NEW YORK

First published 2015
by Routledge
2 Park Square, Milton Park, Abingdon, Oxon, OX14 4RN, UK

and by Routledge
711 Third Avenue, New York, NY 10017, USA

Routledge is an imprint of the Taylor & Francis Group, an informa business

© 2015 Taylor & Francis

All rights reserved. No part of this book may be reprinted or reproduced or utilised in any form or by any electronic, mechanical, or other means, now known or hereafter invented, including photocopying and recording, or in any information storage or retrieval system, without permission in writing from the publishers.

Trademark notice: Product or corporate names may be trademarks or registered trademarks, and are used only for identification and explanation without intent to infringe.

British Library Cataloguing in Publication Data
A catalogue record for this book is available from the British Library

ISBN 13: 978-1-138-80899-7

Typeset in Minion
by RefineCatch Limited, Bungay, Suffolk

Publisher's Note
The publisher accepts responsibility for any inconsistencies that may have arisen during the conversion of this book from journal articles to book chapters, namely the possible inclusion of journal terminology.

Disclaimer
Every effort has been made to contact copyright holders for their permission to reprint material in this book. The publishers would be grateful to hear from any copyright holder who is not here acknowledged and will undertake to rectify any errors or omissions in future editions of this book.

Contents

Citation Information vii
Notes on Contributors ix

1. Introduction: Performing the Self: women's lives in historical perspective 1
   Katie Barclay and Sarah Richardson

2. Performing the Self, Performing the Other: gender and racial identity construction in the Nanteuil Cycle 6
   Victoria Turner

3. Writing the Self: the journal of Sarah Stoddart Hazlitt, 1774–1843 21
   Gillian Beattie-Smith

4. Writing Women's Histories: women in the colonial record of nineteenth-century Hong Kong 35
   Jane Berney

5. Barbara Leigh Smith Bodichon's Travel Letters: performative identity-formation in epistolary narratives 49
   Meritxell Simon-Martin

6. 'A notable personality': Isabella Fyvie Mayo in the public and private spheres of Aberdeen 63
   Lindy Moore

7. 'The Subject is Obscene: No Lady Would Dream of Alluding to It': Marie Stopes and her courtroom dramas 77
   Lesley Hall

8. Body and Self: learning to be modern in 1920s–1930s Britain 91
   Charlotte Macdonald

9. Performing the Political Self: a study of identity making and self representation in the autobiographies of India's first generation of parliamentary women 104
   Annie Devenish

10. Eve Drewelowe: feminist identity in American art 119
    Lindsay E. Shannon

11. Women Activists: rewriting Greenham's history 134
    Elaine Titcombe

CONTENTS

12. The Changing Face of Exhibiting Women's Wartime Work at the Imperial War Museum   154
    Alyson Mercer

13. Concluding Thoughts: performance, the self, and women's history   169
    Penny Summerfield

Index   177

Citation Information

The chapters in this book were originally published in *Women's History Review*, volume 22, issue 2 (April 2013). When citing this material, please use the original page numbering for each article, as follows:

Chapter 1
Introduction: Performing the Self: women's lives in historical perspective
Katie Barclay and Sarah Richardson
Women's History Review, volume 22, issue 2 (April 2013) pp. 177–181

Chapter 2
Performing the Self, Performing the Other: gender and racial identity construction in the Nanteuil Cycle
Victoria Turner
Women's History Review, volume 22, issue 2 (April 2013) pp. 182–196

Chapter 3
Writing the Self: the journal of Sarah Stoddart Hazlitt, 1774–1843
Gillian Beattie-Smith
Women's History Review, volume 22, issue 2 (April 2013) pp. 197–210

Chapter 4
Writing Women's Histories: women in the colonial record of nineteenth-century Hong Kong
Jane Berney
Women's History Review, volume 22, issue 2 (April 2013) pp. 211–224

Chapter 5
Barbara Leigh Smith Bodichon's Travel Letters: performative identity-formation in epistolary narratives
Meritxell Simon-Martin
Women's History Review, volume 22, issue 2 (April 2013) pp. 225–238

Chapter 6
'A notable personality': Isabella Fyvie Mayo in the public and private spheres of Aberdeen
Lindy Moore
Women's History Review, volume 22, issue 2 (April 2013) pp. 239–252

CITATION INFORMATION

Chapter 7
'*The Subject is Obscene: No Lady Would Dream of Alluding to It*': Marie Stopes and her courtroom dramas
Lesley Hall
Women's History Review, volume 22, issue 2 (April 2013) pp. 253–266

Chapter 8
Body and Self: learning to be modern in 1920s–1930s Britain
Charlotte Macdonald
Women's History Review, volume 22, issue 2 (April 2013) pp. 267–279

Chapter 9
Performing the Political Self: a study of identity making and self representation in the autobiographies of India's first generation of parliamentary women
Annie Devenish
Women's History Review, volume 22, issue 2 (April 2013) pp. 280–294

Chapter 10
Eve Drewelowe: feminist identity in American art
Lindsay E. Shannon
Women's History Review, volume 22, issue 2 (April 2013) pp. 295–309

Chapter 11
Women Activists: rewriting Greenham's history
Elaine Titcombe
Women's History Review, volume 22, issue 2 (April 2013) pp. 310–329

Chapter 12
The Changing Face of Exhibiting Women's Wartime Work at the Imperial War Museum
Alyson Mercer
Women's History Review, volume 22, issue 2 (April 2013) pp. 330–344

Chapter 13
Concluding Thoughts: performance, the self, and women's history
Penny Summerfield
Women's History Review, volume 22, issue 2 (April 2013) pp. 345–352

Please direct any queries you may have about the citations to
clsuk.permissions@cengage.com

Notes on Contributors

Katie Barclay is a historian of the emotions and family life at the ARC Centre for Excellence in the History of Emotions, University of Adelaide, Australia. She is the author of *Love, Intimacy and Power: Marriage and Patriarchy in Scotland, 1650–1850* (2011). Katie is currently working on a monograph on performances of masculinity in the Irish court system, 1800–1845.

Gillian Beattie-Smith lectures in English in Edinburgh, at The Open University, UK, and The University of the Highlands and Islands, UK, where she is engaged in research on women's identity in their travel literature about Scotland in the nineteenth century. Her work includes papers on Dorothy Wordsworth, Elizabeth Grant, Sarah Hazlitt and Anne Grant. Gillian's earlier research and published work is in the field of education.

Jane Berney is a third year, full-time PhD candidate at The Open University, UK. The title of her thesis is 'The Contagious Diseases Acts in nineteenth century Hong Kong: Imperial Edict versus Local Governance'.

Annie Devenish is a doctoral student in the Faculty of History at Oxford University, UK. Her research focuses on the emergence of gender as a political question within the Indian Parliament of the 1950s.

Lesley A. Hall is Senior Archivist, Wellcome Library, and Honorary Lecturer in History of Medicine, University College London, UK. She has written several books, and numerous articles and chapters, on gender and sexuality in Britain since the nineteenth century, including *Sex, Gender and Social Change in Britain since 1880* (2000: revised and updated second edition 2012), *Outspoken Women: women writing about sex, 1870–1969* (2005), and *The Life and Times of Stella Browne, Feminist and Free Spirit* (2011), and edited a five-volume collection *Marie Stopes: birth control and other writings* (2000).

Charlotte Macdonald is Professor of History at Victoria University of Wellington, New Zealand. She is the author of *Strong, Beautiful and Modern* (2011), with Frances Porter, 'My Hand Will Write What My Heart Dictates' (1996), and 'Between Religion and Empire', *Journal of the Canadian Historical Association* online edition, Spring 2008 (winner of Canadian Historical Association Prize 2009).

Alyson Mercer is a doctoral degree candidate in the Department of History at King's College London, UK.

Lindy Moore is a retired librarian and independent researcher. She has written on Scottish women's and gender history relating to education and women's suffrage and is a contributor to the Oxford DNB. She is currently researching the life and writing of the

NOTES ON CONTRIBUTORS

novelist, evangelical and anti-racism campaigner, Isabella Fyvie Mayo (1843–1914) and her associates.

Sarah Richardson is an Associate Professor of History at the University of Warwick, UK, and has published extensively on women and politics in the eighteenth and nineteenth centuries. Her next monograph is on middle-class women and political culture in nineteenth-century Britain.

Lindsay E. Shannon is a PhD Candidate in American Art History in the School of Art and Art History, University of Iowa, USA. She specializes in late nineteenth and early twentieth-century art and feminist theory. She has curated exhibitions, written essays, and collaborated on projects in this area, including the Eve Drewelowe Digital Collection and the Women's Suffrage in Iowa Digital Collection.

Meritxell Simon-Martin is a PhD candidate at the Centre for the History of Women's Education, University of Winchester, UK. Her thesis examines the significance of letter-writing in the life of Barbara Leigh Smith Bodichon. She is the author of 'Letter-Exchange in the Life of Barbara Leigh Smith Bodichon: the first female suffrage committee in Britain seen through her correspondence', in Claudette Fillard and Françoise Orazi (Eds.) *Exchanges and Correspondence: the construction of feminism* (2010).

Penny Summerfield is Professor of Modern History at the University of Manchester, UK. Her publications include *Women Workers in the Second World War* (1989), *Reconstructing Women's Wartime Lives* (1998) and *Contesting Home Defence* (2007). She has recently published articles on her current project on film and the popular memory of the Second World War in Britain in *Journal of British Studies* (2009), *Journal of Contemporary History* (2010) and *Twentieth Century British History* (2011).

Elaine Titcombe is a History PhD student at the University of the West of England, UK, studying the Greenham Common Women's Peace Camps 1981–2000.

Victoria Turner is a Teaching Fellow in the Department of French Studies at the University of Warwick, UK. Her doctoral thesis concerns representations of Saracens and racial identity in medieval French and Occitan literature across a range of genres from *chansons de geste* to miracle tales and romance.

Introduction: Performing the Self: women's lives in historical perspective

Katie Barclay and Sarah Richardson

This special edition originated in the 19th Annual Conference of the Women's History Network: Performing the Self: women's lives in historical perspective, held on the 10–12 September 2010 at the University of Warwick. Attended by 120 delegates from five continents over three days the conference explored the myriad of ways that women performed selfhood in past societies. The topics ranged across time, from medieval performances of gender and race to representations of the closing of the Greenham Common peace camp in 2002, and across place, incorporating women from Europe, America, Asia, Australia and Africa. The concept of performance is central to a number of fields including anthropology, psychology, linguistics, politics and theatre studies. This multi-disciplinary focus was reflected in the attendance from scholars across a variety of branches of the humanities and social sciences, including literature, art history, theatre studies and sociology. Although performance may be a contested concept, the variety of meanings of the term, across the disciplines, invited participants to view numerous realities and to interpret them in multiple ways. This focus on interdisciplinarity was also mirrored in the plenary papers. Professor of Politics,

Shirin Rai, provided a rich comparison of ceremony and performance in the Parliaments of the United Kingdom, India and South Africa; Professor of English and Women's Studies, Sidonie Smith, applied her theories of performance through autobiography to the writings of Hilary Clinton; and Professors of History, Carolyn Steedman and Penny Summerfield, both reflected on the different methodological approaches to finding (or not finding) selfhood in the past, looking at account books in the eighteenth century and oral histories of the twentieth century.

The papers chosen for the special edition reflect the major themes of the conference, illustrating its chronological, geographical and disciplinary spread. There are two key motifs concerning aspects of performance and the self that run across all the articles: firstly, 'performing the public self' which considers physical performances in politicised spaces and representational forms created for a public audience; and secondly, 'performing the written self' which focuses on the ways in which the written form has been central to performances of self and questions the relationship between representations and performance in texts. Throughout the special edition, the authors apply different methods of thinking about performance to understanding women's lives in the past. They draw upon a multiplicity of diverse source material to explore issues of identity formation, representations and interpretations. The special edition concludes with an overview by Professor Penny Summerfield, reflecting on how the various contributors' articles fit into and advance ideas around performativity and selfhood.

Performance is a key method by which both individual and collective identities are formed, framed and reiterated. This special edition considers the diverse public stages where women played out and shaped their identities.[1] For example, Hall considers the court room—a place of theatricality, witness, authority and contest. Berney further explores the legal context by considering deposition evidence from a young Chinese runaway seeking sanctuary. In comparison, Mercer focuses on the museum, a similar arena where memory, tradition and history meet, a space which recreates and re-enacts past historical events. Visitors share in a performance of a shared past and in so doing both describe and recreate it. Therefore performance does not merely focus on the actors or participants but also on the audience who may be oppressed by what they experience or alternatively be given political agency.

Erving Goffman defined performance as the 'activity of an individual which occurs during a period marked by his continuous presence before a particular set of observers and which has some influence on the observers'.[2] Thus these public stages have audiences as well as actors and participants all of whom help to define, construct and represent individual identities. Daily life, political and religious ceremonies and artistic presentations all consist of well-rehearsed routines, habits and rituals. These have been categorised by Schechner as 'restored behaviours' or the key processes of performing particular roles, actions that people practice and rehearse.[3] It is these 'restored behaviours' which are particularly valuable for historians to capture and to analyse. They help to understand the mutability of human identity and the social construction of the self. For example,

Judith Butler has explored the ways in which the repetition of culturally normative gestures and performances generate a collective understanding of the gendered self.[4] Everyday life involves the continuous evolution of behaviours that individuals adjust to particular social, political and personal circumstances. Some adapt and conform but others resist. The papers in this collection often focus on women who rebelled against accepted social norms: the Victorian woman traveller seeking divorce; the married woman professional artist; or promoters of exercise for modern women.

Performance may therefore be politically empowering for women reacting to the social, political and cultural constraints of their immediate environment. Amelia Jones, a performance art historian, defined performance as the 'culture of narcissism' writing, 'the enacted body/self is explicitly political and social in that it opens out onto otherness and the world in general; in phenomenological terms, this body/self performs itself through its own particular social situation'.[5] Jones viewed performance as a useful analytical tool for understanding the connections between the personal and political role of women. Likewise the political philosopher, Chantal Mouffe, has argued for the importance of positioning the subject in cultural history distinguishing tradition, personal memory, cultural history and traditionalism. Thus women are constructed as subjects through a series of pre-existing discourses and this framed their political actions.[6] The construction of personal identities in the public sphere has a long history as the essays in this special edition demonstrate ranging in time from the medieval period to the late twentieth century.

While performances of selfhood are often associated with physical interactions on the 'stage of the world', the written form also offers an opportunity to perform selfhood. This can take the form of writing for a public audience, as is explored in Moore's discussion of Isabella Fyvie Mayo's novels, Devenish's analysis of political biographies and Titcombe's comparison of published accounts of the Greenham Common experience. Or, it can be found in private writings, such as Beattie-Smith's study of a travel diary and Simon-Martin's investigation of Barbara Leigh Smith Bodichon's correspondence with her family and friends. Writing has frequently been viewed as a 'representational' form, reflecting the self but not constituting it. But increasingly theories of performativity challenge this interpretation.[7] Like in physical performances, the act of writing comes to comprise the self; the self is not a priori to the text, but 'becomes' as it is expressed in written form. Penny Summerfield highlights, through her work on oral history, the need for public discourses to allow people to articulate their experience. Where little or no public discourse exists, people found it difficult to construct a narrative, talking in a stilted, fact-giving style.[8] Even at the level of basic expression, people rely on metaphor and allusions to give voice to abstract concepts, such as emotion.[9] Wider social conventions and discourses offer the language, or cultural scripts, that people use to construct their identities and place limits on how those identities are formed.

It is the act of speaking or writing, where personal experiences are given voice through their incorporation into larger cultural scripts, that constitutes the self.

As Judith Butler explains, performative speech acts are those that 'bring into being what they name'; in the same way, the act of writing creates the author.[10] Moreover, most writing is created in a dialogic relationship with an intended audience, which acts on the text, informing its content and the manner in which the author will express her or himself. As Bossis and McPherson argue in the context of written correspondence, every letter is a collaboration between the writer and the reader, and so has to be understood as portraying more than the identity of one individual.[11] In this way, as Turner's exploration of medieval oral song demonstrates, traditional representation forms can be understood as a cultural performance, as well as a site for discussion and highlighting the performative nature of selfhood. As Simon Martin's article investigates, this action of the audience on the self also highlights the way that the self becomes fractured, with the creation of multiple selves for multiple audiences, demonstrating the relational nature of selfhood.

This fractured or multiple selfhood is increasingly important within feminist theory, replacing the focus on the unified self of the Enlightenment, and thought to better reflect the multiple subject positions of women's lives that have frequently been created in a dialogic relationship, demonstrated clearly in Moore's account of the life of Fyvie Mayo. Moreover, as women have historically been represented as the 'other' or 'different' from the [male] norm, deconstructing the unified nature of the 'norm' is seen to have liberatory potential. As Barbara Bolt argues, it is the 'representationalist mode of thinking that enables humans to express a will to fixity and mastery over the world'. The seeming stability of representation codifies and normalises experience. In contrast, a performative self is constructed in collaboration with difference, drawing on a Deleuzian concept of identity as an effect of difference, with nothing prior to difference itself.[12] As Hélène Cixous maintains, this focus on the self as relational and shifting, where the difference of the other becomes part of the self, allows for a selfhood that dissolves power relationships, rather than reinforcing them.[13] As Beattie-Smith's article in this edition explores, understanding writing as a performative act uncovers the ways that women managed to maintain a sense of self, and even to develop authoritative voices, within structures where they held little formal power. It also allows for more complex understandings of power as difference becomes incorporated into selfhood, even as it defines the self, destabilising binary power relationships in favour of multiple, intersecting and unstable lines of power, and, in so doing, opening up more dynamic, more interesting selves.

Autobiographies, letters, diaries and other forms of personal testimony form a significant portion of the source base used to explore the performance of the self in this collection. But the essays also demonstrate the diversity of texts, images and public records that may be fruitfully interrogated. An artist's signature at the corner of a painting, a display of women's uniforms in a museum over time, deposition evidence and even an analysis of the female body all provide opportunities to explore and describe women's contested identities in the public sphere. This rich diversity reflects recent cultural histories of the self in which historians analyse gendered identities via an eclectic range of material extending beyond the traditional personal narrative. Dror Warhman, for example, assesses costume, masquerades, medals and even apiary manuals to pinpoint the moment of the emergence of the 'modern' gendered self in eighteenth-century England.[14] The essays in this collection are equally innovative and ambitious and demonstrate the potential of such source material for understanding women's roles and identities in the past, as well as the usefulness of theories of performance in allowing such source material to speak.

Notes

[1] For example: George Robb & Nancy Erber (Eds) (1999) *Disorder in the Court: trials and sexual conflict at the turn of the century* (New York: New York University Press); Angus McLaren (1997) *Trials of Masculinity: policing sexual boundaries 1870–1930* (Chicago: Chicago University Press).

[2] E. Goffman (1959) *The Presentation of the Self in Everyday Life* (New York: Anchor Books), p. 22.

[3] Richard Schechner (2002) *Performance Studies: an introduction* (London: Routledge)

[4] J. Butler (1999) *Gender Trouble: feminism and the subversion of identity* (London: Routledge).

[5] Amelia Jones (1998) *Body/Art Performing the Subject* (Minneapolis: University of Minnesota Press), pp. 46–47.

[6] Chantal Mouffe (1993) *The Return of the Political* (London: Verso).

[7] Butler, *Gender Trouble*, pp. 182–183; Barbara Bolt (2004) *Art Beyond Representation: the performative power of the image* (London: IB Tauris).

[8] P. Summerfield (2004) Culture and Composure: creating narratives of the gendered self in oral history interviews, *Cultural and Social History*, 1, pp. 65–93.

[9] L. Baxter (1992) Root Metaphors in Accounts of Developing Romantic Relationships, *Journal of Social and Personal Relationships*, 9, pp. 253–275; L. Pollock (2004) Anger and the Negotiation of Relationships in Early Modern England, *Historical Journal*, 47, p. 573.

[10] Peter Osborne & Lynne Segal (1994) Gender as Performance: an interview with Judith Butler, London, 1993, *Radical Philosophy*, 67, pp. 32–39.

[11] M. Bossis & K. McPherson (1986) Methodological Journeys through Correspondences, *Yale French Studies*, 71, pp. 63–75.

[12] Gilles Deleuze (1994) *Difference and Repetition* (London: Continuum).

[13] Sal Renshaw (2009) *The Subject of Love: Hélène Cixous and the feminine divine* (Manchester: Manchester University Press).

[14] Dror Wahrman (2006) *The Making of the Modern Self: identity and culture in eighteenth-century England* (New Haven: Yale University Press).

Performing the Self, Performing the Other: gender and racial identity construction in the Nanteuil Cycle

Victoria Turner

This article focuses on the Old French Nanteuil Cycle of chansons de geste, *investigating the nature of medieval identity and its connection to gender, race and religion. The Nanteuil Cycle repeatedly uses disguise as a means of crossing gender boundaries, which allows the repositioning of identity and simultaneously reveals the arbitrariness of cultural categorisation. Although cross-dressing heroines abound in medieval literature, the fourteenth-century* Tristan de Nanteuil *contains instances where cross-dressing is both gendered and racialised, stretching the malleability of identity to the point that it seems physical form can be altered at will. The article discusses the distortion of genealogies in the Cycle effected by the challenges to the social matrix produced by disguise, with a new relational framework where wives may become fathers and mothers become husbands.*

Questions of gender and race are frequently considered in parallel within medieval literary studies, providing a means to explore the inclusion or exclusion of a given community.[1] Perhaps nowhere is this more apparent than in instances where seemingly fixed social conventions become blurred—cases of cross-dressing, transposition or transformation. The anonymous medieval French Nanteuil Cycle of *chansons de geste*, or epic poems, is no exception to this in its many depictions of social crossings that leave Saracen as Christian, friend as foe and woman as man. The term *chansons de geste* here refers to orally performed epic works, following their definition by Sarah Kay as 'representations of the conflictual character of French history, in a mode and with a narrative shape not shared by vernacular historiography';[2] through their depiction of societal frictions, these texts offer a resource for considering community definition and division. The Nanteuil Cycle is thus a group of *chansons de geste* than span over a century, grouped together for their continuing focus on the descendants of Doon de Nanteuil.[3] Reflecting such generic uncertainty, concepts like 'race' and 'gender' are not unproblematic for medievalists, and continue to pose significant issues of definition and temporal specificity. This study therefore seeks to reconsider these notions side by side through an analysis of constructed literary identities.

Historians of medieval 'race' have recently focused on the appropriateness of using modern terms such as 'race' or 'ethnicity'. In the Middle Ages, as William Chester Jordan reminds us, a 'race' could be constructed through 'other characteristics than its biological "unity"' and these characteristics themselves often changed over time.[4] He cautions against ignoring our own cultural baggage as scholars and promotes instead the term 'ethnic identity' to refer to a process of individual reflection and development, where modern 'race' would seem to imply a teleological connection to modern questions of apartheid and slavery.[5] Though the concept of identity as a process would sit well with the performative aspect under discussion here, the term 'ethnic identity' seems equally problematic to apply to the Saracens of epic literature. However valid the attempt to avoid the application of modern notions of race to medieval situations, the modern understanding of race as 'an inherited biological feature' and ethnicity as simply 'cultural differences between groups' would nonetheless seem to unsettle 'ethnic identity' as a suitable lone term for medieval scholarship.[6]

Medieval notions of divisions between different peoples were in a constant state of fluctuation that defies succinct terminology. Geraldine Heng concludes that 'racialising discourses' in medieval romance represent an 'impulse to differentiate' when a community strives for self-definition.[7] Similarly, Kinoshita highlights that the Saracen may actually mould the identity of the Christian community rather than represent an 'other'; she argues that as Saracens only really differ from Franks in their religion, 'the Saracens, then, should be understood not as a race but as a culture'.[8] The use of the term 'Frank' in the Nanteuil Cycle usually refers to 'men from northern France', rather than necessarily denoting the 'aggressive western Christian' of the *Chanson de Roland*.[9] 'Saracen' however, continues to be a particularly debatable epithet, following Cohen's observation that 'there were no real Saracens in the Middle Ages' and Debra Higgs Strickland's description of them as 'imaginary' figures who are nonetheless commonly 'followers of Islam' in literature;[10] in the case of the current study, this latter usage, though common, is not exclusive. Saracens from Armenia appear in *Tristan de Nanteuil* for instance, suggesting that the term here is rather used to denote 'everything inimical to the fragile Christian selfsame' so that 'the Saracen contained within reductive flesh the diversity of the Eastern world'.[11] If the term Saracen could simultaneously denote both religion and race, how then are we to encompass these multifaceted markers of alterity within a workable vocabulary? A term such as 'racial-religious' identity may suffice, as in a modern vocabulary, the limited connotative currency of the word 'Saracen' prevents us from strictly following medieval referential conventions.[12] This combined term would also follow Akbari's assertion that the conflation of racial and religious elements is a defining feature of medieval representations of alterity, in contrast to the Early Modern preponderance on physiognomic features.[13]

Medieval gender is similarly problematic where avoiding modern conventionalisms are concerned, as 'the *chansons de geste* are less committed to a categorical view of gender than their critics'.[14] Steven Kruger for instance has highlighted the need to consider medieval sexuality in terms of 'both the dominant construction and those entities against which it defined itself', which involves linking 'excluded sexualities' to other 'excluded or disfavored identity positions'.[15] He goes on to posit that 'medieval categories of sexuality, religion and race are deeply interimplicated'.[16] Taken specifically in relation to the social milieu of the *chansons de geste*, this would extend Simon Gaunt's call to investigate not only their tendency to exclude women, but also to take into account the gendered 'value system' of the genre as a whole.[17] Though the early *chansons de geste* may present a 'monologic' construction of gender by promoting a masculine ideological framework, later texts that rework such ideologies could perhaps be termed rather *heterologic*, owing to their display of performatively gendered identity through disguise.[18]

Such processes of gender identity formation are also visible in constructions of racial-religious identity in the Nanteuil Cycle. In the first complete text, *Aye d'Avignon*, the Saracen's identity is a counterweight to that of the Christian hero and positions him as the antidote to Frankish social corruption rather than as a threat from abroad.[19] This racial-religious identity is shaped by those around him, so that he is able to perform varying social roles that range from protector to avenger. This is in contrast to the seeming fixity of female social identity. In comparison, the last text, *Tristan de Nanteuil* (from around 1350) incorporates characters who cross social divisions, in this case, women who dress as men; as these gender crossings sometimes involve racial identity shifts, this text provides an ideal arena in which to consider the interplay of medieval gendered and racial identities.[20] By gauging the relative success of the disguises used by women and men across the Cycle, this study seeks to unite these conventionally determined attributes, as while gender crossings in medieval literature have frequently been the subject of scholarly attention, cases of both racial *and* gendered crossings have yet to be fully explored.[21]

This may be achieved through the framework of performativity analysed by Judith Butler, which provides a means of conceptualizing multiply constructed identity. Butler's depiction of the performative process and countering of normative binaries has most commonly been confined to questions of gender and sexuality in medieval studies;[22] I do not attempt here merely to transpose Butler's theory of gender performativity onto race, as she herself cautions against this, but will instead discuss the differing potential for racial or gendered identity to be constructed within a paradigm of performativity.[23]

For Butler, performativity is a system through which to discuss 'the variable cultural construction of sex, the myriad and open possibilities of cultural meaning occasioned by a sexed body'.[24] She emphasises that gender is not merely a 'cultural inscription' upon a given body, but is in fact 'the very apparatus of production whereby the sexes themselves are established'.[25] Gender is not passively conferred upon a given individual by virtue of biological form but an active process: it is assumed by performing in a certain manner, by conforming to (or deviating from) a confined, conventionalising system.[26] Yet the performative process may itself reveal the arbitrariness of this system, as by repeating the conventional, we expose its artifice, and consequently recognise that other forms of identity may be similarly constructed. Cross-dressing and disguise may therefore unveil rather than conceal identity formation, as they confuse any attempt to distinguish a supposedly 'real' identity performance (such as a biologically female body acting according to feminine behavioural norms) from mimicry (as is achieved by a drag queen). Butler states for instance that:

> If the inner truth of gender is a fabrication and if a true gender is a fantasy instituted and inscribed on the surface of bodies, then it seems that genders can be neither true nor false, but are only produced as the truth effects of a discourse of primary and stable identity.[27]

In the Nanteuil Cycle, the instances of multiple gendered identities created through disguise may mean that other aspects of medieval identity, such as race-religion, are far more fluid and discursively determined than is often assumed.[28] Visible through their acts of cross-dressing, the identities of 'Saracens' or 'Franks' are formed through the perpetual interaction of a variety of cultural and physical features, such as religion, clothing, skin colour, and customs; this state of flux renders identity unstable and context-dependent. It is therefore performatively exploitable, as it is not only liable to shift over time, but also able to be consciously constructed through behaviour and dress, moving beyond the purely physical or visual spheres. Characters may forge new familial and genealogical ties, altering their racial and gendered adherence and even biological forms.

This performative reading of gender and racial-religious identity will challenge Jacqueline de Weever's presentation of the medieval epic landscape of *chansons de geste* as founded upon a series of binary oppositions of 'Latin Christian/Oriental pagan, white/black, orthodoxy/heterodoxy, truth/error', which ultimately divide Saracens as either black or white skinned.[29] She views the literary tradition as fundamentally destabilised by the chaotic distortion of marking community through skin colour. The present study will eschew such a prioritisation of the body in the racial representations of the Nanteuil Cycle, where Saracen identity may be defined just as easily through behaviour, religion, and language as through physiological markers.[30] As such, I follow recent trends in scholarship treating the Saracen and Islam in European literature: Suzanne Conklin Akbari underlines the importance of situating the Saracen along 'a continuum', where Saracen identity 'partakes in both the binarism of religious alterity and the spectrum of bodily diversity', as the result of 'religious and ethnic difference'.[31] Considered alongside the performance of racial and gendered identity, the Saracens discussed here extend Akbari's 'continuum' of race to include religion, which may even be specifically doffed and donned in the depicted machinations of disguise.

To aid the reader, the important events of the texts are as follows: in *Aye d'Avignon*, Aye is kidnapped from her Frankish husband, Garnier, by a traitor (Berenger), who flees on a merchant ship to Majorca, the kingdom of the Saracen Ganor. Ganor falls in love with Aye and protects her from the traitor, with the help of Aye's own husband who is in disguise as a mercenary. When Ganor leaves for pilgrimage to Mecca, Aye is rescued by her husband, who betrays Ganor's trust and returns to France. Upon arriving home, Ganor is distraught. He travels to France disguised as a pilgrim and kidnaps Aye's son Gui to raise him as his own. Years later Ganor and Gui must return to France to rescue Aye from more traitors who have killed her husband and wish to marry her. Ganor and Aye are finally married and return to Majorca leaving Gui his father's lands.

Tristan de Nanteuil begins with Gui and his wife Aiglentine being shipwrecked and separated from their young son Tristan, who is brought up in the forest by a wild deer. Tristan subsequently meets and falls in love with Blanchandine, the daughter of the Saracen ruler Galafre. To live with Tristan undiscovered by her relations, Blanchandine disguises herself as a knight. In a parallel plotline, Majorca is attacked by Saracens and Aye must disguise herself as a Saracen knight to remain unharmed, whilst Ganor and their sons are captured.

The Dissident Damsel

Aye is clearly depicted as the damsel in distress in *Aye d'Avignon*: kidnapped from her husband, taken to a foreign land and imprisoned in a tower of ladies whilst men fight over her, she is cast as a Helen of Troy and Ganor as a love-struck Paris, allowing himself to be destroyed for love of a woman (v.1721). Passed from man to man, Aye is very much the passive object in this text and this is reflected in her inability to alter her identity, which remains fixed throughout. Her passivity is clear as she laments that she will be dishonoured or mistreated by the traitor Berenger (v.1514) and falls at Ganor's feet when he swears not to relinquish her to treacherous Saracens in Spain (v.1733). Later, when Ganor, disguised as a pilgrim, steals her son Gui from Nanteuil, Aye merely exclaims aloud, rather than acting or commanding action from her followers:

> Oh those Saracens, how they are deceitful!
> Who could protect themselves from such enchantment? (vv.2554–5)[32]

Although seeming to establish the Saracen as 'other' and fundamentally different to the Christian Franks, Aye's speech here is actually a mirror image of Ganor's own lament when Garnier takes Aye from him:

> Oh those Christians, how they are treacherous!
> Who could protect themselves from such a snare? (vv.2305–6)[33]

These parallel incidents of deception suggest that there is little consistency in the way Christians and Saracens may be identified, as they can each be equally duped. By replicating Ganor's expression, Aye's comment suggests that racialised behavioural traits may be transferrable and non-racially specific, thereby diminishing the descriptive power of such traits as identity markers. The fact that Aye reveals racial identity to be performative renders her an example of Gaunt's dualistic *chanson de geste* woman: although she disrupts male bonding (causing the trust between Ganor and Garnier to be broken for instance), she also indicates a potential 'critical impulse' in the text by signaling the flaws of racial identifications.[34] Here, this exposes that identity is performative and so may be deliberately manipulated—even if she is unable to do so herself. Aye's passivity in *Aye d'Avignon* may however be contrasted with Ganor's activity, for whereas Aye accepts her son's fate, Ganor actively pursues Aye to France. Whilst the racial-religious difference between the two victims of deceptions involving cross-dressing is levelled, their gendered identity remains stable with Aye still a passive object of desire.

In *Tristan de Nanteuil* over a century later, however, we see a very different representation of Aye d'Avignon, where she has a clear voice and presence and is able significantly to alter her racial and gendered identity. She pretends to be a Saracen knight, Gaudion, who is a kinsman of the Saracen ruler, exploiting both racial and gendered epic norms.[35] Unfortunately the original description of her transformation being lost, we learn of her disguise in her later account to Ganor and her sons. She explains that by taking part in battles and tournaments her prowess was such that the king kept her at court and never suspected anything amiss (*Tristan* v.3059–3062).

Aye does not merely conceal her physical, visible appearance through disguise, she also replicates behavioural conventions, such as when she praises the Saracen gods (v.1924). By following culturally normalised behaviour, Aye performs a religious identity that conforms to the expectations of her Saracen allies and her disguise is therefore successful. Her ability to behave according not only to Saracen custom, but also to specifically knightly and therefore masculine norms guarantees the success of her ruse; her racial, religious and gendered identities are temporarily aligned. Even her genealogical, inherited identity is now rendered unimportant by her ability to fight with a sword (v.2088–9)—it is the identity she has personally constructed through replicating behaviour that establishes her social position and worth. As Michèle Perret has noted, the expectations formed from visual appearances are capable of hindering our perception of reality: 'c'est bien l'attente créée par les signes extérieurs qui permet que la réalité ne soit pas discernée et qui fausse la perception'.[36] Since Aye both looks and acts the Saracen warrior, no one thinks to question her. Interestingly, although Aye has managed to create not only a new racial but also gendered identity, she is often referred to as 'Dame Aye d'Avignon' rather than as her alter ego 'Gaudion', even when she is mid-battle (v.2785–7); her biologically determined identity is preserved throughout, as she is never fully represented as a man. Aye's successful transformation 'makes explicit the contrast between biology and socially gendered performance' and it is this revelation that also exposes the potential for identity, both racial-religious and gendered, to be performative and thus deliberately malleable.[37] In contrast to the earlier *Aye d'Avignon*, in this text Aye is able to temporarily perform in a way that contradicts her biological identity.

However, the fundamental difference between racial and gendered identity in this Cycle appears in the success of this construction. Whereas Aye's racial-religious identity as Saracen seems to be taken as a given, her gender is eventually betrayed through her physical form. When she visits her family in prison, she is recognised through her biologically feminine features such as the lack of a beard (v.3028). The physical body is consequently undeniable and so is the stumbling block for Aye's assumed identity, betraying her disguise. In her discussion of the Saracen queen Bramimonde in the *Chanson de Roland*, Kinoshita has shown that her conversion to Christianity actually reinforces the Frank-Saracen division, as she performs 'part of a scripted role' requiring 'women's silent acquiescence'.[38] Yet Aye's cross-dressing ploy involving religious disguise has the opposite effect: as a Christian-turned-Saracen-turned-Christian, she reveals racial-religious identity categorisation to be inherently false—her gender being the constant against which her race-religion is defined. Although ideological conventions may be temporarily exploited due to the citationality of behaviour or dress, the body ultimately proves revelatory when disguise involves gender crossing. This is in contrast to racial and religious identity shifts as enacted by Ganor, which above all rely upon a less definitive catalogue of markers.

The Christian Saracen

Ganor's use of cross-dressing in *Aye d'Avignon* is more subtle and differs in its manner, tone and purpose from that of Aye. When Ganor travels to France in search of Aye, he does this in the guise of a Christian pilgrim from France; his disguise is therefore racial and religious, as opposed to involving gender crossing, which alters the nature of his manipulation of identity.[39] Racial identity is shown to remain consistently fluid, dictated more by behavioural display than inherited physiognomy or genealogy.

Even before his literal use of disguise, Ganor's identity is performative. Despite having white skin and a face that is bright like fine gold, Ganor initially adheres to Saracen convention by displaying a materialistic, rather than courtly, attitude towards Aye.[40] He offers to take Aye as his wife by purchasing her from Berenger in the same way that he would claim a good horse that arrived in his lands (v.1482–4). Berenger now seems to have become Aye's heroic protector, as he replies 'miex voudroie estre mort'—I would rather die (v.1486). Ganor's white body is therefore nullified by his display of Saracen behaviour, demonstrating the illusion of visible identity by revealing how a 'common' racial-religious identity may be perceived.[41] He is clearly an ambiguous figure, blurring the boundaries between self and other for the Christian characters: just after he offers to buy Aye for instance, he becomes a perfectly chivalrous knight, calming Aye's fears of being dishonoured (which would conform to the conventional image of the lecherous

Saracen) by declaring matrimonial intentions (v.1518 and v.1601). Ganor's behaviour here is thus set in stark contrast to Berenger's earlier attempt to rape Aye (v.1229–2) and establishes the Saracen, rather than the Frank, as the courtly suitor.[42]

Bridget Byrne has discussed the importance of visual recognition in concepts of race, which may be produced by 'a particular kind of seeing' as could be suggested here by Aye's initial reaction to Ganor; she extends Butler's analysis of performativity so that 'visual differences are to "race" as sex is to gender':[43]

> 'race' needs to be understood as an embodied performative. That is, the repeated citation of racialised discourses and, importantly, the repetition of racialised perceptual practices produces bodies and subjects that are raced ... 'Race' is in the eye of the beholder.[44]

Aye's difficulty in recognising Ganor's honourable nature, however, is centred upon the incongruity of his visible form and performative identity. Just as Aye's disguise revealed that sex may not necessarily be indicative of gender in *Tristan de Nanteuil*, so Ganor shows in *Aye d'Avignon* that visual appearance is not always reliable; his Saracen identity was initially suggested to Berenger and Aye through his display of mercenary behaviour. All it takes therefore, to reposition this identification is a shift of behaviour, suggesting that, as is possible with gender, performance may rework racial-religious identity as well as confirm it.

Like Aye's Saracen and gendered disguise in *Tristan*, Ganor's subsequent cross-dressing ploy is successful: when he meets Aye in France, although he is familiar, she does not recognise him and believes his explanation that he had been at her wedding.[45] His choice of pilgrim's garb is not especially unusual, as such people travelled widely and similar disguises frequently appear in medieval literature;[46] however, what is striking is that his successful disguise involves a Saracen becoming a Christian, and an exemplary one at that. He concocts a false lineage as a knight who travelled to Rome as penance for killing a relative, and this is easily accepted by Aye, who thinks him a 'bien prodonme'—a very worthy man (v.2430). A coherent identity is perceived by Aye, as his physical, biological body and behaviour are aligned, even though technically this is supposed to be a ruse; whilst his initial and thus 'true' identity provoked anxiety for its obvious incongruity of origins, behaviour and appearance, his assumed identity is unquestioningly accepted.

Although Ganor's cross-dressing unveils his underlying Christian identity, it functions differently from Butler's gender cross-dressing through drag. His purpose is to maintain his ploy rather than to openly reveal the troubling illusion of identity. This occurs in gendered identity performance at the moment when reality and illusion collide and involves the realisation that 'if the "reality" of gender is constituted by the performance itself, then there is no recourse to an essential and unrealized "sex" or "gender"'.[47] As we saw with Aye, such a revelation occurs in cases of cross-gender disguises, since these must always come to an end. Yet, for Ganor, his guise as Christian pilgrim is part of a gradual move towards his integration into Frankish social structure as father to Gui and husband to Aye. We might expect this disguise to exploit racial and religious conventions and thus expose the artifice of Ganor's performance. However, given his courtly behaviour and attractive physiognomy, it is his initial Saracen identity which seems incongruous to a Christian identity that retrospectively appears better to correspond to Ganor's physical appearance.

Ganor's disguise therefore has a lasting, positive effect upon society. It allows him to remove Gui from the web of treachery that led to his father's death and also provides Ganor with a new wife and genealogy by connecting him to the Nanteuil dynasty, and ultimately to Charlemagne, Aye's uncle. He has managed to establish a new, forward looking genealogy that replaces any inherited one, making his position in society, just like his identity, one that is personally constructed as opposed to innate. Yet while he exposes the potential for conventional genealogy to be overturned, Ganor does not upset social order. Firstly, in his role as surrogate father to Gui, he maintains the boy's true identity throughout his upbringing, only assuming an openly paternal role upon the death of Gui's biological father (v.3468). Secondly, the disguise that allows Ganor to kidnap Gui is not really a deception, but rather founded upon the correlation of pre-existing elements of his identity, such as his physical appearance and his courtly attitude as discussed above. In this respect, whereas men in the Nanteuil Cycle are able to show different facets of the same self and thus socially reposition themselves, women are obliged to establish multiple selves, with different names, different behaviour and most importantly, different genders. This is especially the case for Aye's granddaughter Blanchandine, whose physical body is transformed in the process of her disguise, which instead of simply shifting her identity, creates an entirely new self.

The Divinely Different

In *Tristan de Nanteuil*, alongside the cross-dressing of Aye and Tristan, there is also that of Blanchandine, the wife of Aye's grandson, Tristan. In order to avoid being imprisoned in Armenia, Blanchandine dresses as a knight and joins the court of a Saracen Sultan. The Sultan's daughter, Clarinde, falls in love with Blanchandin (as she is now called) and wishes to marry her/him. Although Blanchandin manages to delay this, they ultimately marry, yet she is obviously unable to consummate the union. Clarinde is frustrated by her husband's reluctance and so, being suspicious, holds a public bathing scene to expose Blanchandin. However, at the last moment, Blanchandin is saved by a stag, which distracts everyone and gives her chance to escape to the forest where an angel appears and offers to transform her into a man (vv.16146–7). Thinking Tristan dead, Blanchandine agrees and is able to publicly expose a male body.

As with Aye, Blanchandine troubles the body as the site of gender identity. Her gendered behaviour at court was clearly very successful, especially in attracting the sultan's daughter. Yet her undeniable physical form threatens once again to betray the ruse, as a messenger sent to look for her recognises that she is a woman (v.15650); supernatural intervention is necessary to maintain her new, male self.

Her disguise does not simply exploit her pre-existing identity, but is actually the impetus behind the creation of a completely new being: she has a new name, new partner, new social position and most importantly, a new body.[48] When Doon, Tristan's half brother, comes to help Blanchandine, he encounters Blanchandin in the forest just after the transformation and still refers to her as 'Dame', to which Blanchandin replies that he is not a woman (v.16234 and v.16239). Clearly, even when performed and physical genders are aligned, the resulting identity is not necessarily easy to determine, as Doon thinks Blanchandin is still a woman. As Peggy McCracken comments, the transvestite in medieval literature frequently represents:

> a profoundly troubling spectacle to an aristocratic society founded and maintained by dynastic marriage and succession because ambiguous gender threatens the disruption of dynastic structures—a woman dressed as a man cannot engender a child.[49]

Conversely, through her transformation, Blanchandine is now no longer a transvestite, but a new character, as 'a miraculous regendering of the body' has occurred.[50] Rather than a body performing an identity, this is a gender performance that causes the transformation of the physical body.

Blanchandin in his new role is able to father a child with Clarinde, creating a new genealogical line and as Campbell has noted, 'the performance of genealogy is thus distinguished from that of gender'.[51] Though able to assume a male gendered role as knight, Blanchandin remained unable to assume a male genealogical role as father. Unlike Ganor, whose racial-religious identity shifts directly result in the establishment of a new genealogy, Blanchandine must be wholly man and woman to become both mother and father. This is only achievable through divine means. Gender identity is thus recognised by an ability to reproduce: as a sterile 'man', the disguised Blanchandine possesses two partial identities, being reproductively a woman yet visibly male. Her impotence reflects the restriction caused by the genealogical passivity of women in society, as she is unable to take on an active role as progenitor. To assume a creative role in the dynastic drive of this Cycle rather than a reflective, diagnostic role common to women, a unified male being must be produced, suggesting a prioritisation of the paternal in familial relations.[52]

Conclusion

In the Nanteuil Cycle, the performative nature of social conventions enables characters to exploit expectations of dress, behaviour and form in order to reposition themselves. Although this applies to both male and female figures, the success of these transpositions depends upon the nature of the changes involved. Whereas changes in racial-religious identity seem to be easily believed in cases of disguise, when gender is implicated, biological form will out; in essence, whilst race-religion constantly fluctuates and may be performed and sustained through numerous factors, gender may only be temporarily so. This is because the physical body remains unchanged in this process of identity formation, which hinders the performance of a crucial genealogical role: the production of offspring.

Male characters do not exploit the performativity of gender identity in the Cycle; rather they use racial-religious disguise alone and manipulate associated behavioural and visual conventions. Often, they already possess qualities needed for the disguise, which hinders the dissociation of a performance from an inherited identity. For female characters, however, disguise necessitates the exploitation of gender along with racial-religious identity, doubly making them cross-dressers. Like the off-stage drag act, these women have a 'disquieting effect' as they blur the imaginary and the real; this new 'modality of gender' produces anxiety for those around them (such as Clarinde), whilst suspicions of a false racial-religious identity are never raised.[53] Racial-religious identity is therefore performative in a different sense from that which Butler intends: though it can exploit specific conventions of otherness (such as dress, behaviour or skin colour), it also relies upon the convention that alterity itself is unstable.[54] Whereas Butler's performativity rests upon a socially imposed compulsory heterosexuality,[55] there seems to be no one equivalent concept of compulsory race-religiosity. Though Christianity may ultimately be a compulsory attribute for admirable figures, there is no single racial equivalent, and since these go hand-in-hand as mentioned above, this identity is shown to be both polyvalent and context-dependent in the Cycle.[56] In contrast, gender is a performative construction based upon the deployment of certain expected social roles, and so any attempt to disguise this must ultimately be unveiled.

Significantly, whilst there are numerous examples of men using racial or religious disguise both within the Nanteuil Cycle and in other medieval works, the same cannot be said for women.[57] Disguises for women almost always involve gender; a Christian princess does not choose to disguise herself as a female Saracen for instance. Cases where women do enact a racial-religious disguise tend to involve a Saracen woman rather than Christian—perhaps, in the manner of Ganor, to highlight the incongruity of their performed identity.[58] The lack of female racial-religious disguise may also reflect the fact that fixing racial-religious identity for medieval women was less socially significant; Kinoshita notes that women often married across such borders, altering their identity as necessary, suggesting that race-religion is only really brought to the forefront for women when gender crossing is involved.[59] Women may therefore provide a canvas upon which to sketch out racial-religious identities only at the point where their gender renders their affiliations crucial; whilst they were generally regarded as easier to assimilate into cultures, male alterity was altogether more threatening, perhaps explaining the prominence of male racial-religious disguise.[60]

A change of racial-religious identity for women is therefore not significant enough to provide concealment through disguise, showing the labels 'Frank' and 'Saracen' to be unreliable. For men, however, a change of role, race and religion may be effective enough without a change of gender, and establishes their identity positions (eg. Saracen ruler or Christian pilgrim) as distinctly recognisable and therefore imitable as a disguise. As such, women are never able to sustain their assumed male gender in the Cycle, unless their biological make-up is changed through supernatural means like Blanchandine.[61] Whether racial or gendered, medieval identity is far from clear-cut in this Cycle; while divisions between Christians and Saracens are fluid however, gendered divisions are ultimately reaffirmed, leaving women stripped of their disguises and performing once more according to the conventions of a masculine ideological system. Even if medieval society therefore seems to recognise that race-religion may be both uncertain and changeable, biological gender is a determining factor of social relationships; it defines the future of a family so that a unified identity must be produced to ensure the continuity of chronicle and of lineage—in short, of the 'geste'.[62]

Notes

[1] I briefly use 'race' here to broadly encompass differences in religion, culture, language, behaviour, physiognomy and geographical provenance; see below for the use of this term within contemporary medieval studies.

[2] Sarah Kay (1995) *The Chansons de Geste in the Age of Romance* (Oxford: Oxford University Press), pp. 8–9. In recognising the fluidity of medieval generic division, I also follow Kay's image of the texts in this genre as 'manifesting the same kind of variation as is found in a family'—that is, not necessarily all have the same traits. For general discussion of the *chanson de geste*, see the entry by W. Kibler in W. Kibler & G. Zinn (eds) (1995) *Medieval France: An Encyclopedia* (New York & London: Garland). Kibler notes that the earlier poems date from the early twelfth century and there were efforts as late as the fifteenth century to preserve the genre.

[3] In the *chanson de geste Gaufrey*, Doon de Nanteuil is said to be a son of Doon de Mayence, hero of the early rebellious vassal cycle (see Kibler, *Medieval Encyclopedia*, pp. 658–659). Kibler (p. 196) also notes that one of the earliest recognitions of grouping *chansons de geste* into cycles appears in the prologue to the thirteenth-century *Girard de Vienne*.

[4] W. C. Jordan (2001) Why "Race"?, *Journal of Medieval and Early Modern Studies*, 31(1), p. 165.

[5] Ibid., p. 168.

[6] R. Bartlett (2001) Medieval and Modern Concepts of Race and Ethnicity, *Journal of Medieval and Early Modern Studies*, 31(1), p. 39.

[7] Geraldine Heng (2003) *Empire of Magic: medieval romance and the politics of cultural fantasy* (New York: Columbia), p. 71.

[8] S. Kinoshita (2006) *Medieval Boundaries* (Philadelphia: University of Pennsylvania Press), p. 5.

[9] Robert Bartlett (1993) *The Making of Europe: conquest, civilisation and cultural change 950–1350* (London: Allen Lane) pp. 101–105; for the use of the attribute 'Frank' in the *Chanson de Roland*, see Kinoshita, *Medieval Boundaries*, p. 28.

[10] J. J. Cohen (2003) *Medieval Identity Machines* (Minnesota: University of Minnesota Press), p. 202; Debra Higgs Strickland (2003) *Saracens, Demons & Jews: making monsters in medieval art* (Princeton: Princeton University Press), p. 165.

[11] Cohen, *Medieval Identity Machines*, pp. 190–191.

[12] Heng, *Empire*, p. 234 uses this term to recognise the inseparability of these categories.

[13] Suzanne Conklin Akbari (2009) *Idols in the East: European representations of Islam and the Orient, 1100–1450* (Ithaca and London: Cornell University Press), p. 155.

[14] Kay, *Chansons de Geste*, p. 35. Kay specifically highlights the dangers of assuming a binary sexual or gender identity as 'gender can be contingent or provisional'.
[15] Steven Kruger (1997) Conversion and Medieval Sexual, Religious and Racial Categories, in K. Lochrie, P.McCracken & J. Schultz (Eds) *Constructing Medieval Sexuality* (Minneapolis: University of Minnesota Press), p. 159.
[16] Kruger, Conversion, p. 160.
[17] Simon Gaunt (1995) *Gender and Genre in Medieval French Literature* (Cambridge: Cambridge University Press), p. 22.
[18] Gaunt, *Gender*, p. 23; Gaunt cites the example of Guibourc, a Saracen princess in the *Chanson de Guillaume*, whose actions simultaneously reinforce the hero's masculinity and display his weakness. This would exemplify gender performativity (acting like a man) subverting the masculine textual ideology, especially as she is a converted and white-skinned Saracen princess—an embodiment of the performative nature of racial identifications.
[19] S. J. Borg (Ed.) (1967) *Aye d'Avignon: chanson de geste anonyme* (Genève: Librairie Droz). All further references are to this edition.
[20] K. V. Sinclair (Ed.) (1971) *Tristan de Nanteuil: chanson de geste inédite* (Assen: Van Gorcum & Comp n.v.). All further references are to this edition. The remaining texts of the cycle, *Parise la Duchesse* and *Gui de Nanteuil* will not be included in this study, as neither contain specific examples of disguise.
[21] For discussion of the medieval gender cross-dresser, see Vern L. Bullough & Bonnie Bullough (1993) Cross Dressing and Social Status in the Middle Ages, in V. & B. Bullough *Cross Dressing, Sex, and Gender* (Philadelphia: University of Pennsylvania Press), pp. 45–74; Valerie Hotchkiss (2000) *Clothes Make the Man: female cross dressing in medieval Europe* (New York: Garland); for *Tristan de Nanteuil* specifically, see Kimberlee Campbell (2007) Acting Like a Man: performing gender in *Tristan de Nanteuil*, in E. Doss-Quinby, R. Krueger & E. Jane Burns (Eds) *Cultural Performances in Medieval France* (Cambridge: D. S. Brewer), pp. 79–90.
[22] See for example, S. Salih (2001) *Versions of Virginity in Late Medieval England* (Cambridge: DS Brewer).
[23] Judith Butler (1990 reprinted 2008) *Gender Trouble* (New York and London: Routledge), p. xvi.
[24] Ibid., p. 142.
[25] Ibid., p. 10.
[26] I use the words 'performed' and 'performance' according to Butler's concept of gender performativity as a 'doing' of gender—a 'ritualized, public performance' that is not necessarily linked to dramatic performance; rather the projection of an identity to others. The revealed citationality of this identity performance is the performative. See Judith Butler (1990) Performative Acts and Gender Constitution: an essay in phenomenology and feminist theory, in Sue Ellen Case (Ed.) *Performing Feminisms: feminist critical theory and theatre* (Baltimore: John Hopkins University Press), p. 277.
[27] Butler, *Gender Trouble*, p. 186.
[28] Concerning performativity and race, see Ann Pellegrini (1997) *Performance Anxieties: staging psychoanalysis, staging race* (New York and London: Routledge).
[29] Jacqueline de Weever (1998) *Sheba's Daughters: whitening and demonizing the Saracen woman in medieval French epic* (London and New York: Garland Publishing Inc), p. xvii; for the Saracen princess motif in epic, see: P. Bancourt (1982) *Les Musulmans dans les chansons de geste du cycle du roi* (Aix-en-Provence: Université de Provence) and Kay, *Chansons de Geste*.
[30] Akbari, *Idols*, pp. 160–161: 'skin color was just one in a whole range of corporeal features that were used to distinguish between peoples of various nations'.
[31] Ibid.

[32] 'Haÿ gent sarrazine, conm este[s] souduiant!/Qui se seüst garder de tel enchantement?' All English translations are my own unless stated otherwise.
[33] 'Ahi! Gent crestienne, con par estes felon!/Qui se seüst garder de tel subducion?'.
[34] Gaunt, *Gender*, p. 69.
[35] I refer here to generic expectations of the *chansons de geste* tradition rather than a social norm of heterosexuality. For the anachronism of applying normalised heterosexuality to the medieval period, see Karma Lochrie (2005) *Heterosyncracies: female sexuality when normal wasn't* (Minneapolis: University of Minnesota Press).
[36] Michèle Perret (1985) Travesties et Transsexuelles: Yde, Silence, Grisandole, Blanchandine, *Romance Notes*, 25(3), p. 333 : 'the expectations created by exterior appearances are what allow reality to go unnoticed and which distort perceptions' (my translation).
[37] Campbell, Acting Like a Man, p. 85.
[38] Kinoshita, *Medieval Boundaries*, p. 43.
[39] For medieval racial cross-dressing, see Robert Clark & Claire Sponsler (1999) Othered Bodies: racial cross-dressing in the *Mistere de la Sainte Hostie* and the Croxton *Play of the Sacrament, Journal of Medieval and Early Modern Studies*, 29(1), pp. 61–87.
[40] Kinoshita, *Medieval Boundaries*, p. 184 notes the unreliability of skin colour in medieval society; yet Akbari, *Idols*, p. 156 underlines the difference between those Saracens portrayed with white rather than black skin.
[41] Akbari, *Idols*, refers to this common Saracen identity.
[42] Ellen Rose Woods (1978) *Aye d'Avignon: a study of genre and society* (Genève: Librairie Droz), p. 33.
[43] Bridget Byrne (2006) *White Lives: the interplay of race, class and gender in everyday life* (Abingdon and New York: Routledge), p. 21.
[44] Ibid., p. 16.
[45] It is significant that although he creates a new lineage, Ganor does not assume a new name, which is also the case for Tristan when disguised as a Saracen. For the women who cross-dress, a new name is key to their ruse: Aye becomes Gaudion and Blanchandine emasculates her name to Blanchandin.
[46] Other examples of pilgrim disguise can be seen in the insular romance, the *Romance of Horn* and in Thomas' *Tristan*. See Jane Bliss (2008) *Naming and Namelessness in Medieval Romance* (Cambridge: DS Brewer).
[47] Butler, Performative Acts, p. 278.
[48] Blanchandine's transformation also affects her textual function, as she tells Doon that she can now avenge Tristan's death (v.16275), suggesting that revenge is a male behavioural act that cannot simply be performed in the same way as other knightly duties (although since Tristan is not dead, the plot unfolds differently).
[49] Peggy McCracken (1994) The Boy Who Was A Girl: reading gender in the *Roman de Silence, Romanic Review*, 85(4), pp. 517.
[50] Ibid.
[51] Campbell, *Acting Like a Man*, p. 89.
[52] See Gaunt, *Gender* for the role of women as indicators of problems in the male social order.
[53] Butler, Performative Acts, p. 278.
[54] For an overview of medieval alterity see J. J. Cohen (1999) *Of Giants: sex, monsters and the Middle Ages* (Minneapolis: University of Minnesota Press).
[55] Judith Butler (1997) *The Psychic Life of Power* (Stanford: Stanford University Press), p. 144.
[56] See Kinoshita, *Medieval Boundaries*, p. 184.
[57] Other male racial and/or religious disguises include Daurel in *Daurel et Beton*, who poses as a jongleur and Guillaume d'Orange in *La Prise d'Orange* who pretends to be

a merchant. Female disguises include Silence in *Le Roman de Silence* who lives for years as a man, and Nicolette in the romance *Aucassin et Nicolette*, who returns to Aucassin by disguising herself as a minstrel.

[58] See for instance Maugalie in *Floovant*, mentioned by De Weever, *Sheba's Daughters*, and Nicolette in *Aucassin et Nicolette*.

[59] Kinoshita, *Medieval Boundaries*; In 'Cross Dressing', Vern and Bonnie Bullough discuss the relationship of gender cross-dressing and social status in the medieval period, arguing that such cross-dressing was more acceptable for women than men; it showed that women were trying to better themselves and imitate men, whereas for men, it meant that they lost status and were suspicious, perhaps trying to gain access to women. This perhaps explains why there are few examples of men disguising themselves as women.

[60] Akbari, *Idols* p. 4 discusses the different conversion potential of the Saracens; Sylvia Huot, (2007) *Postcolonial Fictions in the Roman de Perceforest: cultural identities and hybridities* (Cambridge: DS Brewer) touches upon the cultural assimilation of marginalised figures such as giants or wild-men.

[61] An extension to this division between sexes could be to consider disguises enacted specifically by Saracen women, who, though seeming to challenge conventional hierarchies, often reinforce the Frankish colonial agenda. See Kinoshita, *Medieval Boundaries*.

[62] R. Howard Bloch (1983) *Etymologies and Genealogies: a literary anthropology of the French Middle Ages* (Chicago and London: University of Chicago Press), pp. 93–94.

Writing the Self: the journal of Sarah Stoddart Hazlitt, 1774–1843

Gillian Beattie-Smith

This paper is concerned with Sarah Stoddart Hazlitt and her text, Journal of My Trip to Scotland, *written in 1822 and first published by Le Gallienne in 1893. The journal was written during a three-month trip to Scotland and Ireland as Sarah awaited the progress of divorce proceedings from her husband, the essayist, William Hazlitt. The article looks at the journal in its context as travel writing of the Romantic period and examines Sarah's identities performed in the text.*

On 14 April 1822, Sarah Stoddart Hazlitt sailed from London to Scotland. She had been sent to Edinburgh by her husband, William Hazlitt, to secure a divorce to free him to carry out his plans to marry the daughter of his landlady. The journey, the affair, the reasons for the divorce and its proceedings were the source of William's *Liber Amoris* and Sarah's *Journal* of a trip to Scotland. This essay considers the *Journal* as a text which gives an insight into the life of Sarah Stoddart Hazlitt and discusses the self which is created and performed in that text.[1] Written as a personal diary, the *Journal* first appeared in full as an appendix in the 1894 Le Gallienne text of William Hazlitt's *Liber Amoris* as 'Mrs Hazlitt's Diary.' In 1959, it was republished in Bonner's edition of *The Journals of Sarah and William Hazlitt*.[2] Stoddart's *Journal* has received little attention as an independent work, but rather has been used in discussions of William's life and character.[3] The

Journal is Sarah's only published work. It records her time spent in Scotland and Ireland between April and July 1822 while seeking and awaiting the divorce from William.

Sarah Stoddart's travel writing was produced as she walked and as she travelled. It is a record of her days, of her thoughts and reflections. Stoddart's text as a journal is of the Romantic confessional literary genre, a genre which encompasses travel literature, memoirs, diaries and journals. Confessional writing was a genre which grew in popularity from the end of the eighteenth century, following Rousseau's *Confessions*, and was adopted by many writers of the Romantic period.[4] At the time of Stoddart's writing, there were many similar texts, for example, Mary Wollstonecraft's *Letters Written during a Short Residence in Sweden, Norway, and Denmark* (1796), which moves between descriptions of people and landscapes and her affair with Gordon Imlay. Confessional genre writing may be said to be produced in response to change and to encounters with difference. In his biography of William Hazlitt, Grayling observes, '*Liber Amoris* was ... intended to be a psychological study, and a cautionary tale'.[5] Together the two texts, William's *Liber Amoris* and Sarah's *Journal of My Trip to Scotland* form 'a cautionary tale' of the affairs of the heart of Sarah and William Hazlitt. However, as independent texts, they are 'psychological studies' of self.

The location of Stoddart's journal as an appendix to *Liber Amoris* has meant that Sarah's life and writing have only been discussed in the context of William's. Sarah's journal has not been valued as autonomous Romantic writing, but rather as a supplementary text whose purpose was to offer justification for *Liber Amoris*. Sonia Hofkosh calls into question traditions of judgement which position a woman's writing and 'the status of the woman and her conversation ... [as] the husband's private possession'.[6] Stoddart was the subject of her own narrative. The *Journal* is Romantic and conforms to the 'paradigms of romanticism'.[7] For example, it has a walking tour as an organising framework and, through it, the journal reproduced Stoddart's engagement with the landscape, the social conditions of those she encountered and highlighted her concern for social reform. René Wellek suggests three criteria for Romantic literature: 'imagination for the view of poetry, nature for the view of the world, and symbol and myth for poetic style'.[8] Stoddart's journal engages the reader's imagination in her view of the world and her performance in it. She created landscapes with the language of poetics, of verbal and visual imagery, and the symbol and myth of Scotland.

Eagleton contends that from a Romantic perspective, the purpose of creative writing was 'gloriously useless, an end in itself, loftily removed from any sordid social purpose'.[9] He argues that any text can have an aesthetic function if the reader's purpose is its aesthetic use.[10] However, it could equally be argued that the *Journal* does have a 'sordid social purpose': the journal is a record of where Stoddart travelled. It is a record of her journeys, literal and metaphorical. Furthermore, the details of her financial situation, of her income and her expenditure, the records of conversations with lawyers and others connected with the divorce have the air of being recorded as evidence, which might be drawn upon should she have difficulties securing the divorce and a financial settlement. Such entries were not aesthetically distanced from the subject, nor literary in their function, and may be seen to have a 'social purpose'. On the other hand, they also have a creative function in their establishment of Stoddart's identity in the subjective and contrasting locations in which she tours. Stoddart's journal is her performance as a Romantic writer; as an independent traveller; as a woman. This article considers the selves she performs in her text.

Sarah Stoddart Hazlitt

Sarah Stoddart Hazlitt was part of a circle which included Romantic writers such as Wordsworth, Coleridge and Southey, and essayists and radical philosophers like William Godwin. The lives of many of the circle were recorded by the unconventional writers, brother and sister, Charles and Mary Lamb, in their correspondence with their friends.[11] The circle encompassed many of the great professional writers and thinkers of the nineteenth century. Mary Lamb describes Sarah's letters as those which are 'very, very precious ... the kindest, best, most natural ones I ever received'.[12] Sarah was a close and old friend of Mary; Hazlitt met Charles Lamb through Godwin. Mary's letters show Sarah to be frank and open in the information she shared with her and give an insight into her life which, like that of many in her social circle, did not conform to the social norms for women of the period. Before her marriage, Sarah had several lovers in England and in Malta, where she lived with her brother, Sir John Stoddart, the Chief Justice of Malta. Her 'Lovers' were remarked upon by Mary: 'You surprise and please me with the frank and generous way in which you deal with your Lovers, taking a refusal from their so prudential hearts with a better grace and more good humour than other women accept a suitor's service'.[13] Sarah and William were introduced by the Lambs and they had known each other for several years before he proposed to her.

Sarah was 'unconventional, a well-read, intelligent, independent woman' and in her journal, she created the persona of a self which illustrated that unconventional nature and which corresponded with how she behaved and was viewed by her circle.[14] Her expenditure, for example, indicates that within two days of arriving in Edinburgh she had 'subscribed to Sutherland's Library for one month, 4s 6d', highlighting her need to read and to have intellectual stimulation.[15] Sarah recorded that Alexander Henderson, who accompanied William on excursions to visit collections of paintings in Scotland, had taken her for an artist because of her knowledge of and ability to discuss the paintings at Dalkeith House.[16] Sarah actively presented herself as a frank and open character. In describing a conversation with Hazlitt at Dalkeith House, Stoddart commented that Hazlitt used to admire 'plump' women, but that Hazlitt's amour, Sarah Walker, was 'as thin and bony as the scrag-end of a neck of mutton'.[17] She considered that the woman in the portrait was 'more to his taste'. Sarah recorded, 'he fancied it was like her. I said it was much nearer my form in the thighs, the fall of the back, and the contour of the whole figure; he said, I was very well made.' In her contrast of her own body with that of her husband's paramour, Stoddart used conversational forms as a performance of her unconventional and direct character. It also illustrated the intimacy that remained between Hazlitt and Stoddart, in spite of the divorce proceedings.[18]

Sarah conformed to few of the social expectations of a woman of the period and was renowned for her outspokenness. In her journal, she referred to the judge at her divorce hearing as 'a prodigious grave Ass' for example,[19] and Grayling remarks that she 'to the distress of her stiff brother ... enjoyed fun and paid little heed to etiquette'.[20] She had extra-marital affairs and Stoddart herself provided us with evidence of them in the journal. She reported Hazlitt's remarks that she 'had [her] intrigues too, and was quite as bad [as William for having affairs], and that [she] was no maid when he married [her]'.[21] She cited an affair with a Mr Thomas and commented on Hazlitt's jealousies of her affairs. Her non-conformity, her frankness, and her intellectual qualities were attractive to Hazlitt. Nonetheless, Charles Lamb recognised that there was 'love o' both sides'.[22] They married on 12 May 1808.

Marriage and Separation

By 1817, Hazlitt had achieved fame as a writer, but William and Sarah were living apart.[23] In August 1820, at his London lodgings, he saw and became infatuated with Sarah Walker, the daughter of his landlady. Hazlitt's infatuation was regarded by those who knew him as an 'insane passion' with which he 'fatigued every person whom he met by expressions of his love'.[24] When Hazlitt asked Sarah for a divorce, she was pragmatic and agreed.[25]

In England, until the Divorce Act of 1857, divorce was only available by a prohibitively expensive act of parliament.[26] In Scotland, however, the laws of marriage and divorce, influenced by Calvin, incorporated equality of sexual fidelity in marriage, which meant a woman could divorce an adulterous husband through the civil courts.[27] For a divorce to be heard in the Scottish courts, a forty-day residency qualification was required. Hazlitt and Stoddart travelled separately to Scotland to take up the required residency and Sarah sued for divorce. On 4 February 1822, Hazlitt arrived in Edinburgh and began arrangements for a divorce. It was as he embarked on his journey to Scotland that he began to write *Liber Amoris*.[28] Sarah Stoddart arrived in Edinburgh on Sunday 21 April 1822 and began her journal. The divorce was granted in June 1822.[29]

In order for Sarah Stoddart to have grounds for divorce, it had to be established that Hazlitt had committed adultery and it was agreed he would meet with a prostitute. William and Sarah colluded in the arrangements, which were made in secret. Sarah had been advised by friends that if she and Hazlitt were found to have colluded in the evidence for the divorce, the penalty would be imprisonment or penal transportation. Sarah was deeply concerned and recorded in the *Journal* her fears about signing an oath of calumny which she discussed with Cranstoun, the barrister, on Monday 22 April, the first business day after she arrived in Edinburgh. She compared two versions of the oath: one she obtained herself from a law stationers and another she was given by Gray, her solicitor.[30] Stoddart copied out both versions in her journal as if to understand them more fully. She 'certainly had scruples about taking the oath', which she aired to William Ritchie, the editor of the *Scotsman*, and to Adam Bell, the go-between and witness for Stoddart and Hazlitt.[31] Stoddart's frankness about her finances in her journal and her grave concerns about signing the oath are confessional in nature, but are private and personal, not obviously intended for another reader.

The personal reflections were pragmatic. The self she performed in private in her journal reaffirmed those concerns she discussed with the barrister, the solicitor, the agent and the editor of the *Scotsman*. The repetition to herself in writing of her concerns emphasised the gravity of her situation and the weight placed on her thoughts by the oath of calumny and the contrived actions required for the divorce. The written performance affirmed her fears and served as a self in text with which to rationalise them.

Performance and the Travel Writer

Stoddart's text is also a travel journal. Travel writing is an idealist and ideological discourse whose essential theme is the nature of self representation in places of difference. The writer's gaze is not only a record of what is observed, but is also a performance of values, of class, gender and the human condition.[32] As a travel writer, Stoddart observed, reflected and recorded from a preconceived position of herself and from that position, she performed the subjective selves which emerged in the physical and social locations in which she travelled. She established difference between herself and the other in those locations and that difference created and performed a self which she idealised in those locations. For example, she emphasised the social differences she observed between the English and the Scottish rural poor. Such comparisons not only performed her social and national identity, they also suggested ideologies of social reform which connoted the 'paradigms of romanticism'.[33] For example:

> An old highlander whom I met near the town, seeing me fatigued, carried my basket for me and went out of his way through the town, to show me the inn I had been recommended to. Indeed I found them much more civil and attentive than people in the same station in England, though they are much worse fed, and the cottages or huts in which they live are wretched in the extreme, mostly composed of loose stones without any cement or mortar, and a hole in the roof instead of a chimney to let the smoke out.[34]

The use of these paradigms served to create a self as a Romantic writer. Her use of figurative language is particularly notable. She used hyperbole and the comparative—'much more civil', 'much worse fed', 'a hole ... instead of a chimney'. This technique exaggerated her observations to emphasise the extent and original nature of her experience.

In her discussion of the travel writer's anxiety not to repeat what other travel writers have written, Chard argues that 'intense responses endorse the traveller's status as an eye-witness; expressions of "private sentiments" emphasise very strongly that the traveller has actually gone in person to observe the object described'.[35] In the example above, Stoddart gave her own opinion with 'I found' and emphasised it with 'Indeed'. She asserted her experience and her writing as personal and original and in this way performed herself as travel writer. However, hyperbole in travel writing exaggerates not only the personal experience, but also the sublime.[36] The sublime and the beautiful operate in hierarchical opposition: the sublime is associated with ruggedness, vast scale and fear and the beautiful is associated with the small, smooth, and gently rounded. The use of landscapes contrasting the sublime and the beautiful emphasise the travel writer's establishment of self through difference and subjectivity. Stoddart used the sublime to perform a self subjected and diminished by the scale of the landscape, but equally a self which was strengthened by it. For example, on 1 June on the Carse of Gowry:

> you enter by degrees on the Highlands; at first merely naked hills and downs, they rise slowly into importance, and after a time assume a very picturesque and variegated form, though never the grandeur of Loch Katrine; but the road winds for miles through woods of lofty trees, with detached parcels of cultivated grounds, interspersed with gentlemen's houses and cottages beneath you, which, as the evening began to close in, had an awful and somewhat terrific effect.[37]

In this example, Stoddart built from diminished descriptions of 'at first', 'merely', 'naked' and the female binary oppositional position of softness of 'downs', to the masculine sublime. She used the adverbial forms of 'rise slowly' and 'after a time assume' to increase the sublime height to 'lofty'. She placed both herself and the reader in the highest and most sublime position in the landscape and performed herself above and looking down on the social and the familiar of 'cultivated' and the 'gentlemen's houses and cottages', which are 'beneath' her and the reader 'you'. Thus Stoddart performed herself in an hierarchical position in the landscape, distanced from the signs of society. She performed herself located in the sublime, masculine, location which she rose to by her progress through the landscape. She expressed fear of this location in 'awful' and 'terrific' and, moreover, introduced a sense of the uncanny in making the cultivated and the familiar the objects of her fear.[38] However, the emotion is hedged by 'somewhat' and is limited by only occurring 'as the evening began'. Fear was therefore reduced and restricted and her performance was one of an assured and assertive self. Furthermore, the familiar, the social and the everyday were given connotations of oppression in the writing by their rising 'importance' and Stoddart's need to have the 'cultivated' described as 'detached'. Chard argues that travel offers an escape from the familiar and that travel writing displays the writer's 'sense of liberation from the oppressive limitations of the familiar'.[39] Stoddart's 'sense of liberation' was evident in her treatment of the familiar and the social, over which she asserted her hierarchical position.

Gender expectations and place

Stoddart performed different selves in the city and the countryside. The city was a place of people, where she was not alone, and, although this should suggest a place of familiarity, of safety in society, the city is rather a place of social relations which are built on power and exclusion.[40] For Stoddart, the power is vested in the courts dealing with her divorce, in Hazlitt who controls her financial position, and in their agents in the divorce, who take their instructions from Hazlitt. There is for Stoddart, therefore, greater isolation in the city than there is in the country. The city is not a familiar place to her, but one which imposes an authority to which, as can be seen from her unconventional character, she would not have wished to conform. McDowell argues:

> Places are made through power relations which construct the rules which define boundaries. These boundaries are both social and spatial—they define who belongs to a place and who may be excluded, as well as the location or the site of the experience.[41]
> But, as Judith Okely asserts, 'different groups inhabiting the same spaces can create and shift boundaries by subtle means'.[42]

The boundaries were not shifted by subtle means for Stoddart, however. The city was the space of divorce. She was confined to private and discreet conversations, with Hazlitt and his agents, in the internal spaces of their private homes where she was regarded, not as an independent person, but as a possession of a man who no longer wanted her. There was no shifting of boundaries; in fact boundaries to which Stoddart was unaccustomed were enforced. The space and the people with whom she shared it, enforced her exclusion from public space, not only by means of the social mores and binary distinctions of the nineteenth century, but also by excluding her from contact with Hazlitt during the divorce proceedings. In the city, she was confined to private, internal spaces, to dependence, and to powerlessness. Judith Butler proposes that 'the body is not a "being" but a variable boundary, a surface whose permeability is politically regulated, a signifying practice within a cultural field of gender hierarchy and compulsory heterosexuality'.[43] There are several examples recorded by Stoddart in the journal which highlight the gender hierarchy and her subjectivity to the gender performance imposed on her in the city where she was known to be awaiting divorce. Her dealings with the agent, Adam Bell, for example, illustrate his disregard for her as a woman and act as a signifier of his hierarchy. Her encounters with him reveal her justifiable dislike and mistrust of the man, but also display a notable tolerance and patience when he first cursed her, then entered her bedroom and demanded a kiss: behaviour, which by any standards of time or place, is gender hierarchical.[44] Bell's actions can be seen to be reflecting a sexual double standard where Stoddart's role as a divorcing woman was seen to diminish her moral character and left her vulnerable to sexual assault.[45] Furthermore, following this incident, Bell's actions and contempt for Stoddart were not contradicted by either his wife or his son, which indicated a wider disregard for her social position. The attitude toward Stoddart of William Ritchie, the editor of the *Scotsman*, also illustrated the gender hierarchy. He considered that she should 'marry again' and that she could not remain a single woman and that she 'must needs marry'.[46] Stoddart's recording of the attitudes, however, asserted her opinion and contrasts it with the prevalent views of women's status and value. Indeed, she recorded her opinions of such ideologies, thus performing her difference and her contrasting radical thinking.[47]

In the countryside, Stoddart was not known. She was travelling at the time of year when the Scottish rural practice of exchanging servants and of hiring female itinerant labour was ongoing.[48] This allowed her to move freely in the countryside. She was outside; she was in a public space usually associated with the masculine. It offered independence, power and authority—manly qualities during the era.[49] The city was a closed social space and, in this way, may be read not only as a safer place for a woman, but also as an internal space, a confined space, and therefore a space associated with the feminine and with female authority. Yet, it held less authority for Stoddart than the external, public, masculine space of the countryside—a space which connotes neither the feminine nor the familiar. The masculine, public space of the countryside became the location of self autonomy for Stoddart. The feminine, internal space of the city diminished her authority. Her performance of self in the countryside was the performance of an independent woman. Her performance in the city was one of dependence on the courts and her husband; a space in which her husband's character and performance of identity subjugated her. It was a subjective position from which she sought distance—both cognitive and physical, but the divorce was to be secured by Hazlitt's adultery and so Stoddart was required to accept her subjective position. For example, the solicitor, Mr Gray, sought witness statements about Hazlitt and commented the people were 'the lowest, abandoned blackguards'. Stoddart replied that 'many people had been surprised that he preferred such society to mine; but so it was'.[50] Her concluding statement indicated her pragmatic acceptance of her role. The city might also be said to have been a dangerous and masculine place for Stoddart due to its association with prostitution. Her establishment of distance, achieved by travelling to the countryside, may be seen therefore to have held a liberation from the subjectivity that the city enforced.[51]

The Language of Self and Other

Stoddart's assertion of independent self in the country and subjugated self in the city can also be seen in her performance of herself as either subject or agent in discourse. Stoddart asserted herself as the agent of discourse in the country, but as its subject in the city. This is evidenced by her use of different methods of reporting speech and conversations in the city and in the country. In the city, her conversations are all reported, indirect speech whereas, in the country, most of her conversations are recorded in direct speech. She used inverted commas and reproduced the dialect speech quite accurately. For example, she reproduced conversations in which she was referred to by her conversant as English and therefore different:

> ' I walked 170 miles three weeks ago.' 'Gude sauf us! Ye're no a Crieff woman?' 'No, I am English.' 'Aye, an what part o' England?' 'London.' 'Ou aye, I thocht ye war no a Scotswoman. That's a lang way aff.'[52]

The native or local language, the distinctiveness of individual speech, and the patterns of language which might indicate culture, social order, and geographic location, functioned to perform signs of otherness and to establish Stoddart's identity in the text.

Although English was the language of Stoddart's text and was her native language, on her travels it was variants of English that she heard and recorded and she was able to reproduce the language she heard very accurately. Her recordings of what she heard acted as her evidence of close interaction with the other, not in an emotional, hyperbolic, sense, as Chard might argue, but as a linguistic encounter and a linguistic performance of her engagement.[53] Whereas Chard argues that it was the language of the writer which was used by the traveller to prove their experience, Stoddart proved her experience by importing into her text the words and language of the local people she encountered. She reproduced their words in her writing, producing palimpsestic layers of language and perception which created a performance of engagement—not merely a hyperbolic description of encounter. Stoddart's direct engagement with the language performed a self outside of the city who took personal risk and who asserted herself through those risks. At the same time, the rendition of Scots in its colloquial form also reinforced difference through demarcating class and regional variations, that within the context of the period, reinforced her social and class position as a member of the elite.

The incorporation of the language of the other into a travel text is a performance of another self in another place. It is an accommodation with the other and is evidence of shifting identity.[54] Stoddart's own performance of her variable identities in different locations is indicated by use of indirect and direct speech. When she used direct speech to record the voices of those in the countryside, the inverted commas separated the language of the other from the language of her self, reinforcing difference and separation; whereas, when she repeated Hazlitt's words, for example, they were incorporated into her own text and thus became her own. Richard Sha's discussion of verbal sketching is useful here.[55] He argues that nineteenth-century women sketched and copied the visual and the verbal to subvert the gender boundaries of artful expression which imposed limitations on the extent and depth of women's expression. By sketching, that is producing or copying, their visual and verbal observations in part and not in whole, they were able to explore masculine gendered spaces.

This was a technique, it may be argued, which Stoddart employed when she repeated the curses of others and of Hazlitt. She took parts of what others said and reproduced them as her own work, but yet kept them incomplete, fragmented. They were also framed in a context which made them permissible.[56] Stoddart placed Hazlitt's curses in the field or framework of a discussion of Hazlitt's friend, W. G. Patmore, and their agent, Adam Bell, for example, but introduced the topic of Hazlitt's paramour, Walker, in juxtaposition and in such close proximity to their names that she was able to curse Walker as a 'lying son of a bitch', through repeating Hazlitt's curse of Bell. By situating the cursing in the context of the speech of another and in the context of a discussion with another, it becomes permissible as if it were a performance of the other and not a shifting into the language of the other. Another example, again in reference to Sarah Walker, was her repetition of Hazlitt's words to which she then added her own remark for which Hazlitt's provided justification and contextualization. She reported, 'he thinks Patmore has had her ... I myself think it by no means unlikely'.[57] Stoddart's uses of 'flaming' illustrate the pragmatics of linguistic proximity, the contextualizing importance of intertextuality and the non-linear nature of journal writing.[58]

Conclusion

Stoddart was not submissive; evidence of her character suggests she was intelligent, independent and assertive.[59] It is likely that Stoddart would have sworn obedience to her husband in her nineteenth-century marriage vows and the laws governing the status of women in marriage would also have meant the she became the legal property of her husband. Stoddart was, therefore, subject to the coercions of nineteenth-century law in her performance as wife. However, like many women of her social class, her legal position was counterbalanced by her property ownership and some financial independence.

She did not have to grant Hazlitt a divorce. Yet, she showed few regrets; indeed she commented to Ritchie that she and Hazlitt 'had certainly been in a very uncomfortable state for a long time' and, furthermore, in a conversation with Hazlitt about Sarah Walker following the divorce, she explained that she had suspected his infidelity with Walker, but she had only ever asked for what she wanted.[60] There was feminine subordination in granting Hazlitt's request for a divorce. However, there was also a performance of pragmatism, perhaps reflecting her own non-conformity within marriage and her social location in a group which actively questioned traditional forms of marriage.

Stoddart performed her identity by means of her self determination in the landscape. She established liminal positions in which she was able to perform her self of difference. In her encounter at Crieff, for example, she was able to perform herself as an English woman, different from the working Scots men and women and thus performed her cultural and social position. By creating physical distance between her business in the city and her pleasure in the countryside she was able to perform her different selves in those locations: a subjective self, encountering change from married to divorced woman, and a reflective self engaged in her observations of the land and its people. In her records of expenditure and of her discussions with Ritchie, Bell and Hazlitt, she recorded the difference in attitudes of the men she encountered and herself towards her right to financial support. Ritchie urged her to remarry, Bell considered her undeserving and Hazlitt directed her to her brother for loans. The difference in attitudes she showed in the conversations enabled a performance of her as assertive and determined and not to be coerced. Her language choices in describing people, such as the judge at her divorce, show her to have been outspoken in her opinions and blunt and yet she showed a different woman, a woman with respect for the law, in her concerns about the oath of calumny. The positions of difference that Stoddart created enabled her performance of an independent, unconventional woman to be established and identified clearly in contrast with places of culture, gender and ideology.

Sarah Stoddart Hazlitt produced a travel journal which conformed to the paradigms of Romantic literature, combining the exploration of the external space of the landscapes and the internal space of self in the process of change of identity from a married to a divorced woman. Her *Journal* was a private record of experience in public spaces. She recorded the verbal and the visual of the scenes and the people she encountered and she commented unreservedly. In her walking, she imprinted her physical self through her footprint placed on the landscapes of town and country and performed and discovered her different selves in the changing locations. She illustrated the boundaries of social, geographic and gendered space through her language, her observations and her journey. Stoddart's *Journal*, by its published location as an appendix to Hazlitt's text, has diminished the text and the woman to a performance of William Hazlitt's masculine identity. A recontextualization of the text as her story establishes the *Journal* as an autonomous Romantic text, which created a performance of the independent self of a woman of strength and determination.

Notes

[1] All references to the *Journal* are to 'Journal of My Trip to Scotland', published in the Le Gallienne edition of William Hazlitt (1894) *Liber Amoris or the new pygmalion with additional matter now printed for the first time from the original manuscript*, Richard Le Gallienne (Ed.) (London: Elkin Matthews). 500 copies of the edition were privately printed by subscription: 400 for British and 100 copies for American subscribers. The journal is introduced by Le Gallienne as 'Mrs Hazlitt's diary', but is identified as, 'Journal of My Trip to Scotland'. To distinguish her from her husband, Sarah, who was known as Sarah Hazlitt after her marriage, is identified here by her maiden and married names, Stoddart Hazlitt, which is abbreviated to Stoddart.

[2] Willard Hallam Bonner (Ed.) (1959) *The Journals of Sarah and William Hazlitt 1822–1831*, University of Buffalo Studies, 24(3) (Buffalo: University of Buffalo), pp. 171–252.

[3] A notable exception is Betty Hagglund (2010) *Tourists and Travellers: women's non-fictional writing about Scotland* (Bristol: Channel View Publications).

[4] Jean Jacques Rousseau (1782) *The Confessions*, trans. W. Conyngham Mallory, available at http://philosophy.eserver.org/rousseau-confessions.txt [last accessed 9 July 2011]. Another example of the genre is Thomas De Quincey (1886) *Confessions of an English Opium-Eater* (London: George Routledge and Sons; first published 1821). Available at Project Gutenberg: http://www.gutenberg.org/files/2040/2040-h/2040-h.htm [last accessed 9 July 2011]. Recommended reading: Susan M. Levin (1998) *The Romantic Art of Confession: De Quincey, Musset, Sand, Lamb, Hogg, Frémy, Soulié, Janin* (London: Camden House).

[5] A. C. Grayling (2000) *The Quarrel of the Age: the life and times of William Hazlitt* (London: Weidenfeld & Nicolson), p. 293.

[6] Sonia Hofkosh (1998) *Sexual Politics and the Romantic Author* (Cambridge: Cambridge University Press), p. 115.

[7] Ibid., p.116.

[8] René Wellek (1963) *Concepts of Criticism*, ed. S. G. Nichols Jr. (New Haven: Yale University Press), p. 326.
[9] Terry Eagleton (1983) *Literary Theory: an introduction* (Oxford: Blackwell), p. 28.
[10] Ibid., p. 11.
[11] E. V. Lucas (Ed.) (1935) *The Complete Letters of Charles and Mary Lamb* (London: Dent and Methuen), 3 Vols.
[12] Lucas, *Letters*, vol. 1, p. 372.
[13] Ibid., pp. 374–375.
[14] Grayling, *The Quarrel of the Age*, p. 117.
[15] *Journal*, p. 243.
[16] *Journal*, pp. 318–319
[17] *Journal*, p. 328.
[18] For further discussion of intimacy after marital separation, see Katie Barclay (2011) Intimacy and the Life Cycle in the Marital Relationships of the Scottish Elite during the Long Eighteenth Century, *Women's History Review*, 20(2), pp. 189–206.
[19] *Journal*, p. 299.
[20] Grayling, *The Quarrel of the Age*, p. 117.
[21] *Journal*, p. 326.
[22] Lucas, *Letters*, vol. 2, p. 39, quoted in Grayling, *The Quarrel of the Age*, p. 118.
[23] Grayling, *The Quarrel of the Age*, pp. 242–243.
[24] Bryan Waller Proctor (1877) *An Autobiographical Fragment* (London: George Bell), p. 180.
[25] During their marriage, Hazlitt had had several affairs. Patmore commented that 'he was always in love with somebody or other' (Grayling, *The Quarrel of the Age*, p. 261). Sarah and William remained friends after the divorce. Their closeness and frankness with each other is evident in their exchanges recorded by Stoddart in the journal. Sarah read everything he wrote and kept cuttings of his essays. It was she who wrote his death notice for *The Times* and there is evidence (Grayling, *The Quarrel of the Age*, p. 344) to suggest that it was Sarah who had his tombstone raised and wrote the encomium, which closes with the words, 'This stone is raised by one whose heart is with him, in his grave.'
[26] Mary Lyndon Shanley (1993) *Feminism, Marriage and the Law in Victorian England* (Princeton: Princeton University Press), p. 22.
[27] Alan Soble (Ed.) (2006) *Sex from Plato to Paglia: a philosophical encyclopedia* (Westport: Greenwood Publishing), vol. 1, p. 862. The Study Panel of the Free Church of Scotland (1988) *Marriage and Divorce: a report of the study panel of the Free Church of Scotland* (Edinburgh: The Free Church of Scotland), p. 11.
[28] Hazlitt stayed at Renton in the Borders of Scotland, where he worked on a second volume of *Table Talk*. Grayling, *The Quarrel of the Age*, p. 275.
[29] Stoddart secured a settlement and an income. Under the terms of the divorce, Hazlitt agreed to pay all his son's expenses but it was to be paid to Sarah. £150 per annum was agreed (*Journal*, p. 255). Custody of children under English law was always granted to the father (See Shanley, *Feminism*); however, the agreement records that Sarah was to have 'free access to him at all times' (*Journal*, p. 255). Stoddart retained her property and her original independent income both after the marriage and after the divorce (See Grayling, *The Quarrel of the Age*, pp. 117, 121, 139).
[30] *Journal*, pp. 243–244.
[31] *Journal*, p. 245.
[32] For further discussion, see T. Young (1994) *Travellers in Africa: British travelogues, 1850–1900* (Manchester: Manchester University Press) and S. Morgan (1996) *Place Matters: gendered geography in Victorian women's travel books about South East Asia* (New Brunswick: Princeton University Press).

[33] Hofkosh, *Sexual Politics*, p. 116.
[34] *Journal*, p. 282.
[35] Chloe Chard (1999) *Pleasure and Guilt on the Grand Tour: travel writing and imaginative geography 1600–1830* (Manchester: Manchester University Press), p. 108.
[36] Further reading: E. Burke (1987) *A Philosophical Enquiry into the Origin of Our Ideas of the Sublime and the Beautiful*, ed. J. T. Boulton (Oxford: Basil Blackwell; first published 1757-59); I. Kant (2003) *Observations on the Feeling of the Beautiful and the Sublime*, trans. John T. Goldthwaite (Berkeley: University of California Press; first published in 1799); F. Ferguson (1992) *Solitude and the Sublime: romanticism and the aesthetics of individuation* (London: Routledge)
[37] *Journal*, p. 282.
[38] J. Strachey (trans) (1955) *The Complete Psychological Works of Sigmund Freud, Vol XVII (1917–1919): an infantile neurosis and other works* (London: Hogarth Press). The idea of the uncanny is raised by Freud in a discussion of the devices used by writers and story-tellers to create uncertainty in the reader about whether something real or familiar has sinister properties. The function is to raise a sense of fear of what might be hidden in something known.
[39] Chard, *Pleasure and Guilt*, p. 186.
[40] D. Massey (1991) A Global Sense of Place, *Marxism Today*, 24–29 June; N. Smith (1993) Homeless/Global: scaling places, in J. Bird, B. Curtis, T. Putnam, G. Robertson & L. Tickner (Eds) *Mapping the Futures: local cultures, global change* (London: Routledge), pp. 87–119.
[41] L. McDowell (1999) *Gender, Identity, and Place: understanding feminist geographies* (Cambridge: Polity Press), p. 5.
[42] Judith Okely (1996) *Own or Other Culture* (London: Routledge), p. 3.
[43] Judith Butler (1999) *Gender Trouble*, 2nd edn (London: Routledge), p. 177.
[44] *Journal*, pp. 294–295.
[45] See K. Barclay (2011) Sex and the Scottish Self in the Long-Eighteenth Century, in Jodi Campbell, Elizabeth Ewan & Heather Parker (Eds), *Shaping Scottish Identity: Family, Nation and the World Beyond* (Guelph: Guelph Centre for Scottish Studies).
[46] *Journal*, pp. 245, 334.
[47] See, for example, *Journal*, p. 334, for her response to Ritchie and her response to Bell's suggestion of how she might live in Edinburgh and earn a living as a tutor.
[48] *Journal*, p. 284.
[49] See A. Clark (1995) *The Struggle for the Breeches: gender and the making of the British working class* (London: Rivers Owen); M. McCormack (2005) *The Independent Man: citizenship and gender politics in Georgian England* (Manchester: Manchester University Press).
[50] *Journal*, p. 258.
[51] For further reading, see for example: Laura Gowing (2000) 'The Freedom of the Streets': women and social place, 1560–1640, in Paul Griffiths & Mark Jenner (Eds) *Londonopolis: essays in the cultural and social history of early modern London* (Manchester: Manchester University Press), pp. 130–153; Anu Korhonen (2008) To See and To Be Seen: beauty in the early modern London street, *Journal of Early Modern History*, 12, pp. 335–360; Brian Cowan (2001) What was Masculine about the Public Sphere? Gender and the coffeehouse milieu in post-restoration England, *History Workshop Journal*, 51, pp. 127–158.
[52] *Journal*, p. 283.
[53] Chard, *Pleasure and Guilt*.
[54] For a discussion on Accommodation Theory see Howard Giles, Justine Coupland & Nikolas Coupland (1992) *Contexts of Accommodation: developments in applied sociolinguistics* (Cambridge: Cambridge University Press).

[55] Richard C. Sha (1998) *The Visual and Verbal Sketch in British Romanticism* (Philadelphia: University of Pennsylvania Press).
[56] Erving Goffman (1974) *Frame Analysis: an essay on the organization of experience* (New York: Harper & Row).
[57] *Journal*, p. 302.
[58] Flaming is a term used in discourse analysis to refer to the use of adjectival phrases or words, which raise the emotional impact of language. Swearing and cursing are examples. As a feature of language it functions to insult, but its purpose is to provoke response.
[59] See, for example, letters from Mary Lamb to Sarah Stoddart in Lucas, *Letters*, vol. 2, pp. 359–360, and Stoddart's conversation with Ritchie in *Journal*, p. 334, in which she asserts her intention not to remarry.
[60] *Journal*, p. 330.

Writing Women's Histories: women in the colonial record of nineteenth-century Hong Kong

Jane Berney

Women rarely appear in the colonial record and when they do, it is usually as a problematic group. However, just occasionally a woman does appear in her own right. This articles looks at one such instance and uses it to demonstrate how a seemingly isolated piece of evidence can be used to demonstrate the accepted social behaviour of women and men in nineteenth-century colonial Hong Kong and how individuals negotiated their way round these norms to achieve what they wanted through a performance that married the cultural preconceptions of their audience with their own notion of self.

In July 1867, the Governor of Hong Kong, Sir Richard Graves MacDonnell, wrote a frank and uncompromising letter to the British Consul of Canton, D. B. Robertson, explaining that as a British official he was unable to acquiesce in the latter's request to return to Canton a young Chinese woman who had arrived in Hong Kong, seeking sanctuary from an oppressive master. Why the Governor of Hong Kong should act in such a manner is extraordinary in itself, but what makes this incident even more unusual is that the testimony of the woman herself has been preserved in the colonial record: MacDonnell sent to the Colonial Office in London a copy of the woman's statement explaining why she had ran away and why she refused to return to Canton. This is a very rare example of a woman's opinion being asked and considered worth repeating and respecting. As in other locales, the more usual way for a woman to be mentioned in the colonial record in Hong Kong is as a problematic group (such as prostitutes) or via court records. In either case, the actions and words of the women are viewed and recorded from the perspective of the (male) authorities. The issue is made more complicated in Hong Kong as western perceptions of Chinese women are also invoked. This paper both explains what was going on in this particular case and uses it to demonstrate how a seemingly isolated piece of evidence can shed light on Hong Kong society as a whole and how individuals negotiated the public arena of that society by performing the role demanded of them by cultural norms.

On 4 July 1867, a young woman, Tang-San-Ki, was found in a brothel in Hong Kong and brought before the magistrates. This was part of the routine work of the Inspector of Brothels, whose job was to search for unregistered establishments and to arrange for the periodic medical examination of the women working in any brothel, registered or not. The Inspector of Brothels was empowered to so act by the Registrar-General under the aegis of the 1857 Contagious Diseases Ordinance (CDO). The latter was replaced by a revised ordinance in 1867, partly because the Colonial Office in London instructed the Hong Kong government to introduce legislation that followed the 1866 UK Act, but partly because many in Hong Kong believed that the 1857 CDO had become increasingly easy to evade and thus was failing to protect either the military from the scourge of venereal disease or young women from brothel slavery.[1] During the six months or so in which Tang-San-Ki's fate was being discussed, the 1857 CDO was still in operation but the new CDO was the ongoing subject of much heated discussion between the authorities in Hong Kong and London. The 1867 CDO finally came into force on 1 June 1868.

Part of the rationale behind both CDOs was that by inspecting and registering (in the period 1857 to 1867) or licensing (1868 onwards) brothels, the colonial authorities could ensure that any woman was there willingly. It was therefore entirely commonplace for a young woman like Tang-San-Ki to be questioned; her response and the subsequent reaction to her statement were not so commonplace. Her statement was written down by colonial officials who accepted without question her version of events, even when it was subsequently disputed by her master and consular officials in Canton. Thus, the sentiments expressed by Tang-San-Ki and the reaction of the authorities in Hong Kong, Canton and London to her situation can be used to understand the complex relationships between colonised and colonisers, as well as that between metropole and periphery and the protagonists' view of themselves within the context of empire.

Kathleen Wilson has noted that an individual's sense of identity is based upon 'temporally specific ideas about the self and its social location'.[2] Within the context of empire, these ideas are coalesced around notions of difference. It is this notion of difference that underpins the roles played by the British officials in their reaction to Tang. Whilst the roles performed varied with the official position of the protagonist, the underlying assumption remained that the Chinese were different to the British in key respects and that Britishness was defined by these differences. For example the British believed that they 'through superior knowledge and ... high moral standards improved the lot of the native population', in contrast to the Chinese who in the eyes of the British 'lacked moral aptitude and were motivated solely by a desire for self gain'.[3] More pertinently, the position of women within 'oriental' societies was considered proof of the latter's lack of civilization. Practices such as 'sati' in India, foot binding and widow chastity in China were viewed with distaste by the British and provided justification for the imperial project. However, Catherine Hall has noted that the colonists' view of natives was often contradictory as 'they were at one and the same time objects of contempt—effeminate and dependent—and objects of terror and fear, rapists, torturers and murderers'.[4] In Hong Kong, this contradiction was very apparent, as not only were the British outnumbered by Chinese living in the colony, but they were also geographically surrounded by a hostile China, yet most colonists considered themselves superior to the Chinese in every respect.

Tang-San-Ki's statement, as reproduced in the correspondence sent to London, is as follows:

> I am of Canton, and 18 years of age. I am not married.
>
> About five or six years ago my parents sold me for about $50 to a writer of the surname Lee who is employed in the Office of the Chief Justice, Canton. Lee wanted to sell me as a prostitute, I refused. He used to beat me and did not give me enough food.
>
> On the 8th June last I ran away into a house the master of which I did not know. On the same day that man took me to another house, a family house and kept me there for two days. I do not know the name of the Master of that house, but it is Ho-Yin (?) Street, Western Suburbs, a man and woman belonging to that house brought me to Hong Kong by the steamer, and afterwards sold me for $98, to a man (pointing out Lo – a– Kit) who lives in another house. I was put into a Brothel, where I was found last night. I wish to go back to that Brothel. I will not willingly go back to Canton, for my Master ill-treated me very grossly.
>
> I saw the $98 paid for me. It was paid in Lo-a-Kit's house. I lived there two days before I went to the Brothel. Lo-a-Kit paid the money to those who brought me from Canton.
>
> I know a man called A-Tai. I stayed in his house when I first came to Hong Kong. He brought A-Kit to his, A-Tai's house and there made the bargain about me. I do not know the name of its Street, where that house is situate, nor can I take any one to it. I am a stranger. A-Tai told me that the man who brought me here was his relative.[5]

Although the statement was translated from Chinese into English and thus we do not hear Tang-San-Ki's exact words, the statement does provide certain details about her life and more pertinently these are the details of her life-story that she felt comfortable disclosing to an audience of colonial officials and believed that the audience would accept. As Chanfrault-Duchet has argued 'a tension exists between self and society, which is resolved by the narrative presenting a unique self which can also be recognised by society'.[6] The statement was delivered by Tang as a response to a series of questions rather than written down by her as a coherent whole and so in many respects it is formulaic, but the very act of writing it down transformed it into a text and it was this text to which the colonial authorities responded. Moreover it was a text written in English so it became the life-story of Tang as understood by the colonial authorities; their apparent readiness to accept it at face value suggest they may have heard similar stories before and believed them. Thus, the text represented for both parties a truth they were willing to accept. For Tang, even though she was performing a role that the colonial authorities were able to accept as an authentic or 'true' representation of a Chinese woman, she still had to be comfortable with this role as a 'true' representation of her individual self. As a result within her narrative, she had to both highlight her own individual actions (i.e. 'I ran away', 'I refused') and how her life story conformed to accepted norms of behaviour (i.e. 'my parents sold me'). In this way, Tang was able to reconcile her actions in the narrative with her performance before the colonial authorities to create a plausible whole.

The translation was made by Cecil Clementi Smith, a fluent Chinese speaker who had come to Hong Kong under the cadet scheme in 1862 and who by 1867 was the Registrar-General, also known as the Protector of the Chinese. As Registrar-General, Smith was the colonial official who had most direct contact with the Chinese population, as it was him that they were told to approach in the first instance if they had any problems with the authorities.[7] Smith's involvement in the affair was limited to this translation, although he was heavily involved in the drafting of the 1867 CDO and would have been well aware of the issues surrounding its implementation. It is safe to assume that the translation is accurate; the incompetence of translators was a frequent complaint, but not one directed against Smith. The wording used would be subject to the cultural preconceptions of Smith: there is, however, no evidence to suggest that his view of the Chinese or the role of the British in Hong Kong was any different to MacDonnell's or any other colonial official whether in Hong Kong or London.

The statement appears to offer a limited number of facts, beyond that a young woman had run away from Canton and wanted to stay in Hong Kong. However, a closer reading reveals much more about Tang-San-Ki's life and from that one can gain a good deal of insight into the lives of women in China and Hong Kong in the mid nineteenth century. It seems likely she was from a poor family as it was very common for such families to sell their daughters to wealthier families to work as domestic servants when young and possibly as prostitutes when older. When Europeans in Hong Kong protested about this, describing it as slavery by any other name, the Chinese response was that it was a form of charity and better than infanticide which would be the likely fate of unwanted girl babies otherwise.[8] That this was an entirely plausible if tragic outcome was borne witness by many Western travellers to China.[9] Either way, it was not an unusual arrangement, although to be sold at about twelve or thirteen to be a servant was rarer as the more common age was five or six. Girls of Tang-San-Ki's age at the date of her sale were more usually sold to brothel keepers to work as a prostitute or to a wealthy family to be a concubine.[10] Tang-San-Ki's statement does not say what her position in the Lee household was; presumably neither she nor the Hong Kong authorities considered it relevant.

Tang-San-Ki said she 'ran away', indicating that she went of her free will and was not kidnapped. The kidnapping of women to be sold into prostitution was considered to be a problem in China by both the Chinese and British authorities. It was also a crime in both jurisdictions. From Tang-San Ki's perspective, if she had admitted to being kidnapped she ran the risk of being returned to her master in Canton, as she was his property under Chinese law. The expression 'ran away' also suggests that she did not have bound feet, as running would have been impossible, but this could just be an effect of the translation. The evidence regarding bound feet and the poorer classes is inconclusive. Certainly the elite Han Chinese of Canton would have had their feet bound, as is borne out by testimonies of Western visitors to the province who were both fascinated and horrified by the practice.[11] Poorer girls in rural areas were less likely to have their feet bound as the need for them to work in the fields was greater than the need for them to marry into the richer sectors of society, but it was not unknown. John Davis, writing in 1857, commented that 'this odious custom extends lower down in the scale of society than might have been expected from its disabling effect upon those who have to labour for their subsistence'.[12] Edward D. Prime, writing in 1872, estimated that only a quarter of the female population had bound feet; however he also noted that it was 'not altogether peculiar to the higher classes, nor to those who are exempt from labour'.[13] The Qing emperors, who were Manchu and whose women did not bind their feet, tried unsuccessfully to outlaw foot binding.

Although Tang-San-Ki insisted in her statement that she was taken willingly to Hong Kong, whether she was willing to be a prostitute in Hong Kong, or aware that this was her most likely fate, is less clear; she simply stated that she wishes to be returned to the brothel, not Canton. Even though Tang-San-Ki claimed she ran away to avoid being sold into prostitution by her master, her statement was not as contradictory as it might seem. Prostitution and pimping were both made criminal offences by the Yongzheng Emperor in 1723 as part of a wide-ranging attempt by the Qing dynasty to redefine sexual morality within gender norms, rather than by 'status' norms.[14] Prior to this, those of 'mean' status, as opposed to 'commoner' or 'official' status, were considered as sexually debauched by default. 'Mean' status included female slaves who were therefore sexually available to their masters, and 'yue' households, groups of entertainers, including prostitutes, who performed at celebrations. The Qing reforms were a deliberate change in policy, to ensure gender dictated appropriate sexual behaviour rather than status. For example, masters were now required to make female slaves their concubines if they wished to have a sexual relationship with them and arrange for servants to be married, rather than pursue or allow sexual relations with and between slaves on a casual basis. As Sommer explains, 'these measures extended commoner norms of marriage and chastity to servile women and in conjunction with the ban on prostitution, extended the prohibition of extramarital intercourse to all women'.[15] Officials were also encouraged to actively suppress prostitution or face punishment themselves. The laws were extended in 1772 and 1811 by the Qianlong Emperor, but prostitution did not die out.[16] Sommer suggests this is because the selling of sex was not made illegal; the emphasis was on illicit sex. The pimps and matchmakers were punished, but the women were usually treated as victims. As many of them had been sold, they could not be returned to their families so the magistrates found husbands for them.

Sommer's review of court cases has shown that the women's testimonies 'always end with a formulaic plea for mercy and a statement that they are willing to "cong liang"—in a post 1723 context, the term simply meant to quit prostitution and marry'.[17] Given this, Tang's comments were entirely consistent: she was playing the wronged servant and demonstrating the impropriety of sending her back to a master who was willing to transgress (by selling her into prostitution) accepted norms of behaviour. Although the women in the cases unearthed by Sommer express a desire to marry, they would have had no choice in their future husband and once married would have found it almost impossible to leave their husbands. This may well have influenced Tang's desire to run away: she may be the wronged party but the justice system in China may have condemned her, in her eyes, to a fate worse than prostitution.

As such, Tang's statement can be understood as entirely in keeping with the expected performance of a women accused of prostitution: she was a victim and therefore should be saved from an ignoble fate rather than punished. For good measure she adds her master beat and starved her, as if to compound his guilt and heighten her status as a victim. It also fitted in with the view of the colonial authorities with regard to the position of women and servants in Chinese society as a whole. Most colonial officials laboured under the impression that all Chinese women were tantamount to slaves, forbidden to leave their houses and because of their bound feet very restricted in their movements. Research into communities in mainland China are increasingly showing that women could and did work; even with bound feet, elite women could embroider or write poems to earn an income. Other women were extensively employed in the silk factories and cotton mills, as weaving was performed sitting down.[18] Indeed, the Qing attempted to encourage women to work in textiles as an alternative to working in prostitution. As one leading jurist commented, it was inappropriate to condemn women who became prostitutes out of economic necessity if the Imperial State did not provide sufficient opportunities for paid alternatives.[19] There is also evidence to suggest that women in the Canton region were particularly independent. For example, women who worked in the silk industry developed the concept of a 'delayed transfer marriage' through which marriage was either refused, unconsummated or a substitute wife found; others established 'spinster houses' or 'vegetarian halls' where unmarried women could live in safety and ensure that when they died there would be someone to honour them.[20] However, Tang does not seem to have viewed this as an alternative and indeed none of the other parties involved considered it either. Possibly a brothel in Hong Kong was viewed by Tang as a safe haven, her only alternative, as having been sold she could not return to her family.

Notwithstanding the Qing reforms, prostitution seems to have flourished, though, as Yeh has pointed out, it moved from the public to the private arena, particularly in the major commercial centres such as Canton.[21] The active collusion of civic officials was essential for brothels to remain open for business, and this seems to have been readily available. Lee, Tang's master, did not admit that he wanted to sell her to a brothel and as an official he could not without incurring punishment, but that he would be willing to do so seems to be accepted by both Tang and Robertson, the British Consul in Canton who chose to act on Lee's behalf (see below).[22] At the same time, nowhere in the correspondence does Robertson admit that Tang was mistreated by her master or that he could or would sell her into prostitution. Robertson accepted the Chinese view that Tang was her master's property and therefore should be returned to him; how he treated her was irrelevant. In fact Robertson was more concerned that once in Hong Kong, Tang would be a prostitute rather than that a similar fate could be hers if she returned to Canton.

Tang's case was complicated by the fact that she seemed willing to stay and, by implication, work in a brothel in Hong Kong. It is entirely plausible that she was told to say this by the brothel keeper who was, after all, in the room with her when she made her statement. It is highly likely that the brothel keeper was well aware that the local colonial authorities were comfortable with women working as prostitutes provided they were not acting under coercion. Tang confirmed the brothel keeper paid $98 for her and she may well have regarded this as a binding debt: it was customary for prostitutes to be so indebted to the brothel-keeper and in theory they could work their way out of the debt, though many found this to be impossible. The price paid for girls varied from $2 to $200. The brothel keeper would soon gain a return on this investment: the price for deflowering a virgin was $50 to $60, thereafter the price per night started at $2.[23] Tang does not however confirm or deny that she was willing to work as a prostitute; it would seem to all concerned that what she did in Hong Kong was irrelevant to the real issue at stake. It is also worth pointing out that brothels did not solely employ prostitutes: cooks, servants, seamstresses, laundresses, bookkeepers, kitchen staff, restaurant staff and runners were all necessary to varying degrees, depending upon the size of the brothel.[24]

From the colonial authorities' point of view, because Tang said she was quite willingly in Hong Kong and she had not been kidnapped, that would normally have been the end of the matter. She would have been returned to the brothel and registered as a prostitute if applicable. However, her master in Canton, via the local Chinese magistracy, had appealed to the British Consul in Canton, requesting him to contact the authorities in Hong Kong to send her back as she was his property.[25] The Consul, Robertson, wrote to the Governor of Hong Kong and there was a protracted correspondence between the two on the matter. As Consul, Robertson reported to the Foreign Office, not the Colonial Office; his primary role was to liaise with the Chinese authorities on Britain's behalf, particularly with regard to the imposition of import and export duties and extraterritorial law, by which British subjects in the Treaty ports remained bound by British law, rather than Chinese law.[26] Governors of Hong Kong were principally concerned with trade and law and order within the colony and so it is perhaps not surprising that consuls frequently disagreed with the Governors of Hong Kong on the appropriate action to take in the case of disputes between China and Britain or Hong Kong.

Things were made more difficult in this case by the personalities of the two men involved. Robertson by 1867 had been in China for over twenty years at various consular posts and was relatively sympathetic to the Chinese and unsympathetic to Westerners who transgressed the rules. He was equally unsympathetic towards high-handed behaviour by Hong Kong officials or residents. He considered MacDonnell to be ignorant of Chinese customs, unlike himself, and difficult.[27] MacDonnell, as Governor of Hong Kong would have considered himself of equal, if not superior, status to a consular official and this resulted in constant tension between the two officials. MacDonnell was, moreover, authoritarian by nature, indifferent to public opinion, not afraid to state his opinion to officials in London or elsewhere in a forthright manner and, as a qualified lawyer and experienced colonial official, he was confident that his interpretations were correct. Whatever the personalities of the two men, both were reacting to Tang's case in the manner that they deemed appropriate to their position. As the Governor of a British Crown Colony, such as Hong Kong, MacDonnell would have had no hesitation in assuming that he was in a position to determine the fate of the colonised, collectively or individually. Robertson, however, as a British official working in China with the Chinese authorities, presented himself in the role of go-between, the reasonable official deciding the case on its legal merits.

The case became an active dispute between Robertson and MacDonnell, hinging on whether Tang's case should be decided under Chinese or British law. Robertson contended that the girl was clearly kidnapped and must be restored to her rightful owner in accordance with Chinese law.[28] MacDonnell disagreed and on the 22 July 1867, he wrote to Robertson that he:

> has perused your despatch several times, but can extract no other meaning than that as British consul you call upon a British Governor to lay violent hands on a woman found at Hong Kong, and force her to return to a country where a person resides who claims a 'property' in that woman.

MacDonnell claimed this to be an 'extraordinary demand' that had no basis in law. Robertson argued that the principles of international law meant that in this instance Chinese law had to take precedence over British/ Hong Kong law. MacDonnell countered that in accordance with Hong Kong law, the 'only question to consider is the wish of the woman herself'. It would appear that he interviewed Tang-San-Ki herself to ascertain her wishes; although there is no written record of the interview, he told Robertson that she had said that she 'preferred dying to being sent back'. MacDonnell concluded, therefore, that there was 'no room whatever to doubt that she now fully elects to remain here and whilst she conducts herself peacefully she is entitled to and shall receive all the protection which this

Government can afford her'. MacDonnell further added that he would not send her back even if the Emperor of China asked him to do so![29]

MacDonnell did, however, refer the matter to the Colonial Secretary in London, Lord Carnarvon, who referred the matter to Lord Stanley, the Foreign Secretary. The latter sought the legal opinion of the Advocate-General, who concluded that MacDonnell was correct in refusing to return Tang to Canton not just because 'British Law forbids all recognition of rights of property over a human being within British territory', but also because no crime had been committed if there was no evidence of abduction.[30] Both Carnarvon and Stanley accepted the Advocate-General's opinion as definitive and instructed MacDonnell and Robertson to do likewise.

But why did MacDonnell act as he did? His correspondence with London on other matters does not suggest that he was sympathetic to the Chinese or to women in general. Christopher Munn has argued that he was one of the most repressive Governors and quite blatantly introduced legislation that discriminated against the Chinese, particularly with regard to night passes, registration and gambling.[31] When a Chinese delegation petitioned him in 1866 to request that he withdraw the proposals for a registration ordinance, he bluntly refused on the grounds that 'the peculiar habits of the Chinese themselves & the crimes of their countrymen have necessitated the recent legislation'.[32] Furthermore, in the debates in the Legislative council concerning the 1867 CDO, he argued that the original legislation of 1857 needed to be revised and made more stringent because the prostitutes had found ways to avoid inspection due to 'collusion among the Chinese who form more than 19/20 of the population, aided by the corruption of the police'.[33] MacDonnell insisted that brothels should be licensed, rather than just registered, because a license could be revoked and this was a necessary sanction, because of all the abuses that went on in Chinese brothels.[34]

It is tempting to believe that MacDonnell was being mischievous as he clearly did not get on with Robertson. But beyond personal animosity, the authorities in Hong Kong had, since its inception as a colony, been vociferous in their desire to eliminate slavery. This was because the cultural preconceptions of colonial officials maintained that slavery was endemic within China, but could not and would not be tolerated within the British Empire. Indeed, MacDonnell expressed his surprise that Robertson would wish Tang to be sent back as she has escaped 'of her own free will' from slavery.[35] When the first CDO was discussed with the Colonial Office in 1856/7, the then Colonial Secretary, Labouchere, only allowed brothels to be registered as a way of preventing slavery.[36] When in 1866/7 the revised CDO was under discussion, brothel slavery was again an issue and again it was argued that licensing was necessary to prevent slavery.[37] In both cases, the argument was that under a licensing or registration system, all prostitutes had to appear before the Registrar-General and confirm that they had not been kidnapped, or sold into prostitution, and by implication, kept as slaves. In turn the Registrar-General would tell each girl that, under English Law, she was free to leave the brothel if she so wished, irrespective of whether she had been kidnapped or sold. So by listening to Tang, MacDonnell was showing quite clearly to the metropolitan authorities that the system was working. He was also performing his role as a British official within the British Empire, who was doing his best to ensure that British values were being upheld and these included an abhorrence of, and refusal to tolerate, slavery.

MacDonnell's acceptance of Tang's claim that she had not been kidnapped is more surprising, because the authorities were of the view that the kidnapping of women and children was rife. In 1865, Ordinance number 4 'Offences against the Person' was passed and included several clauses detailing the penalties for kidnapping.[38] A year after Tang arrived in Hong Kong, the following proclamation was published in the Hong Kong Government Gazette:

> Whereas the crimes of child-stealing and kidnapping have much increased in this Colony and its Dependencies of late, and a new law has provided for the flogging of offenders convicted of these crimes:—it is hereby notified that if any person shall give such information, evidence or assistance, as that any kidnapper, decoy or child –stealer be thereby convicted and flogged (or being a women shall be convicted only) then such person shall receive a reward of $20 from the Colonial Treasury.[39]

This proclamation is worthy of note, not only because it confirms that kidnapping was a cause for concern, but that the authorities appear to be at a loss as to how to prevent it, other than by imposing harsher regulations. But even these measures proved ineffectual and in 1873 an 'Ordinance for the Protection of Woman and Young Girls' was passed, specifically to stop kidnapping and the 'Po Leung Kok' was established by the Chinese elite with the same aim.[40]

As mentioned above, the prevalence of kidnapping was a concern of the Chinese authorities on the mainland. Robertson was well aware of the problem and so found it easy to believe that Tang had been kidnapped (rather than absconded) and should be returned to her master in China, in accordance with Chinese law. For Robertson, as an employee of the Foreign Office, his major concern was the maintenance of a good relationship with China. Consuls were instructed to 'avoid giving just cause of offence to officials' and it seems likely that this was Robertson's primary concern, and overrode any feelings of disquiet he may have had with regard to the treatment of women within Chinese society.[41] Although he described officials in Canton as 'reasonable and sagacious', he also wrote that the chief fault of the Chinese was 'that of a proud and sensitive people, unwilling to show openly their inward realization that their ancient civilization was paling before a newer one'.[42] Clearly his view of the Chinese was not so different to that of MacDonnell.

MacDonnell did not question whether it was right or wrong for Tang to live in a brothel and work as a prostitute, so long as she had come to Hong Kong willingly and knew that she was free to leave the brothel whenever she wished. This was because the colonial authorities accepted prostitution as a fact of life and only sought to curtail it if it threatened law and order or the health of soldiers.[43] During the discussions in the Legislative council and with the metropole concerning the introduction of the 1857 CDO or its revision in 1867, there was never any suggestion that prostitution should be outlawed. An inquiry in 1878 into the 1867 CDO condemned the workings of the ordinance, but again there was no discussion as to whether prostitution should be curbed or prevented.[44]

Once the metropolitan authorities decided that Tang was free to remain in Hong Kong, she disappeared from the colonial record, as she was no longer a problem. One has to assume that she returned to the brothel, despite MacDonnell telling her she could leave, as there were very few options for a young woman in Hong Kong in the 1860s. There is no evidence of any charitable organisations operating in Hong Kong at this time that rescued and reformed prostitutes, although there was a medical mission and a missionary school for young girls. The 1867 Census records that there were approximately 32,000 Chinese women living in Hong Kong, out of a total population of 117,000. Of these 22,000 lived in Victoria, 3,000 lived in the villages and 7,000 were classified as boat people (Dan/Tanka).[45] The census does not record the occupations of the women, though it does record that there were 174 brothels. For the vast majority, the main occupations would have been within the family, such as child rearing and agriculture, though some could have been teachers in government or missionary schools and there is some evidence of entrepreneurial activity beyond the domestic sphere.[46] Just over a thousand were employed by Europeans. The Dan/Tanka were a distinct ethnic group who lived in boats in the waters of Hong Kong and the women (who did not bind their feet) earned a living transporting people back and forth across the harbour. However, the Tanka were scorned by the Han Chinese as an inferior class consisting mainly of pirates and prostitutes, so it is unlikely that Tang would have sought refuge amongst them.[47]

One alternative to working as a prostitute was to be a brothel keeper, the vast majority of whom were women and not always former prostitutes.[48] Sinn has suggested that brothel keeping in Hong Kong gave Chinese women 'the rare opportunity to assume new roles and develop new perceptions of themselves'.[49] Tang's statement could be interpreted as her attempt to assume such a role, but it is more likely that she was knowingly performing the role expected of her sex, social status and nationality by her audience, the colonial officials in Hong Kong. That these officials accepted the veracity of her statement, apparently without hesitation and continued to do so even when challenged, suggests that her performance was not unusual and conformed to the cultural norms expected of the Chinese by the British colonial authorities. From the British perspective, by accepting Tang's version of events and not her master's, not only were they reinforcing the stereotype of the downtrodden Chinese female and the brutal Chinese male, but also the motif of the superior British male, protecting the vulnerable from the uncivilised, oriental 'other'. That the performance of these roles enabled each protagonist to achieve their own ends, Tang to remain in Hong Kong, MacDonnell to assert the supremacy of British rule over the Chinese, and Robertson to maintain good relations with the Canton officials, does not suggest that the performances were merely a 'show', but that the relationship between colonised and colonisers depended as much upon the acceptance of cultural norms as on force.

Notes

[1] An Act for the Better Prevention of Contagious Diseases at Certain Naval and Military Stations, 29 Vic Cap 35. (The Contagious Diseases Act, 1866).
[2] Kathleen Wilson (2005) Going Global: empire, identity and the politics of performance, *Journal of British Studies*, 44 (January), p. 194.
[3] Ulrike Hillemann (2009) *Asian Empire and British Knowledge. China and the networks of British imperial expansion* (Basingstoke: Palgrave MacMillan), p. 192.
[4] Catherine Hall (2002) *Civilising Subjects: metropole and colony in the English imagination 1830–1867* (Cambridge: Polity Press), p. 62.
[5] Colonial Office, Hong Kong Correspondence, CO129/123 letter number 337, 29 July 1867, National Archives, London.
[6] Marie-Francoise Chanfrault-Duchet (2000) Textualisation of the Self and Gender Identity in the Life Story, in Tess Cosslett, Celia Lury & Penny Summerfield (Eds) *Feminism and Autobiography. Texts, theories, methods* (London: Routledge), p. 61.
[7] Although one wonders how effective this was as on a fairly regular basis the authorities placed advertisements (in Chinese) in the *Hong Kong Government Gazette* reminding the Chinese population of the Registrar-General's role.
[8] Sir John Smale, the Chief Justice of Hong Kong at this time, was a particularly vociferous critic of the practice and petitioned both the Hong Kong authorities and the Imperial government to outlaw the selling of little girls. See also Maria Jashok & Suzanne Miers (Eds) (1994) *Women and Chinese Patriarchy: submission, servitude and escape* (London and Hong Kong: Hong Kong University Press and Zed Books).
[9] Sir John Bowring (1868) *Hwa Tsien Ki, the flowery scroll, A Chinese novel translated and illustrated with notes by Sir John Bowring* (London: WH Allen), passim.
[10] Maria Jaschok (1988) *Concubines and Bond Servants: the social history of a Chinese custom* (Hong Kong: Oxford University Press).
[11] See for example C. F. Gordon Cummings (1900) *Wanderings in China* (London and Edinburgh: William Blackwood & Sons) and Isabella L. Bird (1883) *The Golden Chersonese and the Way Thither* (London: John Murray, reprinted 1967 by Oxford University Press, Kuala Lumpur). Susanna Hoe (1991) *The Private Life of Old Hong Kong* (Hong Kong: Oxford University Press) also refers to the practice being followed by Chinese women living in Hong Kong.
[12] Barbara-Sue White (Ed.) (2003) *Chinese Woman. A thousand pieces of gold* (Hong Kong: Oxford University Press (China)), p. 61. Davis was Governor of Hong Kong from 1844 to 1848 and one of the few able to speak Chinese.
[13] Ibid, pp. 63–64. Prime was an American Doctor of Divinity who visited China in the 1870s as part of a worldwide tour.
[14] The Yongzheng Emperor reigned from 1722 to1735 and was the third Emperor of the Qing dynasty.
[15] Matthew H. Sommer (2000) *Sex, Law and Society in Late Imperial China* (Stanford, CA: Stanford University Press), p. 9.
[16] The Qianlong Emperor reigned from1736 to 1799, the 4th emperor of the Qing dynasty.
[17] Sommer, *Sex, Law and Society*, p. 293.
[18] Recent studies include: Susan Mann (2007) *The Talented Women of the Zhang Family* (London: University of California Press); Helen F. Sui (Ed.) (2010) *Merchants' Daughters. Women, commerce and regional culture in South China* (Hong Kong: Hong Kong University Press).
[19] Sommer, *Sex, Law and Society*, p. 319.
[20] Hill Gates (1989) The Commodization of Chinese Women, *Signs*, 14(4), pp. 799–832.

[21] Catherine Vance Yeh (2006) *Shanghai Love. Courtesans, intellectuals and entertainment culture 1850–1910* (Seattle and London: University of Washington Press).
[22] At least in the correspondence it does not say he does. See Colonial Office, Hong Kong Correspondence, CO 129/124 and CO129/123, National Archives, London.
[23] Elizabeth Sinn (2007) Women at Work. Chinese brothel keepers in nineteenth-century Hong Kong, *Journal of Women's History*, 19(30), pp. 87–111.
[24] Ibid, pp. 99–101.
[25] The correspondence does not explain how Tang's master knew she was in Hong Kong but Robertson's readiness to believe him suggests that it was a common occurrence for Chinese women and girls to end up in Hong Kong, whether voluntarily or not. The Hong Kong authorities similarly do not show any surprise at Tang's arrival in the colony.
[26] By the Treaty of Nanking 1842, the Chinese allowed the British to set up consulates in five treaty ports (Canton, Foochow, Amoy, Ningpo, and Shanghai) and ceded Hong Kong to the British.
[27] P. D. Coates (1988) *The China Consuls. British consular officers, 1843–1943* (Hong Kong: Oxford University Press).
[28] Colonial Office, Hong Kong Correspondence *CO 129/123*, National Archives, London.
[29] Ibid.
[30] Foreign Office, FO 96/305, *Report on the Correspondence between Her Majesty's Consul at Canton and the Governor of Hong Kong with regard to the extradition of a Chinese girl from that colony*, dated 9 October 1867, National Archives, London.
[31] Christopher Munn (2009) *Anglo-China. Chinese people and British rule in Hong Kong, 1841–1880* (Hong Kong: Hong Kong University Press).
[32] As reported in the *Hong Kong Government Gazette*, Government Notification number 170, 17 November 1866.
[33] Colonial Office, Hong Kong Correspondence *CO 129/124 Hong Kong Correspondence*, number 350, 10 August 1867, National Archives, London.
[34] Ibid.
[35] Colonial Office, Hong Kong Correspondence, *CO129/123 Hong Kong Correspondence*, number 337, 29 July 1867, National Archives, London.
[36] Colonial Office, Hong Kong Correspondence, *CO 403/8 Correspondence* 27 August 1856, National Archives, London.
[37] Colonial Office, Hong Kong Correspondence, *CO129 /124 Hong Kong Correspondence*, passim, National Archives, London.
[38] It is also worth noting that it was not until 1861 that child stealing was made a crime in England and Wales, in response to some high profile cases. See P. T. d'Orban (1976), Child Stealing: a typology of female offenders, *British Journal of Criminology*, 16(3), pp. 275–281.
[39] *Hong Kong Government Gazette* 29 Aug. 1868.
[40] Po Leung Kuk translates as 'Protect Virtue Association'.
[41] Coates, *The China Consuls* p. 30.
[42] Ibid, p. 192.
[43] In every discussion concerning CDOs the overriding concern was to protect the military from venereal disease. Protecting women from slavery and kidnapping were secondary concerns and used more as a justification for harsh measures than an end in itself.
[44] *Report of the Commissioners Appointed by his Excellency John Pope Hennessy CMG to enquire into the Workings of the Contagious Diseases Ordinance, 1867* (Hong Kong: Noronha & Sons, 1879).
[45] 1867 Census published in *The Hong Kong Government Gazette* dated 14 March 1868, Government Notification number 34.

[46] Such evidence is mainly derived from court records, so the women are being prosecuted for illegal activities, but it is still work beyond the domestic sphere.
[47] Anders Hansson (1996) *Chinese Outcasts: discrimination and emancipation in late imperial China* (Leiden and New York: EJ Brill).
[48] Sinn, *Women at Work*, passim.
[49] Ibid., p. 105.

Barbara Leigh Smith Bodichon's Travel Letters: performative identity-formation in epistolary narratives

Meritxell Simon-Martin

Barbara Leigh Smith Bodichon was a mid-nineteenth-century feminist, philanthropist and painter. This article examines Bodichon the female traveller as a way of discussing the process of identity-formation in letter-writing. It proposes reading letters through the lens of Judith Butler's theory of gender (1990). Following her concept of performativity, letter-writing is conceived as a performative act of identity-formation. The article argues that, conditioned by the addressee she wrote to, Bodichon gave written expression to her subjectivity in her travel letters via her epistolary persona. This autobiographical gesture acted as one means through which she constituted her identity as a female traveller. In turn, drawing on Butler's notion of subversive repetition, the article concludes that the resulting multiple epistolary 'I's Bodichon developed in accordance with each of her addressees permitted her to venture into her subjectivity as a female traveller—ultimately prompting her epistolary challenge of normative codes.

Best known among women's historians as the charismatic leader of the mid-Victorian women's movement, Barbara Leigh Smith Bodichon (1827–1891) was also a lifelong inveterate traveller. A leisured upper-middle-class artist and philanthropist, she led a nomadic lifestyle, even after the series of strokes she suffered, aged 50 onwards. From an early age, her father, Benjamin Smith, a successful businessman, took Bodichon and her siblings on educative day excursions and holiday trips by train, boat or in their luxurious eight-passenger carriage. During her teenage years she went on painting expeditions with a view to improving her drawing and colouring techniques. Later in life her sketching tours regularly took her to Wales, Cornwall, and the Isle of Wight. Following Victorian fashion she frequented resorts for convalescence. She also travelled around Britain and abroad to visit friends and relatives or simply for the sake of sightseeing and getting to know other cultures. Married to Eugène Bodichon, a French army surgeon she met in Algiers, she lived between England and Algeria. In her home country, she divided her time between her different interests: the woman question, philanthropy and painting. In Algeria, she primarily developed her artistic facet, though she never fully disconnected from her other social endeavours.[1]

Bodichon was also a prolific letter-writer. Letters provided her the means to be in touch with her family and friends wherever she went. Letter-exchange worked as a social and psychological medium: it had communicational uses, forged interpersonal bonding, and functioned as an emotional outlet for self-expression. Most significantly for the purposes of this study, in her letters Bodichon articulated her subjectivity as a female traveller. This article explores her epistolary travel writing as a source of self-construction, drawing on the letters she wrote during her journeys. Traditionally, historians have treated letters as recordings of factual information about a person's life, as if the raw experiences and true emotions of letter-writers were captured in them. Most recently, referentiality, authenticity and sincerity in letter-writing have been revised. Reflecting current autobiographical theory, writing a letter is now conceived as a mediated act of self-projection where, conforming to historically-specific letter-exchange conventions, the writer constructs multiple personae determined by the addressees s/he is writing to.[2] Letter-writing is understood as a site of struggle and empowerment where the writer negotiates different subject positions.[3] Similarly, women's travel writing, be it published autobiographies, travelogues or letters, is examined as a space for identity-formation which involves discourse reappropriation in the form of textual strategies.[4]

A representative example is Pauline Nestor's study of Bodichon's travel letters. In her article, Nestor explores the potential of leaving England for nineteenth-century middle-class women in terms of self-formation. According to her, Bodichon 'took her impetus to travel' from a 'sense of discontent' and found in 'the unprecedented opportunities for travel' new options for her: to turn 'one's back on home and convention' in search for 'new and less oppressive circumstance in the beyond'.[5] Thus, Bodichon's travelling acted as a 'transformative experience' that gave her more freedom and 'a startling and critical perspective on her former life'.[6] In turn, Bodichon conveyed her experiences as a traveller in her letters. This self-projection took the form of an epistolary self that was 'at once authoritative and fearless'. Referring to her American honeymoon voyage,

Nestor claims that Bodichon's sense of courage when refusing 'prohibitions, attending church services as the only white person, travelling with negroes in the segregated cabins of the paddle steamer, [and] attending a slave auction on her own' gave her the impression that she was entitled 'to speak with authority and superiority of vision'.[7]

Bodichon's epistolary travel writing is fragmentary, which makes any reading inevitably tentative.[8] Notwithstanding, the diverse nature of her (piecemeal) epistolary voice raises questions about the significance of letter-writing in the process of self-formation. This article suggests that throughout her life Bodichon forged her identity as a female traveller by countless means, including life choices and daily habits. Simultaneously, she projected an articulation of her identity in letters by way of her epistolary persona which was constitutive of her self-formation. In order to unpack this written identity-formation, Bodichon's epistolary narratives are read through the lens of Judith Butler's performative theory of gender, via Sidonie Smith's notion of *autobiographical performativity*.[9] Following Smith's theoretical project, Bodichon's letter-writing is understood as a performative act of identity-formation whereby the self is (partially) comprised through epistolary self-narrating. On that account, letter-writing is not an expression of the self. Instead, the self-narrating subject is an effect of the autobiographical act; it is constituted through the act of letter-writing. Thus, as performative autobiographical acts, travel letters function as a source of self-construction, operating simultaneously with numerous other forms of self-formation. That being so, Bodichon gave written expression to her subjectivity in her travel letters and this autobiographical gesture acted as another means through which she constituted her identity as a female traveller. In Butler's conceptual vocabulary, Bodichon *acted out* her identity through the signifying practice of epistolary self-narrating via her epistolary 'I'. Reading letter-writing as a performative autobiographical act teases out the process of self-formation in the epistolary medium and claims letter-exchange as a source of female agency, where an apparently anodyne and trivial custom turned out to be a disruptive practice. Ultimately, this performative understanding of personal correspondence is offered as an alternative to self-expressive interpretations of letter-writing—such as Nestor's—whereby the narrating subject is implicitly understood to exist prior to the autobiographical act.

Autobiographical Performativity: Bodichon's Epistolary Identity as a Female Traveller

Bodichon's epistolary self-projection as a female traveller is slightly disruptive of current understandings of the term. She did travel abroad, including to North-America, Canada, Europe and North-Africa. To a certain extent, her travel writing is comparable to the works by renowned female travellers such as her friend Marianne North. In her letters, some published in article format, Bodichon expressed what it meant for her to be a female traveller in the form of descriptions of her sightseeing tours, painting sessions and anecdotes. In addition, she gave voice to her impressions as a (foreign) visitor by writing detailed accounts of cultural sites and local customs as well as practical information about accommodation and travelling. Given that she was constantly moving from place to place, both around Britain and outside the country, her travel letters also reveal her voice as a nomadic Victorian. Her epistolary travel writing acted as a space where she created meaning from her nomadic lifestyle and reconciled her 'fragmented' self. In her travel letters, Bodichon worked out her self-understanding not only as a woman living between her Algerian and English homes but also as a leisured person who regularly rented temporary accommodation in seaside and countryside resorts and frequently stayed at her relatives' and friends' places. Letter-exchange permitted her to bridge the gap that distance created between her and the people for whom she cared and the social projects in which she was engaged. Thus, she enquired after the health, doings and whereabouts of her loved ones, asked for and conveyed information about common acquaintances, gave accounts of her own routine and endeavours, and informed about when and where she was travelling so that letters could be forwarded. Likewise, Bodichon managed to run her philanthropic projects and be part of the women's rights campaigns by means of letter-writing. In her letters she included articles for the *English Woman's Journal* and the Kensington Society and enclosed cheques to finance campaigns. Moreover, she made use of letters to gain support and raise money for her social endeavours, including setting up a fund for American Dr Elizabeth Blackwell to 'come to England for the purpose of opening the medical profession to women'.[10] Ultimately, in the process she carved out her epistolary identity as a female traveller, which, as we have seen, coexisted alongside her lived identity and was constitutive of her self-formation.

In her letters, Bodichon's projection of herself as a female traveller was determined by the recipient she wrote to. As dialogical acts, letters intrinsically involve an addressee: the epistolary 'you', which determines the epistolary narrative strategies adopted by the epistolary 'I'. That is, the addressee implicitly dictates the content, tone, form, and handwriting the letter-writer employs. In the words of Elizabeth MacArthur:

> [l]etter writers inevitably construct personae for themselves as they write, and if they are involved in a regular exchange they construct personae for the correspondent and plots for the story of the relationship as well. They become co-authors of a narrative in which they, or rather epistolary constructions of themselves, also play the leading roles.[11]

Bodichon corresponded with a wide range of people, which included family members, close friends, acquaintances, and feminist, philanthropists and artistic colleagues. She adapted her epistolary narrative to each of her addressees, developing multiple epistolary 'I's. In Butler's conceptual vocabulary, she *enacted* an epistolary articulation of her identity in accordance with each epistolary 'you'.[12] Her textual strategies consisted in bringing out certain aspects of her subjectivity and concealing others. That is, Bodichon was constituted by numerous identities: a leisured traveller, a woman, an artist, a philanthropist, an educationist, a feminist, a neighbour, an English citizen, an illegitimate child, a daughter, a wife, a friend and so on. In her epistolary narratives she 'played' with these facets and presented different combinations and 'versions' of them—sometimes these were only subtly distinct. In virtually all her epistolary travel writing, including her published articles, Bodichon wrote in her characteristic lively style. Yet, she adapted the format and the tone in which she approached recipients appropriately. To close friends and relatives she wrote in a rather random conversation-like manner, hardly using punctuation marks, and drawing sketches.[13] In her formal travel letters, she wrote more structured texts, using a neat hand-writing and adding date, greeting, closing and signature.[14] Through doing so, she projected nuanced portraits of herself—which reach us today in the form of a manifold (piecemeal) epistolary voice.

In her epistolary travel writing addressed to her family, Bodichon invariably presented herself as an intrepid visitor, fearless of 'snakes',[15] 'foul filth',[16] boats 'crowded with a disreputable looking set of people',[17] and 'earthquakes, locusts, fever, [and] insurrections'.[18] To them she expressed the exhilarating experiences of witnessing the 'grand and awful sight' of Vesuvius erupting;[19] sailing the Mississippi, with its 'everlasting woods on either side' and the 'houses floating down on rafts';[20] 'coming through the rapids' in Canada;[21] painting an alligator 'with the vilest demon eyes' tied down in her drawing-room;[22] wandering around Algiers, with its 'dark arched' passages 'with mysterious doors leading into darker passages';[23] or being stuck 'in a dirty room waiting for the train' for five hours, only accompanied by 'picturesque creatures' ('5 Guardia Civil, 5 women, a cat, a little dog & 2 big dogs & lots of fleas') which 'made a whole series of Goya's eaux fortes'.[24]

In her travel letters to her sisters (Bella and Nanny) and female confidantes, Bodichon explained juicy anecdotes and intimate secrets. At the age of 23, Bodichon and her best friend Bessie Parkes embarked on an unchaperoned trip around continental Europe. To her sisters, she reported her unsuccessful encounters with young Germans in a self-mocking tone. The latter were half appalled half amused by their outfits—which consisted of comfortable loose-fitting short skirts, thick-soled boots and blue-tinted spectacles.[25] During her first trip to Algeria in 1856, she confided her interest in Dr Bodichon to her close friend Marian Evans (novelist George Eliot). She described him and sketched the back of his head, covered by a mass of thick black hair, writing underneath: the 'French *philosophe* ... will not wear a hat because he says the hair if cultivated to grow like fur, is the best defence against the sun'.[26] After a short and unorthodox courtship, Bodichon announced their intention to marry. Her family tried to dissuade her, horrified by the prospect of her marring such a singular man, seventeen years her senior. Offended at finding out that her brother had inquired about her fiancé behind her back to an unknown Frenchman, she wrote infuriated to Parkes: 'Can you think of anything more undignified than that Ben should go to a stranger, and a person who is held in no respect, to ask questions about a man everyone respects?'[27]

After her marriage to the French doctor some months after, Bodichon described her conjugal life in her travel letters with the view of making sense of her new marital status and reassuring her family. During their ten-month honeymoon trip across America and Canada, she gave accounts of their household arrangements and daily routine. She assured her maternal aunt, Dorothy Longden, that she needed 'not be afraid of the Doctor not taking care of' her.[28] He was in charge of housekeeping: cooking 'little things beautifully'[29] like 'queer fish, gumbo soup, roast grey squirrel, boiled wildcat, [and] omelette of alligators' eggs'.[30] As she did during their voyage to Brittany to visit Dr Bodichon's relatives four years later,[31] she projected a positive image of her husband, conveying his 'kindest regards to everyone'[32] and encouraging them to write him 'a scrap' back, which he would 'always answer'.[33] Indeed, throughout her married life, Bodichon used letters to smooth out the tense relationship between her husband and her family, who never fully approved of him. Only to Evans, who had a cordial relation with him, did she confide her marital difficulties, being persuaded that Evans was 'the most likely person in the world to help' her.[34]

Bodichon was born into a politically and philanthropically engaged family. Both her father and grandfather were Liberal politicians; her father was the founder and main benefactor of an infants' school in London, and her paternal aunt, Julia Smith, participated in abolitionist and free trade activities during the 1830s and 1840s. Following the family's tradition, Bodichon presented herself to them as a committed citizen, embracing the advance of justice and democracy. Thus, during her continental tour, while she confessed her failed love affairs with young men to her sisters, Bodichon dramatically expressed her views about the political situation in Austria to her paternal aunt, who had previously introduced her to female modes of participation in political campaigns. In a rather dramatic tone, she wrote to her:

> I did not know before, how intense, how completely a part of my soul were all feelings about freedom and justice in politics and government. I did not think, when I was so glad to go in Austria, how the sight of people ruled by the sword in place of law, would stir up my heart, and make me feel as miserable as those who live under it.[35]

Similarly, while she reassured her maternal aunt about her marital happiness, in her honeymoon letters to the Leigh Smiths, Bodichon wrote long passages giving her opinion about American society:

> This is really a free country in the respect of having no privileged class—excepting the class of white over black. White men are free in America and no mistake! ... One is so little used to freedom, real freedom, even in England that it takes time to understand freedom, to realize it.[36]

As part of her interest in social reform, during her voyages Bodichon combined cultural sightseeing with philanthropic 'touring', visiting prisons, refuges for destitute girls, hospices, and schools. During her convalescence trip to Italy in 1854, while she described the spectacular eruptions of Vesuvius to her maternal aunt, in her letters to family friend Annie Buchanan Bodichon added her opinion about the level of schools in Rome.[37] In a burst of indignation and exasperation she commented:

> The teachers of schools make a country. Here, alas! Ignorant or wicked priests are the teachers for the most part, where there are any. I have had dreams of freedom and republics for Italy, but my hopes are less and less now I see how tight is the grasp in which the people are held. At Rome the despotism is of the worst kind—a spiritual despotism.[38]

Furthermore, as a women's rights activist, while she kept her American colleagues updated of the steady progress of her feminist projects,[39] Bodichon confided to some of her best friends the inner difficulties she encountered in making them prosper. Against a background of clashing temperaments and opposing feminist outlooks at the heart of Langham Place, Bodichon spoke favourably of the often recalcitrant Emily Davies, 'a solid sterling good young woman with a great capacity for learning, shy & not generally pleasing but one who always gains her ends'; she defended Maria Rye, the secretary of the Middle-Class Female Emigration Society, against 'stupid complains [sic]' she 'never listen[ed] to';[40] and she criticised Parkes for writing of the success of the *English Woman's Journal* 'in such a wild way' and 'exaggeration' that she was 'disgusted' and 'hardly [knew] what to make of her'.[41] Finally, to some of her feminist colleagues, such as suffragist Helen Taylor, Bodichon wrote courteous businesslike letters that kept her engaged in the women's movement in spite of the distance.[42] As these examples illustrate, Bodichon presented herself as a female traveller in a slightly different way to each of her correspondents, adapting her epistolary 'I' accordingly. Each epistolary enactment revealed a nuanced articulation of her subjectivity.

Subversive Repetition: Identity Resignification in Bodichon's Epistolary Self-formation

As we have seen, Bodichon verbalized a versatile self-projection as a female traveller through the epistolary medium by virtue of the multiplicity of correspondents to whom she wrote. This section argues that, in the process, letters acted as a space where Bodichon individuated her subjectivity as a female traveller. For this purpose I draw on Butler's notion of *subversive repetition,* in collaboration with Smith's understanding of autobiographical writing as a site for resistance.[43] Following Butler's theoretical project, I suggest that the intrinsic failures that occur in an identity injunction—to be a female traveller—and the simultaneous discursive routes through which it takes place—the set of gendered prescriptions associated with being a female traveller—permitted Bodichon to reappropriate normative discourses and forge her individuality. In the process, she engaged critically with discursive traditions, including prevailing notions of femininity. Nonetheless, hers was a counter-hegemonic viewpoint within limits. For her standpoint was also caught by certain colonialist assumptions, contributing to 'malestream' discourse on 'otherness'. In turn, I argue that Bodichon's epistolary challenge of gendered understandings of being a traveller was prompted by her versatile articulation of her identity. That is, the act of staging nuanced self-projections in accordance with each correspondent permitted her to explore her subjectivity as a traveller. Each set of correspondences sent to one particular addressee created a new scenario where she ventured into different self-portraits. Ultimately, writing to such a variety of epistolary 'you' maximised her opportunities for identity resignification. Indeed, letter-writing, an apparently innocuous practice, turned out to be a fertile source of female agency.

Against gendered expectations and without self-justification, Bodichon projected herself as an intrepid tourist voyaging out of personal curiosity and for the sake of pleasure. Most often travelling accompanied by a female friend while her husband remained in Algeria, during her trips she also embarked on excursions on her own. In Spain, she visited Burgos Cathedral, kneeling down for prayers 'with 80 or 100 women all in black veils' without anybody noticing her and in Madrid she attended the 'dull & stupid' backstage preparations' of a bullfight accompanied only by 'a man servant'.[44] By travelling to Spain, France, and Italy with the purpose of discovering new landscapes, cultures and people; by setting out on sketching tours while her husband went on long walks for 'twenty or thirty miles all over the country'[45] or 'was sent for to visit the sick';[46] by travelling back to England every spring, very often without him, to keep up with her philanthropic and feminist projects, Bodichon presented herself as a woman who asserted her right to personal self-fulfilment. Indeed, formally, she displayed the image of a respectably married woman, which contributed to counterbalancing the effects of her illegitimate birth. In her private letters, she acted out the role of an independent woman at the heart of her marital union.

Bodichon regarded herself as an accomplished watercolour painter, an enthusiastic philanthropist and deep-rooted feminist. Dismantling prejudices against women as valid sources of expertise, she projected herself as knowledgeable in aesthetics and social matters. In doing so, she was placing herself within an already established tradition. For, as Betty Hagglund shows in her study of female travel writing about Scotland, British women had been using the written medium to assert their authority as experts since at least the late eighteenth century.[47] As an artist, Bodichon displayed an 'emotional response' to the beauty of the landscapes she encountered, projecting a relational interaction with them as invigorating places – a sensibility culturally associated with female nature.[48] For instance, riding around the Roman Campagna, the 'horseback views, wild and dashy', inspired her with the 'most vivid ideas for pictures'.[49] At the same time, she adopted the 'masculine'—and thus authoritative—subject position of describing and judging the aesthetic value of cultural sites from an omniscient and commanding standpoint. For example, she considered that Spanish tiles could not 'be compared with the old tiles of Algiers'. For they are 'very much more modern' and 'often ugly in colour'. She recognised that '[o]f course, the mosaic pottery in the Alhambra is beautiful & the few little tiles one sees with the shield & the motto are good'. But she believed that 'for exquisite design' visitors should go to Algiers. Eventually, impressed by the 'richness & picturesqueness' of Spanish monuments but deploring the poor state of the buildings as a result of 'ignorance, stupidity and greed', Bodichon decided she was 'quite reconciled to England buying up everything for the South Kensington Museum'.[50] Indeed,

Bodichon's travel letters reveals her writing within a mindset that took for granted British middle-class superiority.

As a philanthropist, Bodichon reported on her charity endeavours to her American colleagues, presenting herself as a leading figure in the social reform movement in England forging transatlantic networks. Simultaneously, to closer friends she gave her opinion about particular activities and approaches. Thus, having visited several charitable institutions with the Davenport-Hill sisters in Bristol, she judged 'excellent' the way in which women managed ragged, industrial, and reformatory schools for girls.[51] Nonetheless, she thought children should not be separated from their parents since it broke 'the family life' and made 'the child a solitary unit'.[52]

Likewise, with no sign of self-deprecation, Bodichon presented herself as an experienced traveller—advising correspondents to carry 'a little hand bag & waterproof bath' at every hotel and 'a very big leather box', because 'size is nothing on railways & you can always leave it everywhere at the depots at the station';[53] and an expert in foreign cultures, be it Spain, France, Algeria or America. Having witnessed the reality of slavery first-hand and listened to the slaves' testimonies themselves, in her American letters she tore down myths about this institution in an authoritative tone. She denounced not only the slave owners but also 'all in America who would exclude the dusky skinned from the light of knowledge and the blessings of freedom which here all the white race so abundantly enjoys'.[54] She was disdainful of the publications by other female social commentators, like Amelia Murray and Frederika Bremer, which she regarded as 'very poor books on a rich subject'. For '[t]he two ladies lived with ladies and polite gentlemen and saw nothing of the life of the lowly I have seen during my nine weeks in New Orleans... their opinions are founded on very insufficient data', she concluded assertively.[55] Ultimately, Bodichon published a series of articles on each of her areas of expertise, mainly in the *English Woman's Journal*, establishing herself as an authority.[56]

In the eyes of Victorian society, Bodichon's outlook verged upon eccentricity and was occasionally condemned. However, she seems to have taken certain delight at this. Unapologetic for compromising her femininity, during her outdoor painting sessions she wore comfortable clothes, appropriate boots, a big hat and a pair of blue glasses. As during her European tour, her attire did not go unnoticed in America. She complained that she had never seen 'such utter astonishment as is depicted on the faces of the populace' when she 'return[ed] from a sketching excursion'.[57] She once even frightened off a group of black children: '"I do not eat niggers," I said—so they came up to me and one said, "Why, it's a woman!" "Why do you wear boots?" "Because it is wet!" "Why do you wear spectacles?" "Because I can't see without" "Why do you wear a hat?" "Because I can't carry a parasol!"', she reported amused.[58] Southern women found her outfits embarrassing, especially her leather boots, which were considered 'monstrous', and her wardrobe, 'shabby and triste'. Her 'linen dresses' and 'little plain bonnet and plain ribbon' were despised to the point that many ladies refused to walk with her. They offered her 'flower garden bonnets' but she declined, privately dismissing their 'stupid extravagance'.[59] In Algeria, Bodichon hosted salons every Saturday and gave parties where she invited her 'curious' neighbours, 'Nuns, Arabs, Jews, & farmers from Italy, Spain & Malta'.[60] She found it 'exceedingly delicious' 'to hear French people tell their scandalous stories'. And she confessed that she had 'a profound relish for a bit of this kind of life'.[61] But her marriage arrangement and leisured routine devoted to painting were not always approved of by certain members of the communities with whom she socialised. She complained:

> Our life here is very quiet & hard working & one would have thought perfectly inoffensive to any one on earth, but it is not so! The little foolish circles of French & English talk in the most absurd manner about us & find us very offensive.

'Have you read Mill "On Liberty"?', she asked her recipient. 'It delights us. I wish all these people could read it. To a certain extent we live on his principles!' she replied slightly condescendingly.[62]

During her journeys, letters were 'precious' gifts to Barbara Bodichon, who always rushed 'at the postman in a frantic state', expectant of fresh news.[63] In her epistolary travel writing, she forged her individual identity as a female traveller through her manifold epistolary 'I' by reason of the wide range of addressees with whom she corresponded. Understanding identity-formation as a *performative* mechanism, this epistolary articulation was constitutive of her process of self-formation. During her trips, Bodichon carved out her identity as a female traveller. Simultaneously, she *acted out* her identity in her epistolary travel narratives. The epistolary 'I's she constructed in accordance with each of her addressees coexisted alongside other forms of self-formation—namely Bodichon's lived identities, the 'flesh-and-blood' woman who experienced the voyages. As Nestor suggests, travelling was a transformative adventure that provided Bodichon with new and exciting opportunities for self-fashioning. Alternatively, by reading identity-formation through Butler's theoretical project, Bodichon's epistolary voice can be understood not as an expression of her lived identity—as it is implicit in Nestor's study—but as a narrative construction that coexisted alongside it. Thus, Bodichon's eventual contingent self was as much the result of her travelling as the effect her epistolary self-projection.

We will never know how Bodichon actually acted out her identity as a female traveller during her lifetime. This is one of the limitations of personal correspondence as historical evidence.[64] Given that her epistolary enactment was constitutive of her self-formation, we can suppose a correlation existed between her epistolary and lived self-projection. But, as we have seen, her epistolary 'I's did not always emerge entirely consistently but in a complementing, overlapping or slightly opposing manner. A comparable tension can also be assumed to exist between her lived identity and her epistolary self-presentation. A humble reminder of the limits of historical inquiry—this surmise will nonetheless remain unproven.

Notes

[1] Biographical data is drawn from Pam Hirsch (1998) *Barbara Bodichon: feminist, artist and rebel* (London: Chatto & Windus).

[2] See for example Sidonie Smith & Julia Watson (1998) *Women, Autobiography, Theory. A reader* (Madison: University of Wisconsin Press); Sidonie Smith & Julia Watson (2001) *Reading Autobiography: a guide for interpreting life narratives* (Minneapolis: University of Minnesota Press).

[3] See for example Rebecca Earle (Ed.) (1999) *Epistolary Selves. Letters and letter-writers, 1600–1945* (Aldershot: Ashgate); Margaretta Jolly (2008) *In Love and Struggle. Letters in contemporary feminism* (New York and Chichester: Columbia University Press); Sara Crangle (2005) Epistolarity, Audience, Selfhood: the letters of Dorothy Osborne to William Temple, *Women's Writing*, 12(3), pp. 433–451; Martyn Lyons (1999) Love Letters and Writing Practices: on *ecritures intimes* in the nineteenth century, *Journal of Family History*, 24(2), pp. 232–239; Martyn Lyons (2003) French Soldiers and their Correspondence: towards a history of writing practices in the First World War, *French History*, 174(1), pp. 79–95; Karina Williamson (2003) The Emergence of Privacy: letters, journals and domestic writing, in Ian Brown (Ed.) *The Edinburgh History of Scottish Literature*, Vol. 2 (Edinburgh: Edinburgh University Press), pp. 57–70; Mireille Bossis & Karen McPherson (1986) Methodological Journeys through Correspondences, *Yale French Studies*, 71, pp. 63–75; Patricia Meyer Spacks (1988) Forgotten Genres, *Modern Language Studies*, 18(1), pp. 47–57; Maire Fedelma Cross & Caroline Bland (Eds) (2004) *Gender and Politics in the Age of Letter-Writing* (Aldershot: Ashgate); Katie Barclay (2011) Intimacy and the Life Cycle in the Marital Relationships of the Scottish Elite during the Long Eighteenth Century, *Women's History Review*, 20(2), pp. 189–206; Susan Whyman (2009) *The Pen and the People: English letter writers, 1660–1800* (Oxford: Oxford University Press); Amanda Gilroy & W. M. Verhoeven (Eds) (2000) *Epistolary Histories: letters, fiction, culture* (Charlottesville and London: University Press of Virginia). Other relevant works on diaries and life writing are Suzanne Bunkers & Cynthia Huff (Eds) (1996) *Inscribing the Daily: critical essays on women's diaries* (Amherst: University of Massachusetts Press) and Marlene Kadar (Ed.) (1992) *Essays on Life Writing. From genre to critical practice* (Toronto: University of Toronto Press).

[4] See for example Shirley Foster & Sara Mills (Eds) (2002) *An Anthology of Women's Travel Writing* (Manchester and New York: Manchester University Press); Caroline Franklin (Ed.) (2005–2006) *Women's Travel Writing, 1750–1850* (London: Routledge); Kristi Siegel (Ed.) (2004) *Gender, Genre, & Identity in Women's Travel Writing* (New York: Peter Lang); Jennifer Bernhardt Steadman (2007) *Travelling Economies: American women's travel writing* (Columbus: Ohio State University Press); Sidonie Smith (2001) *Moving Lives: twentieth-century women's travel writing* (Minneapolis: University of Minnesota Press); Kathryn Walchester (2007) *Our Own Fair Italy: nineteenth-century women's travel writing and Italy, 1800–1844* (Bern & Oxford: Peter Lang); Sara Mills (1991) *Discourses of Difference. An analysis of women's travel writing and colonialism* (London & New York: Routledge).

[5] Pauline Nestor (2005) Negotiating a Self: Barbara Bodichon in America and Algiers, *Postcolonial Studies: Culture, Politics, Economy*, 8(2), p. 156.

[6] Idib., p. 158.

[7] Ibid., p. 159.

[8] Only a fraction of the letters she wrote is extant and most are undated and/or incomplete. The bulk of her personal correspondence consists of letters addressed to her.

[9] In *Gender Trouble*, Butler develops a performative reading of gender identity on the premise, adapted from Nietzsche, that 'there need not to be a "doer behind the deed," but that the "doer" is variably constructed in and through the deed' (p. 195). Following this postulate, she puts forward her thesis of *performativity*, whereby gender is understood to be an effect of incessant reiterated acting. Butler questions 'the fixity of gender identity as an interior depth that is said to be externalized in various forms of "expression"' (p. 202). Instead, she conceives gender identity as a signifying practice that operates through reiteration and constitutes the subject. Judith Butler (1990) *Gender Trouble* (New York and London: Routledge). Smith proposes a *performative* reading of self-narrating as a way of unpacking the implications of the autobiographical project in terms of identity-formation and agency. She contends that 'autobiographical telling is not a "self-expressive" act' where 'self-identity emerges from a psychic interiority, located somewhere "inside" the narrating subject', and is 'translated into the metaphorical equivalence in language'. For, in her view, '[t]here is no essential, original, coherent autobiographical self before the moment of self-narrating'. Instead, the interiority (the self that is said to be prior to the autobiographical expression) is 'an *effect* of autobiographical storytelling'. Drawing on Butler's concept of *performativity*, Smith argues that autobiographical storytelling is a performative occasion through which discourses permeate the autobiographical subject by means of reiteration. In other words, autobiographical narrative, understood as a performative act, constitutes interiority. Thus, for Smith, autobiographical storytelling becomes one means through which the subject believes to be a 'self': Sidonie Smith (1995) Performativity, Autobiographical Practice, Resistance, *a/b: Auto/Biography* Studies, 10(1), pp. 17–19.
[10] To Marian Evans, [Algeria], 25 December [1859], Beinecke Library, Yale University, George Eliot and George Lewes Collection, Box 7.
[11] Elizabeth J. MacArhur (1990) *Extravagant Narratives: closure and dynamics in the epistolary form* (Princeton: Princeton University Press) p. 119.
[12] As other epistolary studies have underlined, an epistolary 'you' could make reference to a group of people. Unless specified, the letter was expected to be read by third parties. This implies that Bodichon bore in mind the practice of collective reading when she adapted her epistolary 'I' to each epistolary 'you'.
[13] For example, letter to Marian Evans, Alger, 21 November 1856, GCPP Bodichon 4/20.
[14] For example, letter to Lord Shaftsbury, London, 26 July [1862], Women's Library, London Metropolitan University, Autograph Letter Collection, General Women's Movement.
[15] Diary, [Savannah], 28 February [1858], Joseph W. Reed (Ed.) (1972) *An American Diary 1857–1858* (London: Routledge & Kegan Paul), p. 121. During her American voyage, Bodichon wrote a series of letters, some addressed to particular recipients and others to her family generally. She also kept a diary, addressed to her family, which she sent as she travelled.
[16] Diary, Mobile, 17 February [1858], Reed (Ed.), *American Diary*, p. 111.
[17] Ibid., p. 112.
[18] To Marian Evans, Algiers, 11 January 1868, Beinecke, Box 7.
[19] To Dorothy Longden, [Rome, winter 1854–1855], Burton, *Barbara Bodichon 1827–1891* (London: J. Murray), p. 78.
[20] Diary, [Mississippi River], 8 December [1857], Reed (Ed.), *An American Diary*, p. 58.
[21] Diary, Montreal, 26 May [1858], Reed (Ed.), *American Diary*, p. 148.
[22] Diary, New Orleans, 27 December [1857], Reed (Ed.), *American Diary*, p. 73.
[23] To Bessie Parkes, [Algeria], [November 1856], GCPP Parkes 5/175.
[24] To Marian Evans, [Spain, 1867–1868], Beinecke, Box 7. Only a compiled copy of the letters Bodichon wrote to Evans during her Spanish trip is extant. The text looks like

a manuscript ready to be edited for publication. This means this copy may be a slightly modified version of the original letters Evans received. The published article, a further edited version of the manuscript, is 'An Easy Railway Journey in Spain', *Temple Bar*, February 1868, Vol. 25, pp. 240–249.

[25] To Nanny and Bella Leigh Smith, [Germany 1850], Burton, *Barbara Bodichon*, p. 34.
[26] To Marian Evans, Algiers, 21 November 1856, Beinecke, Box 7.
[27] To Bessie Parkes, [Algeria, April 1857], Hirsch, *Barbara Bodichon*, p. 127.
[28] To Jo Gratton (relative), New Orleans, 21 December [1857], Reed (Ed.), *An American Diary*, p. 67.
[29] Diary, New Orleans, 27 December [1857], Reed (Ed.), *American Diary*, p. 71.
[30] To Jo Gratton, New Orleans, 21 December [1857], Reed (Ed.), *American Diary*, p. 67.
[31] Travel diary sent to her Leigh Smith family as letters, Brittany, 3–27 June 1861, GCPP Bodichon 8/4.
[32] To Benjamin Smith and Nanny Leigh Smith, Savannah River, 13 March [1858], Reed (Ed.), *American Diary*, p. 127.
[33] To Benjamin Smith, [Savannah], 3–4 March [1858], Reed (Ed.), *American Diary*, p. 123.
[34] To Marian Evans, [Algeria], 25 December [1859], Beinecke, Box 7.
[35] To Julia Smith, [Austria, 1850], Burton, *Barbara Bodichon*, p. 33.
[36] Diary, [New Orleans], 27 December [1857], Reed (Ed.), *American Diary*, p. 72.
[37] She was the daughter of James Buchanan, Bodichon's tutor. The Buchanans ran Benjamin Smith's infant school in London.
[38] To Annie Buchanan, Sorrento, 17 May 1855, GCPP Bodichon 4/12.
[39] Marcus and Rebecca Spring, Dorothea Lynde Dix, Charles Henry Brainard, and Caroline Wells Healey Dall for example.
[40] To Emily Blackwell, [Algeria], 11–13 February 1862, Schlesinger Library, Harvard University, Elizabeth Blackwell Collection, Box 13 Folder 185.
[41] To Marian Evans, [Algeria], 26 April [1859], Beinecke, Box 7.
[42] To Helen Taylor, Paris, 2 November 1866, London School of Economics, Mill-Taylor Collection 12/49.
[43] Butler's performative reading of gender identity accounts for individuals' capacity for agency. Far from being caught in a spiral of normative repetitions, individuals are capable of identity transgression through subversive reiterations. For '[t]he injunction *to be* a given gender produces necessary failures, a variety of incoherent configurations that in their multiplicity exceed and defy the injunction by which they are generated. Further, the very injunction to be a given gender takes place through discursive routes: to be a good mother, to be a heterosexually desirable object, to be a fit worker, in sum, to signify a multiplicity of guarantees in response to a variety of different demands all at once'. Accordingly, it is through these failures and concurring manifoldness that disruptive re-enactments of norms are possible. Butler, *Gender Trouble*, p. 199. Following Butler's notion of *subversive reiteration*, Smith states that, in like manner, 'the autobiographical subject finds him/herself on multiple stages simultaneously'; s/he is trapped in multiple demands—to which they simply fail to fully conform. Since these 'multiple calls never align perfectly' but 'create spaces or gaps, ruptures, unstable boundaries', transgression becomes possible. Based on the analysis of published autobiographies, she concludes that autobiographical writing permits self-narrating subjects to make and unmake identities. Smith, Performativity, pp. 20, 30.
[44] To Marian Evans, [Spain, 1867–1868], Beinecke, Box 7.
[45] To Jo Gratton, New Orleans, 21 December [1857], Reed (Ed.), *American Diary*, p. 67.
[46] To Anna Jameson, Algiers, 21 April 1859, GCPP Bodichon 4/16.
[47] Betty Hagglund (2009). *Tourists and Travellers Women's Non-fictional Writing about Scotland, 1770–1830* (Bristol; Buffalo, NY: Channel View). What is particularly

striking in Bodichon's case is that she was remarkably unapologetic about her assertive tone.

[48] Foster & Mills (Eds), *An Anthology of Women's Travel Writing*, pp. 178–179.
[49] To Dorothy Longden, [Rome, winter 1854–1855], Burton, *Barbara Bodichon 1827–1891*, p. 75.
[50] To Marian Evans, [Spain, 1867–1868], Beinecke, Box 7.
[51] Florence and Rosamund Davenport-Hill were two Unitarian social workers from Bristol.
[52] To Marian Evans, Bristol, 3 April 1868, GCPP Bodichon 4/10.
[53] To Marian Evans, [Spain, 1867-1868], Beinecke, Box 7.
[54] Diary, [Augusta], 14 March [1858], Reed (Ed.), *American Diary*, p. 131.
[55] Diary, [New Orleans], 11 February [1858], Reed (Ed.), *American Diary*, p. 99.
[56] A comparative analysis between Bodichon's epistolary self-projection and her voice as an author is beyond the scope of this study. But, very briefly, in her articles she wrote in a more detached style, excluding personal anecdotes and references to family and friends. She described cultural monuments, social customs and social reform endeavours, putting forward her self-projection as an expert.
[57] Diary, [New Orleans], 21 January [1858], Reed (Ed.), *American Diary*, p. 87.
[58] Diary, [New Orleans], 5 January [1858], Reed (Ed.), *American Diary*, pp. 77–78.
[59] Diary, [New Orleans], 21 January [1858], Reed (Ed.), *American Diary*, p. 87.
[60] To Anna Jameson, Algiers, 21 April 1859, GCPP Bodichon 4/16.
[61] To Marian Evans, Algiers, 21 November 1856, GCPP Bodichon 4/20.
[62] To Anna Jameson, Algiers, 21 April 1859, GCPP Bodichon 4/16.
[63] Diary, [Boston, 3–5 June 1858], Reed (Ed.), *American Diary*, p. 155.
[64] In her study of intimacy and life cycle in marital relationships as expressed in letters, Katie Barclay reaches a similar conclusion. She highlights that the way 'a marriage functioned when performed through correspondence and over distance may have very little in common with how a couple behaved when together'. Barclay, *Intimacy and the Life Cycle*, p. 193.

'A notable personality': Isabella Fyvie Mayo in the public and private spheres of Aberdeen

Lindy Moore

Isabella Fyvie Mayo (1843–1914) was already well-known as an author when, towards the end of the nineteenth century, she began performing in public within the local civic sphere. She gave talks, chaired public meetings and wrote to the correspondence columns of the local press at a time when such activities were still relatively rare for women. In itself this introduced an apparent tension between her public actions and her stated view of woman as above all the home-maker. Moreover, although some of her performances were gender-related and took place within female associational networks, most were not. Mayo also challenged class and race ideologies and hierarchies, as she allied herself with the local trades council and trades unions, and with Black and Asian peoples in criticism of racism and imperialism. This article examines how Mayo's moral and religious convictions enabled her to retain her respectability despite some controversial platform presentations.

In 1878 thirty-five-year-old Isabella Fyvie Mayo and her son moved from central London to Aberdeen, in north-east Scotland. The daughter of a baker whose business went into debt after his death and widow of a young lawyer, Mayo supported herself financially by taking in boarders and by writing for evangelical religious and family periodicals, as she had done before and during her brief marriage.[1] She lived in rented accommodation and it was not until she was over forty that she was able to begin saving for her old age. By 1910, then in her late sixties, she had bought a small house and had an annual income of £150.[2] This article examines how, despite this modest background, Isabella Fyvie Mayo acquired the cultural capital and confidence, through literary writing, public activities and an intense religiosity to become 'a notable personality' in the public and civic spheres of her new home city.[3] It considers the public domain Mayo had to negotiate, and reveals that the evangelical Christianity which motivated her was subsequently influenced by Tolstoyan religious and political humanitarianism, leading her to adopt more radical views and to perform in a more outspoken and controversial way in public.

Public and Private Spheres

The term 'public' is used here to define interaction with individuals outside Mayo's personal kinship, friendship or neighbourhood networks.[4] This interaction might be direct, through platform appearances and speeches, or indirect, either through reports mediated by the local press, or by published authorship, in the newspapers, periodical press or as complete works aimed at unknown individuals (though often consisting of an imagined community). Whereas the concept of the 'public' sphere was initially defined as a coming together of individuals with middle-class economic and social ideologies, creating a 'public opinion' centred around political, administrative and economic culture in contradistinction to a private, civic and familial sphere, more recent research suggests a more nuanced and dynamic relationship within urban society of multiple 'publics' and counter-publics.[5] The nineteenth-century civic arena consisted of a network of relationships within the city, linking official municipal positions and those semi-official and voluntary institutions that would be listed in the local directories. Urban society's sense of its civic self, largely shaped by the local press, was especially important in Scotland due to the absence of a national parliament and the substitution of local politics, education, church and legal institutions as centres for debate on the identity of the nation into which women could sometimes insert themselves.[6]

The 'private' sphere was not a synonym for the 'domestic' sphere or for 'woman's sphere', but the imagery was often used in this sense in nineteenth-century discourse, particularly in didactic writing. This led to the much quoted trope of 'separate spheres', which if not a reflection of reality (men clearly lived and sometimes even worked at home and women did paid work and sometimes voted in public) could, it has been suggested, create a 'virtual' separation which was powerful enough to influence the gendered identities, actions and interactions of women and men.[7] Anne Summers suggests that within the public arena there were gendered public spheres based on parallel economic systems of paid/professional and unpaid/untrained labour. Eleanor Gordon and Gwyneth Nair found that in Glasgow, middle-class women had created their own 'public worlds' in physical space as well as 'metaphorical "social circles"', while Megan Smitley has suggested the creation of a 'feminine public sphere' of Scottish women's woman-centred associational activities in philanthropy, temperance, politics and suffrage, which existed alongside the hegemonic male sphere of the political, legal and economic institutions.[8]

A contributory role to this 'feminine public sphere' was played in Aberdeen by the Aberdeen Union of Women Workers. Formed as an umbrella organisation for philanthropic activities in 1883 under the title Aberdeen Ladies' Union, by 1900 it formed part of an influential national and international movement.[9] In 1888, the Union, led by Lady Aberdeen, organised the first regional annual conference. Fifteen local associations were represented and there were section meetings on twenty-nine topics, some addressed by women from Edinburgh, London or overseas. Held over three days in the main cultural public building in the city, the conference opened with a public meeting attended by over 1,000 people, nearly all women. The Lord Provost, in his welcoming speech, looked forward to a future benefit from the conference, both for Aberdeen and the whole country. After this confident display of feminine maternalist (and imperial) philanthropy and the satisfactory civic recognition of it as an appropriate part of the national ideology, it is salutary to note that, despite male encouragement on at least two occasions, there were no women candidates for the Aberdeen School Board (formed in 1873) for the first twenty years.[10] Women perceived the culture of the civic political sphere of local government elections and formal public committee structures as less hospitable to their ideologies, social interests and collaborative methods of working than the city's feminine sphere of religious philanthropy.

Religious Beliefs

Much of women's associational activities in Aberdeen centred on the churches. Isabella Fyvie Mayo did not become involved with any of the formal church-based activities because she considered the churches to be condoning a separation of religious belief and daily behaviour, not because of her own lack of faith.[11] On the contrary, like so many women active in public reform movements, her intense religious convictions underpinned all her actions:

> The true joy of existence is real, earnest, intense living ... It involves the unreckoned pouring out of energy fed from divine sources, in love, in labour, in endurance, sometimes in conflict and in indignation, when for God's sake we must bear reproach, and are consumed with the zeal of His house.[12]

Only recently has research begun to investigate the personal meaning of religion for women who moved into areas of public reform.[13] As a nominal Episcopalian, but a non-denominational evangelical in practice, Mayo was another woman whose life illustrates the fundamental importance of religion as a mainspring of action. She found a niche in the popular religious press, writing simple, seemingly conventional, works of fiction based around domestic life, the training and education of children and domestic service, most aimed at 'young people'. When she first arrived in Aberdeen, her literary reputation as a writer for mainstream non-denominational religious family periodicals such as those of the Religious

Tract Society, *The Quiver, The Sunday Magazine, Leisure Hour* and *Good Words* would have preceded her in certain religious and university circles,[14] but her identity was not necessarily known to the wider Aberdeen public(s) as most of her serials and books had appeared under the *alter ego* of her pseudonym, 'Edward Garrett' (a retired City of London merchant who first appeared in 1867).[15] Being a local author may have encouraged reviews of her work in the local press, but it did not mean they were necessarily more favourable.

However, while reviewers frequently criticised her fiction for its lack of action and overly religious and didactic emphasis, at the same time they saw Mayo as the provider of moral and sensible, if conservative, advice, especially for young women.[16] Mayo's emphasis on women's domestic role and her special interest in the position of female domestic servants, their relations with their employers and their moral training, was particularly noted by the local press.[17] In 1892, Mayo turned this interest into practical action with an unsuccessful attempt to establish an organisation, which she hoped would be national in its coverage, the 'Lady Helps' Association.[18] This was aimed, not at working-class servants, but at middle-class women, encouraging them to take up domestic work as a preventative and caring activity, in the same spirit they had taken up nursing.[19] Like many other middle-class women, Mayo brought together her religious, philanthropic, class and gendered interests in welfare activities, such as a Scottish Girls Friendly Society branch in the poorest part of the city and prison work, visiting women in their cells and holding Sunday afternoon services for them.[20]

An admirer of John Ruskin, who she thought would be recognised in the future as the prophet of the present age,[21] Mayo acquired sufficient status and recognition as an authority on issues of informal education and religious training from a Christian Socialist viewpoint to be invited by 'a committee of gentlemen' to stand for the school board in 1885 (she declined) and received official civic recognition in 1892 in the form of an invitation to the Lord Provost's 'at home', attended by 'nearly 800 of the leading ladies and gentlemen of the city and county', where she was exceptional among the female guests in that her status was wholly due to her own efforts, rather than because of her marital or kinship connections, inherited wealth or even an appropriate upper-middle-class status.[22] It was possible for women to acquire sufficient cultural capital, through a combination of publications and public activities, to be seen as local or even national 'experts' in certain areas, expertise temporarily overriding gender subjectivities, but Mayo was unusual in that scholars suggest that this normally also required family connections and wealth in order to provide a supporting network of influential contacts.[23] Moreover by the early 1890s, Mayo's public persona had begun to move in an unexpected direction, when her interpretation of Leo Tolstoy's religious and philosophical writing convinced her that it was her moral Christian duty to speak out publically on matters of personal conscience.

Mayo's discovery of the writings of Leo Tolstoy in late 1887 led to the most substantial break in her perceived ontology of her 'self'. She described the experience using the metaphor of light which she had frequently used to depict religious conversion experiences in her fiction:

> I felt I had encountered a mind under whose sway I realised and understood my own thoughts and feelings as never before. I was conscious of a new light upon all life—a light rising within myself, though kindled by Tolstoy's words.[24]

Tolstoy began writing on religious, ethical, and political themes in the 1880s and from 1886 his works started to appear in English. Mayo immediately read everything available. Many years later she wrote:

> Tolstoy has given me *my true self*—has shown me that where I surrendered my own consciousness of right to conventionality and to the opinions of others, I have done wrong and have suffered loss for so doing. He has given me a new and better world.[25]

Tolstoy not only reinforced her personal approach to religion and ethics, inspired by the life of Christ, he also provided her with a comprehensive, internationally-relevant political framework, a perspective missing from Christian Socialism which has been defined as 'a religious and moral movement intended to make political activity unnecessary'.[26] By the mid-1890s, Mayo considered herself a Tolstoyan anarchist—seeking to promote social revolution through the slow, peaceful process of personal reformation, leading to a free, individual life—and she considered socialism a 'half-way' stage to this.[27] The emphasis on spiritual and moral issues Tolstoy inspired has been described as ethical anarchism.[28] He was one of several writers proposing utopian ideals between 1883 and 1896, years which were lit up by the 'religion of socialism'.[29] However Mayo defined her post-1887 creed as a re-interpretation of her evangelical Christian belief, which she held as fervently as ever. She was not 'converted' to socialism as a religion of humanity, but saw socialist behaviour as a form of practical Christianity.

Public Performance and Private Person

Perhaps as a result of Tolstoy's influence, Mayo began extending her presentations from the (physically) indirect relationship between author and reader through the printed page to the active performance of platform literary readings, lectures, political speeches and sermons. Mayo was an excellent public speaker. 'Terse, forcible speeches, often scintillating with wit and humour, fell from her lips as the veriest commonplaces'.[30] She went on to lecture on subjects such as children's reading habits and career choices, the role of the free public library and the literature of the Bible. But if these educational and welfare presentations, founded in a deep religious conviction, make an understandable persona, they were more contentious when performed to public audiences by an author whose novels and writing on gender seemingly emphasised the role of women as home-makers, rather than as active participants in the public domain. In 1894, only days after a local press review of her latest novel, *Her Day of Service*, had quoted her opinion that women did not need a wider or newer field of action 'but only power and wisdom to enter into full possession of what they have already', Mayo was elected as the first and only woman on the Aberdeen School Board.[31] Thus Mayo's activities created an apparent tension between her advice and her own actions. This was not unusual. The history of middle-class women in Britain and the Empire has shown the dichotomy that so often existed between elite middle and upper-class women's perception of the advice and homilies suitable for the working-class, based on gender, with their perception of their own appropriate actions and claims on the civic space, based on social class and race—a confident belief in Anglo-Saxon moral superiority that extended beyond the social hierarchy in Britain to the colonies and dealings with indigenous peoples.[32] But Mayo's subjectivities were more complex than such an interpretation would suggest. She considered women were and should be pre-eminently homemakers, but she did not see this as a force which limited a woman's freedom of action. Like Josephine Butler, Mayo insisted women must be independent in following their conscience:

> ... when will women learn that the path of duty lies direct between God and their own souls, and that no influence, however venerable and venerated, no opinion, however universal, can make wrong, right, or right, wrong![33]

This reasoning was important in enlarging women's sphere and enabling seemingly conservative, conformist women to act in ways beyond the general parameters of perceived respectability.[34]

Thus, while some of Mayo's performances were gender-related and took place within middle-class feminine associational networks, she rejected the hegemonic ideology of a specific 'woman's mission' based on a presumption of feminine moral superiority which was prevalent throughout the women's movement,[35] preferring mixed-sex organisations, whether religious, welfare or political, where men and women could work together on social issues. She wanted the 'frank and fearless friendship—that priceless *Camaradarie* which can only flourish where men and women seriously work and think together, so that labour and aspiration banish all frivolity and "sentiment"'.[36] Consequently she often broke gender barriers as the 'first' or 'only' woman active in public events. For example, she gave talks to the various non-denominational organisations established to spread religion among the working class in the city, including several, such as the Sabbath School Union, the Pleasant Sunday Afternoon society, the Labour Church and the YMCA, which were predominantly, or entirely, male in management and in some cases, also in membership.[37] Furthermore, she challenged and complicated class and race ideologies and hierarchies, as she allied herself with the local trades council and trades unions, and with Black and Asian peoples. When she did stand for election to the Aberdeen School Board, in 1894, it was not on a middle-class gender ticket, but sponsored by the predominately male working-class Aberdeen Trades Council.[38] Mayo was not seen as a woman's candidate and did not stand as such. She campaigned with four other candidates following a prearranged programme which ignored gender issues. According to a supporter: 'by her own profession she goes to the School Board not as a representative of the female electors, but as an ardent worker in the cause of human progress'.[39] In the election campaign Mayo presented herself as a working woman and therefore a working-class woman:

> The 'Free Press' had been kind enough to make the remark that the Trades Council had selected a lady between whom and the Trades Council there appeared to be no earthly connection. For her own part she hoped she did emphatically belong to the working class. She had never one year in all her life been a lady at leisure, and she, therefore, belonged to the working class, and was much more in her place as a Trades Council candidate than she would be as the candidate of any other section of the community.[40]

Mayo's social class identity was complex and fluid; the daughter of a successful middle-class master baker, the failure of the family business after her father's death left her looking for employment first in needlework and then as a secretarial 'temp', before she managed to pay off the debt and gain a precarious independence as an author.[41] Her subsequent marriage to a lawyer meant in theory she could claim upper middle class identity as the widow of a professional, but her husband's health was so poor it appears to have been Mayo who supported her mother and two older sisters while, as the result of the 'criminal folly of a relative', a family estate John Mayo should have inherited had to be sold.[42] In Aberdeen, Mayo's literary reputation and network of middle-class university and evangelical friends would have given her social status, but she was still referred to in some circles as having been 'just an envelope-addressing girl'.[43] Whether she genuinely considered herself as working-class by the mid-nineties or simply identified with working-class people is not clear.

In addition to her school board candidacy, Mayo worked with the trades council in recruiting members for the Carters' Union, gave a talk on socialism to the Social Democratic Federation (SDF), and chaired a Sunday concert in aid of striking operative engineers, this last an action which, with its additional challenge to the ritual of strict Sabbath observance, unsettled religious as well as gender, and class identities. Her platform performance was provocative as she invoked images of violence and war to define the relationship between workers and employers: the strike was now over, she announced, for human flesh and blood and human courage and fortitude were not fairly matched against the Lee-Metfords and big guns of capital ...[44]

Mayo also introduced international issues to Aberdeen. In 1893, she held a drawing-room meeting and then chaired a public meeting attended by over 500 people, addressed by English Quaker Catherine Impey (1847–1923) founder of *Anti-Caste*, the first anti-racism periodical in Britain, and Ida B. Wells (1862–1931), a pioneering African American campaigner against lynching in the United States, who was speaking for the first time in Britain. Wells placed lynching within a framework of segregation, where white supremacy was maintained at any cost, and black women as well as black men were injured. It was thus both a racial and a gendered analysis. Involving contested issues of rape and miscegenation, this was an extraordinarily sensitive and provocative subject for Mayo to support, as she did, by letters to the press, articles, and fiction.[45]

A ground-breaking national and international anti-racism organisation, the Society (later International Society) for the Recognition of the Brotherhood of Man ([I]SRBM) was formed. Mayo became president, and for the few years of its existence Aberdeen was one of the most active branches, bringing individuals such as West Indian proto-anti-imperialist S. J. Celestine Edwards, African American ex-Senator John Patterson Green and future pan-Africanist J. E. Casely Hayford to the city.[46] In the course of various other public addresses, Mayo described war as large-scale murder, theft and drunkenness, criticised the process of colonisation, suggested the press should describe speculation in South African gold as '"Great Gold Robbery in South Africa"—"Successful Resetting of the Stolen Goods in Great Britain"', defended Muslim culture, giving several talks on her impressions of Egypt which she visited in 1895, accused Rhodes and others of treating Africans in precisely the same way as it had been alleged the Boers had been doing, and told Aberdonians they should turn their attention to India, where Europeans were murdering natives with impunity.[47]

Live performances, press reports, periodical writings, personal contacts with officials and signed letters to the press were some of the ways in which Mayo performed, or was represented, in the civic space. Throughout the 1880s and 1890s, there was also a steady drip feed of literary reviews in the press, which by highlighting only certain aspects of her writing, depending on the reviewer or paper, created and presented an authorial identity seen as appropriate by the media. There were also occasional snips of personal information about her (her health, her planned movements, her family link to Aberdeenshire Fyvie farmers), part of the increasing commodification of celebrities, which effectively invaded her private persona. Mayo herself occasionally blurred the distinction between the public writer (her 'authorship self') and the private person, writing personal dedications in her published books, making self-referential remarks in some of her talks and articles and publishing her recollections.[48] In the home she prioritised family-centred activities rather than those arranged by 'public' organisations, but if Mayo's concept of the home was a space where relaxation, family and personal privacy could be found, it was certainly not one shut away in a separate sphere shielded from the outside world. It was, rather, a precursor of the kingdom of heaven, not a place at all, but 'a consciousness of the presence of God'. Women, natural home-makers, should not leave the home circle, but rather enlarge it by welcoming others into it.[49] Thus in Mayo's own 'domestic sphere', far from shutting the 'public' out of her 'private' life, she developed a lifelong friendship with many of her boarders, held drawing-room meetings, kept an open house for visitors, acted as a centre for the Asian students in Aberdeen and corresponded with individuals worldwide (including Mohandas K. Gandhi from 1911 until her death).[50]

Religious Agency

The extent to which Mayo felt her authority for social and political reform came from and was strengthened by the cultural capital of her evangelical and Christian Socialist writing is indicated in her self-referential use of 'Edward Garrett' in her 1890s anti-racism writing and activities.[51] Mayo was aware of her diverse public identities and used her pseudonymous authorial identity as a means of providing gravitas and status. It brought behind her all the wise, moral,

Christian writing and advice she had given as Edward Garrett, the publicity of his more widely-known name and perhaps, too, something of the character of the man himself—older, male, experienced in worldly matters. Thus she could not be explained away as just another meddling, do-gooder woman. Consequently, when a lynching apologist wrote to the local *Free Press*, he hastened to say that he was not writing maliciously against Mayo herself. 'Edward Garrett' had been an honoured writer in the sober, Calvinistic home of his childhood, from works in *The Quiver*, and *Good Words* and he had only recently read an interesting and beautifully written article in the paper on 'The Poets of the Bible' by Mrs Mayo. But he was nevertheless strongly convinced of the folly of some of her social views, particularly those respecting the Negro.[52] In other words, her critic had to apologise and defer to 'Edward Garrett', before he could proceed to attack Mayo's views on Africans and African-Americans and this inevitably diluted his argument.

Mayo's agency was also partly a result of the change in the available 'publics' with the formation of feminine associational groups and the opening of school board and parish council membership to women. But other activities, such as her co-founding of an anti-racism society at a time of extreme racism, her support for striking trade unionists and her platform opposition to the South African War most certainly addressed counter-publics. Further, she challenged the ritual of school board meetings with her quick response to a fellow board member that 'there are some of us who do not do everything in quite proper form',[53] while a number of her public comments, such as her assertion that James Robertson, a respected professor of religion and chairman of the Aberdeen School Board, 'had been trained in a school of autocracy and privilege, a school which caused a man to think of his fellow-creatures as subject races and next of women as a subject sex', went well beyond the bounds of acceptable middle-class behaviour for a woman, and at several public meetings she was hissed or heckled.[54] So how did her social status and 'respectability' survive in the eyes of the Aberdonian elite as she moved into other, working-class and radical 'publics'?

What Mayo defined as 'the finding of her true self' through the upholding of her own 'consciousness of right', when she adopted Tolstoy's interpretation of biblical and ethical issues, led her to be outspoken in her beliefs regardless of the consequences. Her earnest moral conviction was evident to her audiences, and whatever opinions there were about her views or her methods of expressing them, there was near unanimity about her sincerity, honesty and 'transparent straightforwardness'.[55] Describing an address she had given to the Labour Church, William Diack, secretary of the Aberdeen SDF, recalled 'above all, the personal charm of the speaker—whose whole form seemed transfigured by a strong, spiritual force—riveted the attention of her audience'.[56] Effectively she was preaching and Diack commented: 'I can scarcely think that a more eloquent sermon was delivered that day in all the "Granite City"', thus awarding her a religious authority equivalent to that of the male church ministers. Her address showed how her religious beliefs connected with her radical politics:

Jesus Christ, as he went to his death, clearly expressed one plain wish—'Weep not for me: weep for yourselves and for your children.' Yet all these eighteen centuries the greatest genius of poet and painter, and the sentiment of womanhood, have been poured out on the long-finished, brief physical sufferings which he asked us NOT to weep for; while the horrors of slavery and war, and competition, have maintained the perpetual crucifixion of the Son of Man.[57]

For Mayo 'vital Christianity' was best expressed in 'the brotherhood of all races of men' and 'the cause of international peace'.[58]

While her contemporaneous writing (fiction, poetry and prose) in religious family periodicals was, at least superficially, beyond reproach in terms of conventional conformity, so much so that Mayo used her authorial alter ego 'Edward Garrett' to support some of her more radical opinions, on the platform her religiously-motivated convictions were evident through her performance, and could counter her more provocative comments. As Kathryn Gleadle notes, passion for a cause could cut across gendered (and other) subjectivities.[59] Mayo articulated her public self in many ways, often incorporating several subjectivities simultaneously. She performed as anti-lynching and anti-racism campaigner, as author, biblical authority, evangelical, Christian Socialist, educationalist, 'Edward Garrett', ethical anarchist, hymn-writer, internationalist, pacifist, preacher, philanthropist, pro-Boer, poet, public speaker, school board member, socialist, Tolstoyan, as a cultured woman, a chairwoman, an elderly woman, a voteless woman, a working woman, a home-lover, a feminist and a part of the brotherhood of man; but all her subjectivities were connected by the thread of religious conviction. The diversity of Victorian women's religiously inspired campaigns is only beginning to be recognised. Many religiously motivated women were drawn to feminist woman-centred reforms. Like most women active in reform, Mayo believed woman's 'right' was in duty and service to others but she worked this out in a different way with a different emphasis. A life-long women's suffragist, she did not stand for the school board as a 'woman's' candidate, and criticised the Church for its involvement in colonial misrule, rather than its attitude to women. But when Mayo worked together with men in public, rather than through feminine associational networks, she was challenging the invisible barrier that existed between the hegemonic male and (subordinate) feminine public spheres.

Notes

[1] Isabella Fyvie Mayo (1910) *Recollections of What I Saw, What I Lived Through, and What I Learned, during more than Fifty Years of Social and Literary Experience* (John Murray: London); Lindy Moore (2010) The Reputation of Isabella Fyvie Mayo: interpretations of a life, *Women's History Review*, 19(1), pp. 71–88.
[2] Letter from Isabella Fyvie Mayo to John Murray, 20 July 1910, National Library of Scotland Archive, Acc.12927/362.
[3] William Diack (1939) *History of the Trades Council and the Trade Union Movement in Aberdeen* (Aberdeen: Aberdeen Trades Council), p. 56.
[4] Leonore Davidoff (2003) Gender and the 'Great Divide': public and private in British gender history, *Journal of Women's History*, 15(1), pp. 11–27.

[5] The complexity and value of the concepts of the public/private binary and gendered 'separate spheres' has been discussed amongst others by Craig Calhoun (Ed.) (1992) *Habermas and the Public Sphere* (Cambridge, MA: MIT Press); Leonore Davidoff & Catherine Hall (2002) *Family Fortunes: men and women of the English middle class, 1780–1850*, 2nd edn (London; New York: Routledge); Jane Rendall (1999) Women and the Public Sphere, *Gender & History*, 11(3), pp. 475–488.

[6] Esther Breitenbach & Lynn Abrams (2006) Gender and Scottish Identity, in Lynn Abrams, Eleanor Gordon, Deborah Simonton & Eileen Janes Yeo (Eds) *Gender in Scottish History since 1700* (Edinburgh: Edinburgh University Press), pp. 17–42

[7] Anne Summers (2000) *Female Lives, Moral States: women, religion and public life in Britain, 1800–1930* (Newbury, Berks: Threshold Press), p. 11. For a critique of separate spheres see Amanda Vickery (1993) Golden Age to Separate Spheres? A review of the categories and chronology of English women's history, *Historical Journal*, 36(2), pp. 383–414.

[8] Summers, *Female Lives, Moral States*; Eleanor Gordon & Gwyneth Nair (2003) *Public Lives: women, family and society in Victorian Britain* (New Haven & London: Yale University Press), p. 230; Megan Smitley (2009) *The Feminine Public Sphere: middle-class women and civic life in Scotland, c. 1870–1914* (Manchester & New York: Manchester University Press). See also Simon Morgan (2007) *A Woman's Place: public culture in the nineteenth century* (London & New York: Tauris Academic Studies).

[9] Aberdeen Ladies' Union (1888) *Report of Women's Conference on Women's Work held in The Music Hall Buildings, Aberdeen on 9th, 10th, and 11th October, 1888* (Aberdeen: Wyllie & Son); Aberdeen Union of Women Workers, Aberdeen *Daily Free Press*, 15 February 1900. See also Julia Bush (2007) The National Union of Women Workers and Women's Suffrage, in Myriam Boussahba-Bravard (Ed.) *Suffrage Outside Suffragism: women's vote in Britain, 1880–1914* (Basingstoke: Palgrave Macmillan), pp. 105–131; Moira Martin (2008) Single Women and Philanthropy: a case study of women's associational life in Bristol, 1880–1914, *Women's History Review*, 17(3), pp. 395–417.

[10] A. L. McCombie (1972) *Aberdeen and its First School Board* (Aberdeen: Aberdeen City Council). In 1885 a committee of gentlemen was formed to persuade women to stand and to promote their election as candidates free of expense (Aberdeen School Board election, *Aberdeen Weekly Journal*, 27 March 1885).

[11] Mayo, *Recollections*.

[12] Edward Garrett [Isabella Fyvie Mayo] (1888) Husband and wife. Friendly talks. Concluding paper, *Sunday Magazine*, 17, pp. 826–828, quotation pp. 827–828.

[13] Susan Morgan (Ed.) (2002), *Women, Religion and Feminism in Britain 1750–1900* (London: Palgrave); Susan Morgan & Jacqueline de Vries (Eds) (2010) *Women, Gender and Religious Cultures in Britain 1800–1940* (London & New York: Routledge).

[14] Aberdeen divines such as university professor William Milligan and Principal of the Free Church College, David Brown, were contributors to these publications, and the Professor of Greek, William Geddes (from 1885 Principal of Aberdeen University) befriended her on her arrival.

[15] Edward Garrett [Isabella Fyvie Mayo] (1868) *The Occupations of a Retired Life: a novel* (London: Tinsley, Boston: Littel & Gay, New York: George Routledge & Sons) first published in *The Sunday Magazine for Family Reading* (1867–1868).

[16] Literature, *Aberdeen Weekly Journal*, 13 Apr. 1885.

[17] The Magazines, *Aberdeen Weekly Journal*, 5 Mar. 1888; The 'Ladies' Column', *Aberdeen Weekly Journal*, 20 May 1891, quoting Isabella Fyvie Mayo (1891) Under discussion: 'Young men and maidens', *The Leisure Hour*, 40, (May 1891) pp. 483–488.

[18] 'Lady Helps' Association, *Aberdeen Weekly Journal*, 9 Apr. 1892.

[19] Isabella Fyvie Mayo ('Edward Garrett'), Letter to the Editor, *The Scotsman*, 10 Nov. 1891, p. 7; Isabella Fyvie Mayo (1891–1892) Domestic Service: a problem and a possibility, *The Victorian Magazine*, pp. 343–353; Mayo, *Recollections*.

[20] Scottish Girls Friendly Society, *Aberdeen Weekly Journal*, 18 May 1891; Mayo, *Recollections*.

[21] Edward Garrett [Isabella Fyvie Mayo] (1881–1882) Equal to the Occasion, *The Quiver*, 17.

[22] Lord Provost Stewart's 'At Home', *Aberdeen Weekly Journal*, 26 February 1892. She received a similar invitation in 1899, as one of 300 of the civic elite, to celebrate Queen Victoria's 80th birthday (The Lord Provost's entertainment, *Aberdeen Weekly Journal*, 25 May 1899).

[23] Kathryn Gleadle (2009) *Borderline Citizens: women, gender and political culture in Britain, 1815–1867* (Oxford and New York: Oxford University Press); Martin, Single women and philanthropy; Elizabeth Crawford (2002) *Enterprising Women: The Garretts and their circle* (London: Francis Boutle).

[24] Isabella Fyvie Mayo (Dec. 1905) Modern Influences. III.- Lyof Tolstoy, *The Millgate Monthly*, 1(3), pp. 153–159, here p. 153.

[25] Isabella Fyvie Mayo (Sep. 1911) An afterword on a controversy, *The Open Road*, 9, pp. 181–184, here 181–182. Italics added.

[26] Edward Norman (1987) *The Victorian Christian Socialists* (Cambridge, NY: Cambridge University Press), p. 10; Peter d'A. Jones (1968) *The Christian Socialist Revival 1877–1914: religion, class, and social conscience in late-Victorian England* (Princeton, NJ: Princeton University Press).

[27] Letter from Isabella Fyvie Mayo to the Aberdeen Social Democratic Federation, 18 Oct. 1894, quoted in Diack, *History of the Trades Council*, p. 59. From about 1900 until her death in 1914 she assisted the *Free Age Press* (Christchurch, Hants) in the publication and promotion of Tolstoy's English editions.

[28] Mark Bevir (1996) The Rise of Ethical Anarchism in Britain, 1885–1900, *Historical Research*, 69, pp. 143–165.

[29] W. H. G. Armytage (1961) *Heavens Below: Utopian experiments in England 1560–1960* (London: Routledge and Kegan Paul); Stephen Yeo (1977) A New Life: the religion of socialism in Britain, 1883–1896, *History Workshop Journal*, 4(1), pp. 5–56.

[30] E. D. (July 1914) Isabella Fyvie Mayo: an appreciation, *Our Fellow-Mortals*, 9, pp. 1–2.

[31] Edward Garrett [Isabella Fyvie Mayo] *Her Day of Service* (Edinburgh and London: Oliphant, Anderson & Ferrier, 1894), p. 58, reviewed in Aberdeen *Daily Free Press*, 9 Apr. 1894, p. 3. (First serialised as Edward Garrett [Isabella Fyvie Mayo] (1886) The Stranger within the Gates, *The Quiver*, 21).

[32] Lesley Orr Macdonald (2000) *A Unique and Glorious Mission: women and Presbyterianism in Scotland, 1830–1930* (Edinburgh: John Donald); Antoinette Burton (1994) *Burdens of History: British feminists, Indian women, and Imperial culture, 1865–1915* (Chapel Hill: University of North Carolina Press).

[33] Isabella Fyvie Mayo (1889–1890) Vexed questions, *The Sun. A magazine for general readers*, 3(5), pp. 69–76, here p. 73.

[34] Helen Mathers (2002) Evangelicalism and feminism. Josephine Butler, 1828–1906, in Morgan (Ed.) *Women, Religion and Feminism in Britain*, pp. 123–137.

[35] Edward Garrett [Isabella Fyvie Mayo] (1889–1890) The object lesson for the world: a woman's warning, *The Sun*, 3(9), pp. 131–135; Isabella Fyvie Mayo (1892) 'Looking at Home'. A woman's reflections concerning woman's suffrage, *The Victorian Magazine*, pp. 631–637.

[36] Isabella Fyvie Mayo (1892–1893) 'Good Genius.' Jenny Lind (Madame Goldschmidt), *Atalanta*, 6, pp. 374–382, here pp. 378–379.

[37] The Sabbath School Union was a semi-civic umbrella organisation linking all Presbyterian Sunday Schools in the city. In 1893 60% of pupils and teachers were female,

but none of the 114 supervisors or elected managing committee. Mayo was the first woman invited to give one of the training lectures provided annually for the Sunday school teachers. Her five lecturing colleagues included a university Divinity professor, the principal of the Free Church training college and the editor of the thirteen-volume *Encyclopaedia of Religion and Ethics*. See Jones, *The Christian Socialist Revival* on the Labour Church nationally.

[38] In 1891 the twenty-six member executive was all-male. There were three women out of 141 members on the General Committee.

[39] 'Canvasser' Letter to the Editor, [Aberdeen] *Daily Free Press*, 23 Apr. 1894.

[40] School Board elections, [Aberdeen] *Daily Free Press*, 5 Apr. 1894, p. 6. For how unusual Mayo's approach was at this time see Jane McDermid (2009) School Board Women and Active Citizenship in Scotland, 1873–1919, *History of Education*, 38(3), pp. 333–347 (but note this incorrectly describes Mayo as a former schoolteacher); Jane McDermid (2010) Blurring the Boundaries: school board women in Scotland, 1873–1919, *Women's History Review*, 19(3), pp. 357–373; Patricia Hollis (1987) *Ladies Elect: women in English local government 1865–1914* (Oxford: Clarendon Press).

[41] Mayo, *Recollections*.

[42] *Ibid.*, p. 239, identifies the individual as John Mayo. I. F. Mayo (1886) Dear Old People, *The Sunday at Home*, 33, pp. 305–309 uses the phrase 'criminal folly', p. 307.

[43] Mayo, *Recollections*, p. 111.

[44] Aberdeen Carters' Union, *Aberdeen Weekly Journal*, 16 Nov, 1896; *Aberdeen Weekly Journal*, 26 Oct. 1898; Mrs Fyvie Mayo on sacred concerts, *Aberdeen Weekly Journal*, 7 Feb. 1898.

[45] Aberdeen—Lynch law in America, [Aberdeen] *Daily Free Press*, 25 Apr. 1893, p. 4; Isabella Fyvie Mayo, Letter to the Editor, [Aberdeen] *Daily Free Press*, 27 May 1893, p. 7; Isabella Fyvie Mayo, Letter to the Editor[Aberdeen] *Daily Free Press*, 22 Aug. 1893. On the reception of Wells in Britain see Teresa Zackodnik (2005) Ida B. Wells and 'American Atrocities' in Britain, *Women's Studies International Forum*, 28(4), pp. 259–273.

[46] The Ashanti Question. Meeting in Aberdeen, [Aberdeen] *Daily Free Press*, 26 Nov. 1895, p. 6. For the SRBM and the breakdown of relations between Mayo, Impey and Wells see Moore, The reputation of Isabella Fyvie Mayo.

[47] The Salt of the Earth, *Aberdeen Weekly Journal*, 23 Apr. 1894; The chronicles of our colonies, *Aberdeen Weekly Journal*, 1 Oct. 1894; Mrs Fyvie Mayo on gambling and municipalisation, *Aberdeen Weekly Journal*, 21 Oct. 1895; *Aberdeen Weekly Journal*, 23 Nov. 1895; *Aberdeen Weekly Journal*, 28 Jan. 1896; *Aberdeen Weekly Journal*, 14 Dec. 1896; Extraordinary scenes in Aberdeen. The Stop-the-War crusade, [Aberdeen] *Daily Free Press*, 21 May 1900, p. 5.

[48] Mary Jean Corbett (1992) *Representing Femininity: middle-class subjectivity in Victorian and Edwardian women's autobiographies* (New York: Oxford University Press), p. 56; Isabella Fyvie Mayo (1889–1890) On the Seventh Day, *The Sun*, 3, pp. 504–510; Mayo, *Recollections*.

[49] Mayo, *Her Day of Service*.

[50] Elizabeth Manning (Sep. 1887) Note by the editor, E. Manning, *The Indian Magazine and Review*, 202, p. 553; Alfreda M. Duster (Ed.) (1970) *Crusade for Justice: the autobiography of Ida B. Wells* (Chicago: University of Chicago Press); James D. Hunt (2005) *An American Looks at Gandhi: essays in satyagraha, civil rights and peace* (New Delhi and Chicago: Promilla & Co.). See Gordon & Nair, *Public Lives*, on the public penetration of middle-class homes in Glasgow.

[51] See letters and articles in *Christian World, Clarion, Fraternity, Labour Leader, Labour Prophet and Labour Church Record, The New Age*.

[52] 'Miles', Letter to the Editor, [Aberdeen] *Daily Free Press*, 25 Aug. 1893, p. 3.

[53] Aberdeen School board, *Aberdeen Journal*, 21 Sep. 1894.
[54] Aberdeen School Board election, [Aberdeen] *Daily Free Press*, 13 Apr. 1897, p. 7.
[55] 'Canvasser', Letter to the Editor, [Aberdeen] *Daily Free Press*, 23 Apr. 1894; *Northern Figaro*, 28 Apr. 1894, p. 7; Pleasant Sunday Afternoon Service, *Aberdeen Weekly Journal*, 7 Jan. 1895; Cronwright-Schreiner in Aberdren [sic], *Aberdeen Weekly Journal*, 21 May 1900; Death of an Aberdeen Authoress, *Aberdeen Daily Journal*, 14 May 1914.
[56] William Diack (30 Jan. 1903) Isabella Fyvie Mayo, a famous Scottish authoress, *The Scottish Co-operator*, pp. 93–94.
[57] Mrs. Fyvie Mayo ('Edward Garrett') (1894) 'Labour and worship'. Notes of an address to the Aberdeen Labour Church, *The Labour Prophet*, 3, (July and August), pp. 93, 100.
[58] Mayo, *Recollections*, p. 170.
[59] Gleadle, *Borderline Citizens*, p. 264.

'The Subject is Obscene: No Lady Would Dream of Alluding to It': Marie Stopes and her courtroom dramas

Lesley Hall

Although it is often assumed that Marie Stopes (1880–1958) was put on trial for her promotion of birth control, the cause célèbre which brought her major media attention in 1923 was in fact her own libel suit against the Roman Catholic doctor Halliday Sutherland for his attack against her clinic. This article looks at Stopes performing in the courtroom as a victim of injustice, deserving of remedy, both in this case, and in her earlier case for the annulment of the marriage to her first husband, Reginald Ruggles Gates, on the grounds of his impotence. It is argued that her success in bringing the latter to a successful conclusion led her to an unrealistic assessment of the degree to which she could control the narrative about herself within the context of the courtroom in her libel suit. In both cases, factors external to the courtroom had a significant impact.

Most people in the UK have heard of Marie Stopes (1880–1958), the famous advocate of birth control and author of the pioneering and successful marriage manual *Married Love*. While she was involved in a number of legal actions over the course of her life, there were two courtroom dramas in which she was concerned as a leading performer of particular significance in the trajectory of her career: in fact they may be seen as bracketing its most successful phase. One was the action for annulment of her first marriage in 1916, when her life must have seemed in a very low place, and the second was her libel suit against the Roman Catholic doctor, Halliday Sutherland, in 1923, at perhaps the peak of her fame (or notoriety).

Some people have an idea that this latter widely reported cause célèbre was in fact about Stopes being put on trial for her promotion of birth control and sexual enlightenment.[1] Muriel Box opened her introduction to the published transcript of the case with the sentence 'What crime did Marie Stopes commit?', which suggests that this was a fairly common belief during the 1960s.[2] However, it is not entirely wrong for this case to be remembered as Stopes being on trial, since *Stopes vs Sutherland* did, in fact, come to centre on Stopes herself and questions about the acceptability of her 'New Gospel' proclaiming marital bliss without automatic parenthood.

Friends and legal advisors had cautioned her against pursuing the case: the controversial surgeon and health reformer Sir William Arbuthnot Lane warned her that lawsuits were an 'uncertain luxury', and suggested that 'you and your work are too big to mind paltry criticism'.[3] The case itself, as will be discussed further, was far from an unqualified triumph from Stopes's point of view. Even so, in one sense it formed the apogee of her career, as extensive press coverage (including in periodicals which refused paid advertisements for her clinic) brought her name and her message to audiences unlikely to encounter her books. Her sales soared as never before, more copies of *Married Love* being sold between March 1923 and November than in the first five years since publication.[4] Her already copious correspondence from grateful readers increased dramatically.[5]

How did she get there, how deliberate was her use of the courtroom as a stage to promote herself and her message, and what were the consequences of placing herself on trial in this way? This particular courtroom drama was preceded in Stopes's life by another notorious legal case, her annulment suit against her first husband, Reginald Ruggles Gates, on the grounds of his sexual impotence, which became her foundational myth about her incarnation as a reformer of marriage. In the Preface to *Married Love* she wrote: 'In my first marriage I paid such a terrible price for sex-ignorance that I feel that knowledge gained at such a cost should be placed at the service of humanity'.[6] Stopes's successful negotiation of a far from clear-cut case and her vindication in the form of the dissolution of their marriage, it may be suggested, created expectations about her ability to produce a courtroom performance that would convince legal authorities and institutions, which ultimately proved ill-founded.

Stopes had had a spectacular career, or rather, several careers, by the time of the suit against Sutherland. From the example of her mother, Charlotte Carmichael Stopes, a leading figure in the late nineteenth-century women's movement and a militant suffragette,[7] and also through the encouragement of her father, Henry Stopes, an architect from a wealthy brewing family interested in archaeology, Stopes gained a sense of the possibility of achievement and a faith in her ability to make her own destiny. At University College London, she had a brilliant career both academically—winning the Gold Medal for Botany in her first year—and socially as President of the Women's Debating Society. She took a BSc with double honours (botany and geology) within two years. Her desire to shine was manifest.

She undertook postgraduate study at the Botanical Institute in Munich, the only woman among five hundred men, and completed and defended her PhD thesis (in German) within the year. (Sutherland's snide, post-war, hints in his 1922 attack on her clinic about 'German philosophy' were thus rather misleading.)[8] This led to a remarkably successful scientific career in paleobotany, the study of fossil plants, that would have been remarkable in a man, but for a woman at that period was quite spectacular. Stopes's profile as a successful female scientist was considerable, combining her indubitable achievements with a distinctive femininity of self-presentation: contemporary photographs show her arrayed in flowing garments in romantic poses rather than tailored severity.

Professional success was not paralleled in her emotional life. She had a number of unsatisfactory and inconclusive relationships. In 1910, aged thirty, increasingly desperate to experience marriage and motherhood, she met the Canadian botanist Reginald Ruggles Gates, two years her junior, at a meeting of the American Association for the Advancement of Science. They were married in Montreal soon after. On their arrival in London, Marie issued a circular letter informing friends and acquaintances that she would keep her own name. She had no intention of dwindling into conventional paradigms of wifehood: she also supported the Married Women's Taxation Reform League and opposed the imposition of marriage bars to women's employment.

The marriage initially appeared to be a great success, but rifts soon appeared. There are questions about the marriage and its dissolution which neither the narrative established by Stopes nor the counter-version by Gates, posthumously placed in the British Library, really answer. Her public version was that, concerned at her failure to become pregnant, she had enlightened herself by studying the learned tomes, medical and legal, on problems of sexuality held in the 'Cupboard' of the British Museum Reading Room (to which she had access by virtue of her professional status as a scientist) and discovered that the marriage had never been consummated: thus she successfully sued for an annulment. How ignorant she actually was remains debatable: in 1910 she had written a treatise on marriage (unpublished and now lost), though possibly theoretical and idealistic rather than the practical handbook she eventually produced.[9]

Gates on his part alleged that far from being a naive innocent, Stopes was sexually knowing and had insisted on the use of birth control from the outset of the marriage. She was, he asserted, over-sexed to the point of nymphomania and multiply adulterous. However, his statement on these matters was written nearly fifty years after the events in question, which had clearly rankled bitterly through two further marriages, and it burst forth in response to Keith Briant's adulatory biography of Stopes.[10]

What is clear is that the marriage soon became, at least from Stopes's point of view and, from the tenor of his later diatribe, also from Gates's, a complete disaster area. Letters from Stopes to her solicitor in the autumn of 1913 indicate a women desperately thrashing around to find some legal exit from a toxic relationship. At that date a woman could only divorce her husband for adultery *plus* another matrimonial offence such as cruelty, desertion or sodomy. She could probably have obtained a legal separation on the grounds of cruelty, or Gates's failure to maintain her (she had been the principal breadwinner), but Stopes wanted the marriage utterly dissolved. She was an early instance of a woman explicitly concerned about the sinister ticking of her biological clock: 'I have always passionately desired a baby, &... have already wasted the best five years of my child-bearing life'.[11]

Stopes embarked on this struggle in a state of considerable naivety over the divorce law,[12] but, over the course of the next two years, she must have realised that obtaining a divorce, under the law as it stood, was not a realistic proposition. By the autumn of 1915, she was preparing a statement laying out her evidence for a verdict of nullity of the marriage on the grounds of non-consumption. Meanwhile Gates—who had locked Stopes out of their Hampstead house, and then written to her demanding her contribution towards the rent—had gone to North America on family and professional business.[13] Following the outbreak of the Great War, he wrote to his employers at King's College London indicating that 'he would prefer, in the circumstances, to stay on the other side of the Atlantic'.[14]

Whatever the sexual state of affairs between the couple, there was clearly bitter hostility and a breakdown of all possibility of repairing the relationship. Gates himself only started to take legal action with a view to divorce after Stopes had already set the ball rolling (and it is questionable whether, whatever his later claims, he had evidence that would stand up in court).[15] Annulment was the only way that she could free herself while retaining both her respectability and the chance of a second and better union. There was still the problem that the very fact of identifying non-consummation as an issue demonstrated a degree of sexual knowledge in the complainant that might undermine her claims to respectability. There was therefore a significant issue of reputation management requiring careful negotiation. How very delicate the issues involved were can be seen from the way Stopes dramatized her own story in *Vectia*, the play she based on the debacle of her marriage.

Heron, based on Aylmer Maude, who lodged with the Gateses, is cast in the rather less intimate relation of next-door neighbour, and Stopes very heavily emphasises the absence of romantic feelings between him and Vectia. In the play Heron enlightens Vectia as to why she isn't having the baby she longs for, rather than Vectia taking measures to discover the reason herself.[16] This was surely because a woman actively seeking sexual understanding would have been seen as immoral and unsympathetic.[17] June Rose in her biography of Stopes was inclined to believe that Stopes and Maude did have some kind of affair (and that she did, in fact, learn in rather more practical ways about sex from him than Vectia learnt from Heron), but that Maude had no intention of dissolving his own comfortably semi-detached marriage.[18]

Stopes obtained a rather qualified certificate of virginity from her GP, which read 'In my opinion there is evidence from the condition of the hymen that there has not been penetration by a normal male organ', and informed her lawyers that prior to marriage, on medical advice while travelling in the tropics, she had employed a wide-nozzled vaginal douche apparatus to explain any hymeneal damage.[19] The two doctors appointed by the court examined her in March 1916 (one of whom, ironically, was to publish a hostile article in the special birth control issue of the medical journal *The Practitioner* appearing in the same year as her libel suit was in court: this would almost certainly never have appeared had it not been for Stopes' notoriety).[20] They declared that they had 'examined the parts and organs of generation of Marie Carmichael Gates otherwise Stopes the petitioner and do find that she is a virgin and that she hath not any impediment on her part to prevent the consummation of marriage' and that Ruggles Gates had not presented himself for examination.[21]

This might seem unequivocal evidence for lack of consummation, but Hanne Blank has demonstrated that the determination of virginity was and is by no means a simple and absolute matter of present or absent hymen.[22] Textbooks of forensic medicine available at the period of the case indicate that doctors recognised no single sign that could be taken as definitive proof, and all concurred that the hymen could have been destroyed by a number of non-sexual occurrences (the matter was seldom discussed in any detail in the sections on nullity, usually being found in the chapters relating to sexual assault).[23] The whole question had to be considered contextually, with the woman's own demeanour as a significant element.

Stopes' case was heard on 9 May 1916. The judge seems to have felt a good deal of unease about it, first enquiring whether the case should not be held in camera and then saying 'Ladies, I think, should leave the Court; I think it would be better if any ladies would leave the Court'. He also cut off her detailed descriptions of Gates's conjugal inadequacies: 'That will do'.[24] In spite of his queasiness, Stopes was granted her decree nisi, which was made absolute on 20 November.[25]

Studies of women, crime, and the courtroom have emphasised the extent to which women were obliged to manifest a convincing version of reputable womanhood for success in their cases.[26] It is plausible that Stopes could have persuaded herself that—whatever the undiscoverable technicalities of her relationship with Gates—there had been at the profoundest level no real marriage and no genuine union, and therefore had been able to give an effective performance of ignorant young woman marrying in innocence an impotent man who had deprived her of maternity. This ability to impose her version of events on a situation might well have influenced her decision to sue for libel, seven years later. However, a neglected factor in this equation was Gates's decision to remain in America in 1914, which would, in context, have strongly affected opinions of his essential manliness, or rather, lack of it: 'So everything has been done as far as possible to get this man to come and be examined by the doctor of the

Court'.[27] His failure to appear to defend his masculinity, and for such a reason, would not have encouraged judgement in his favour.

In the limbo between separating from Gates and receiving her annulment, Stopes worked on a non-fictional study of sex and marriage, based on the knowledge she had acquired, and observation of her own sexual feelings as well as discussion with other advanced women. She became very involved in progressive literary and intellectual circles, in which she was well-known and influential. Even so, she experienced difficulties in getting her manuscript published. Finally, through her contacts in the birth control movement, she met Humphrey Verdon Roe, a wealthy young officer in the Royal Flying Corps interested in promoting contraception, who put up the £200 required by the small firm of Fifield and Co to publish her manuscript. Appearing early in 1918, *Married Love* became a runaway best-seller, generating a huge correspondence, followed in November by *Wise Parenthood*, dealing explicitly with contraception (only implied in *Married Love*). Meanwhile, feelings between Stopes and Lieutenant Roe had ripened, and in spite of his pre-existing engagement, they were married in May 1918. By the end of the year Stopes was, to her delight, pregnant. Fast approaching forty, she remained an over-achiever, continuing a hectic round of lecturing, writing, travelling, dealing with her enormous correspondence, dashing off letters to the newspapers, and joining the deliberations of the National Birth Rate Commission, while still pursuing her government-sponsored researches on coal. On 16 July 1919, following a labour under the new Twilight Sleep method of analgesia, her first child, a son, was stillborn. This disappointment did not slow her down.

In 1920, she claimed to have received a direct message from God while sitting under a yew tree near her home, to inform the bishops at the Lambeth Conference of *A New Gospel to All Peoples*, that marital intercourse was not intended solely for the procreation of children: a revelation greeted with silence by the bishops.[28] Early in 1921, she and Humphrey inaugurated a birth control clinic in a poor working class area, Upper Holloway, North London, staffed by trained nurses with a woman doctor available. On 31 May 1921 Stopes made the first move in a campaign to make birth control respectable with a mass meeting at the Queen's Hall London, attended by distinguished medical, political, literary and artistic sponsors. Before a packed audience, she emphasised the positive aim of 'healthy, happy, desired, babies'.[29] Negative though much of the response was, she had breached the silence of taboo.

The very high profile of Stopes's enterprise aroused hostility, in particular among Roman Catholics. Her less than favourable views on doctors and their ignorance and pusillanimity about contraception also aroused antipathy among the medical profession. In 1922, Halliday Sutherland, a Roman Catholic medical man, published a book entitled *Birth Control: A Statement of Christian Doctrine against the Neo-Malthusians*. In this he made several attacks on Stopes personally as well as on birth control generally. He cited exchanges she had had in the pages of various journals alleging that doctors had a mercenary interest in keeping the birth rate high.[30] The passage to which she most objected read as follows:

[T]he ordinary decent instincts of the poor are against these practices, and indeed they have used them less than any other class. But, owing to their poverty, lack of learning, and helplessness, the poor are the natural victims of those who seek to make experiments on their fellows. In the midst of a London slum a woman who is a Doctor of German Philosophy (Munich) has opened a birth control clinic where working women are instructed in a method of contraception described by Professor McIlroy as 'the most harmful method of which I have had experience'. It is truly amazing that this monstrous campaign of birth control should be tolerated by the Home Secretary. Charles Bradlaugh was condemned to jail for a less serious crime.[31]

Stopes initially challenged Sutherland to a public debate, but on receiving no response, issued a writ for libel.[32]

It was nearly a year before the case was heard, during which two other birth-control related *causes célèbres* drew significant public attention. Late in 1922 Nurse Elizabeth Daniels was dismissed from her post as a Health Visitor in Edmonton for giving birth control advice. Early in 1923 the anarchist publishers, Guy Aldred and Rose Witcop, were prosecuted for selling Margaret Sanger's pamphlet, *Family Limitation*. Stopes demonstrated a considerable lack of supportiveness, withdrawing her initial support for Daniels on tenuous grounds, and not only refusing to support the Aldred/Witcop appeal campaign, but writing privately to the Director of Public Prosecutions to condemn Sanger's work.[33] These actions lost her influential support within the growing birth control movement.[34] Stopes possibly resented the attention that was being drawn away from her pending case towards these other victims of persecution. She had already had a public and vituperative exchange with Stella Browne during which she utterly denied owing anything to Sanger, in spite of having been informed by her about the female check pessary in 1915,[35] and vindictively tried to get her solicitor to take legal action against *The New Generation*, in which the claims for Sanger's priority had been made, and against Browne herself.[36]

Convincing the Divorce Court that she was the injured and innocent party in her first marriage may have given Stopes rather too high hopes of the outcome of bringing a libel prosecution and her ability to manage her reputation successfully. The situation was very different: far from being a still relatively young woman deceived (though in far from the usual way) by her husband, Stopes in 1923 was a notorious and newsworthy figure. She had written several best-selling books on subjects still considered very risqué and even pornographic, and she had, of course, set up a birth control clinic.[37] The feelings she aroused in the courtroom, therefore, were not necessarily as sympathetic as she had anticipated. The case also took place in the context of the recent preceding scandals, the Aldred/Witcop case in particular having associated the subject with their anarchist and free love views.[38]

Stopes faced a situation very different from the one she had encountered in the Divorce Court in 1916. Then, the judge had found the whole matter so distasteful that he wanted to hurry through it with as little gory detail as possible, while Gates's unwillingness to leave America while war raged in Europe meant that he put up essentially no defence and that therefore judgement went more or less by default to Stopes. Things were very different in 1923 in the libel case, not only because she was facing a determined defence from Sutherland.

Her own counsel was Patrick Hastings, whose speeches to the court manifested a certain unease about how best to present his client. In his address to the jury, when mentioning the annulment of Stopes's first marriage, he expressed himself glad that they were all male as he would have felt hesitation at discussing such matters to a mixed audience (although women were eligible for jury service there were none on the jury).[39] In his account of Stopes's antecedents, to underpin assertions of her respectability and credibility, Hastings mentioned her father, 'a man of very great culture and of very great research', but was silent as to her equally distinguished mother.[40]

However, he was, with whatever reservations, on her side. The counsel for Sutherland began with the loaded question, meant to suggest a certain equivocal quality to her status, 'I do not know whether you would like me to call you Dr Stopes, or Mrs Stopes, or Mrs Roe'.[41] (*The Times*, which was persistently hostile to Stopes, throughout its reports of the case referred to her as 'Mrs Stopes'.)[42] The judge himself, Lord Justice Hewart, was profoundly antagonistic, intervening in the examination of witnesses and making prejudicial remarks from the bench. Mostly notably he claimed that Stopes must have been making enormous profits from the sale of her books, completely misunderstanding the economics of publishing.[43]

In spite of the stellar line-up of medical witnesses with which Stopes was provided, strong professional support came to the defence of Sutherland's statements. As Box points out in her introduction to the trial transcript, 'the medical evidence from both sides virtually cancelled out', whereas no women were called to testify in support of Sutherland's allegations to having been victims of Stopes's experimentation.[44] In a confusing and muddled conclusion, the jury found Sutherland's remarks justified but not fair comment, and recommended damages of £100, but the judge found for Sutherland, with costs.[45] Stopes appealed, and was granted damages and costs by the Court of Appeal. But Sutherland, with strong Catholic backing, appealed to the House of Lords, which upheld the original verdict, although one Law Lord entered a dissenting verdict that the jury had been misdirected.[46] George Bernard Shaw wrote to Stopes:

> The decision is scandalous, but I am not surprised at it: the opposition can always fall back on simple taboo. The subject is obscene: no lady would dream of alluding to it in mixed society.[47]

This was very far from being the triumphant vindication that Stopes had surely envisaged: the case dragged on at substantial expense, for no clear legal statement of her role as righteous injured party. It was very unlike her annulment, in which she had both gained her freedom and, arguably, revenge on Ruggles Gates by casting him as a pathetic excuse for a husband.

Nonetheless, the outcome was far from entirely negative. Sales of her books soared, much of the press reported sympathetically throughout, and letters of support poured in from all quarters.[48] Even her rivals in the birth control movement paid tribute to the publicity for the cause. C. V. Drysdale of the Malthusian League 'fanc[ied] the popular practical propaganda will fall almost entirely into the hands of Dr Stopes after the publicity she has got for her case'[49] Stella Browne wrote to Havelock Ellis about the 'good adv[ertisemen]t the Stopes case [is] giving the cause'.[50] A more cynical view was (reportedly) expressed by Lord Dawson, a leading light in the medical profession and himself sympathetic to birth control, who was alleged to have 'once told Dr Robert L. Dickinson that she told [him] that she guessed she would have to have a suit soon as her books were not selling sufficiently well. Shortly afterwards she sued the Catholic, Sutherland'.[51]

This case was also the point at which Stopes became increasingly alienated from the wider birth control movement, as well as ever more paranoid about her opponents on the anti-contraception side. While it is true that there was considerable Roman Catholic hostility to her work, and organised Catholic opposition to birth control, the specific personally targeted conspiracies she believed in seem somewhat implausible, such as the plot to have her pet chow Wuffles put down as dangerous.[52]

Why did she embark on the case? Sutherland's book had extremely limited circulation, especially by comparison with her own works, and could have been dismissed as a trivial annoyance, particularly as the author's own biases were so clear. Many people would doubtless have taken this to heart and shrugged off Sutherland's attack, but for all her success and the amount of adulation that she received, Stopes was quite unable to do this. This was a characteristic very evident in her books and papers. She drafted and redrafted irate letters concerning minor misrepresentations of her works and got into extended epistolary brawls—the one with Stella Browne over her debt to Margaret Sanger, already mentioned, escalated from private notes to vituperation in the pages of *The New Generation* and *The Birth Control Review*. Books from her library bear furious scrawled rebuttals on passages to which she objected.[53] She wanted everyone to admit that she was right and to give her the credit she believed her due. She could not let things go.

Stopes had already been engaged in controversy with the old guard of birth control campaigners over the historical role of the free thought movement and the pivotal trial of Bradlaugh and Besant for obscenity. Bradlaugh and Besant had successfully challenged their prosecution in court, and won an acquittal: the jury, while conceding that *Fruits of Philosophy* was an obscene book, agreed that its publishers had been actuated by good intentions.[54] It seems not entirely improbable, from what we know of Stopes and her highly competitive nature, that she wanted to outdo them with a dramatic new epoch-making case in defence of birth control, in which it would be, in her person, triumphantly vindicated.

This scenario gains a certain amount of credibility from Stopes's stage-plays. In several of these a young woman finds herself in an equivocal, though morally justified, position. In *The Race, or Ernest's Immortality* (1918), Rosemary Pexton becomes pregnant by her fiancé, whom her father has refused permission for her to marry, before he leaves for the Front, where he is killed.[55] The eponymous heroine of *Vectia* is subjected to paranoid accusations from her impotent husband.[56] In *Our Ostriches*, Evadne finds that her increasing commitment to birth control estranges her aristocratic fiancé.[57] But they are all positioned as essentially righteous, and vindicated by the events of the plots. They are presented as unambiguously virtuous, and, although threatened, never actually lose anything by taking the stand they do.[58]

In the theatre of the High Court, Stopes must have felt that she would be enacting a similar scenario. Unfortunately, several other scripts were in operation, not merely those of the prosecution and the judge, and the various witnesses called by each side, but also, it may be argued, that of her own counsel, and indeed, the very parameters of the courtroom situation and the constraints of legal procedure and protocol. She was not writing the script nor was she in charge of the production: in several instances early in her own testimony, her desire to explain her position and intentions at length was cut short by her own counsel—'May I stop you there. One is anxious to keep, if one can, within short answers'.[59] In her cross-examination by Ernest Charles, for Sutherland, she had probably not anticipated his strategy of hostile nitpicking questions concerning her statements on various contraceptive methods in various places and in different editions of her books, including those on the gold pin pessary which she no longer recommended, as well on the ways and places in which her books were sold.[60] During her cross-examination by Serjeant Sullivan for Sutherland's publishers, she complained 'My Lord, he keeps on interrupting me'.[61] During the cross-examination of Nurse Maud Hebbes from the Mothers' Clinic, Ernest Charles complained of Stopes 'speaking rather louder than she intends' (i.e. not in a presumably acceptable discreet whisper to her counsel but in a way inappropriately audible to the rest of the courtoom while not formally on the stand and therefore entitled to speak).[62]

Counsel for Sutherland and his publishers made repeated and determined attempts to depict Stopes's books as obscene and inappropriately circulated among the young and unmarried, and birth control as innately dangerous and deleterious. The Lord Chief Justice himself intervened in this cross-examination to ask 'why did it appear to you to be desirable or necessary... to produce a book like this?'.[63] In his summing up, the Lord Chief Justice characterised the proceedings as 'this rather long and disagreeable case'[64] before making his own lengthy (as even he recognised—'Members of the Jury, I have detained you at perhaps excessive length') and prejudiced plea to the jury.[65] This was surely not the scenario envisaged by Stopes.

Nonetheless, the impression that many people did retain from the case was exactly what Stopes wanted: the unjustly victimised but righteous heroine who was fighting for the good of others. But this does not seem to have been enough for Stopes herself, who wanted not just success—and in terms of publicising herself and her cause, and garnering a substantial amount of sympathy for both, the case succeeded outstandingly—but victory and vindication, which she did not achieve. Nor did she achieve a dramatic martyrdom; only a lawsuit which dragged on, inconclusively and expensively and to her ultimate defeat in the House of Lords. This did not discourage her in later years from becoming almost excessively litigious and may even have motivated her to this course.

Over the course of her life, Stopes threw herself into many roles, bringing to them her intense convictions, undoubted personal charisma, and capacity for self-dramatization. However, some of them went over less successfully than others. Her performance as a brilliant yet feminine scientist was based on her genuine abilities as a palaeobotanist, a field in which her achievements included significant and still recognised studies on the composition of coal. Her works on marriage and contraception were adeptly pitched towards specific audiences and found a resonance in many hearts and minds with the illumination they provided on subjects previously hidden in darkness.

However, in other instances her self-dramatization failed to take adequate account of her particular intended audience, or to realise that there were other actors in the scenario to whom she should adjust or adapt her performance. The Anglican bishops ignored her self-positioning as a prophetess in *A New Gospel*, and this is really not very surprising. Other members of the birth control movement were unwilling to act the admiring chorus while Stopes took centre stage. In her libel suit Stopes was not dealing with the characters she had created in her plays, but with other individuals with their own agendas who had narratives about what was going on which ran athwart her attempt to control the story, as did the constraints of legal process. It is possible to conclude that Stopes' performance was insufficiently self-conscious and that she had failed to construct a persona that would successfully carry her through the tribulations of cross-examination by refusing to be rattled by the hostile line of questioning.[66] The outcome of her libel suit suggests both the success, and ultimately the limitations, of her desire to engage in courtroom drama.

Notes

[1] I have certainly had people mention this to me when discussing Stopes several decades later.
[2] Muriel Box (Ed.) (1967) *The Trial of Marie Stopes* (London: Femina), p. 11.
[3] Sir W. Arbuthnot Lane to Stopes, 22 Jan. 1923, BL Add Ms 58566, cited in June Rose (1992) *Marie Stopes and the Sexual Revolution* (London: Faber & Faber), p. 163.
[4] Peter Eaton & Marilyn Warnick (1977) *Marie Stopes: a checklist of her writings* (London: Croom Helm), pp. 23–24.
[5] Rose, *Marie Stopes*, p. 173.
[6] Marie C. Stopes (1918) *Married Love: a new contribution to the solution to sexual difficulties* (London: AC Fifield), p. xiii.
[7] Lesley A. Hall (2004) Stopes, Charlotte Brown Carmichael (1840–1929), *Oxford Dictionary of National Biography* (Oxford: Oxford University Press), online edn, Oct. 2005 [http://www.oxforddnb.com /view/article/53016, accessed 4 Dec. 2010].
[8] Halliday Sutherland (1922) *Birth Control: a statement of Christian doctrine against the Neo-Malthusians* (London: Harding & More), pp. 101–102.
[9] Alluded to in a letter from Maurice Hewlett to Stopes, 20 February or March 1911 [date pencilled on letter, perhaps by Stopes], British Library Additional Manuscripts 59496.

[10] Statement by Reginald Ruggles Gates, 24 Apr. 1962, BL Add Ms 59848.
[11] Marie Stopes, statement of claim to Nullity of Marriage, 21 Sep. 1915, BL Add Ms 586647.
[12] Manuscript (draft) letter from Stopes to Messrs Brown (Brown, Montgomery and Michael of Montreal) 12 Oct. 1913, BL Add Ms 586647.
[13] Ruggles Gates to Stopes, 10 July 1914, and draft of her reply, BL Add Ms 58462.
[14] Marie Stopes, statement of claim to Nullity of Marriage, 21 Sep. 1915, BL Add Ms 586647.
[15] Note that Gates filed divorce proceedings on 15 Oct. 1915 (a fortnight after Stopes's nullity suit was filed), and this was served on her on 3 Nov. 1915, in BL Add Ms 586647.
[16] Marie Stopes (1926) *A Banned Play (Vectia) and a Preface on the Censorship* (London: J Bale & Co.).
[17] See Simon Szreter & Kate Fisher (2010) *Sex Before the Sexual Revolution: intimate life in England 1918–1963* (Cambridge: Cambridge University Press), in particular Ch. 2, pp. 63–112.
[18] Rose, *Marie Stopes*, pp. 84–89.
[19] Marie Stopes: statement of claim to Nullity of Marriage—copy of certificate from her family doctor, 21 Sep. 1915, BL Add Ms 586647.
[20] Sir Maurice Abbot-Anderson (1923) Birth Control as seen by an Open Mind, *The Practitioner*, CXI, pp. 6–13, in which he alleged that birth control clinics 'are at the present time unsavoury and harmful institutions, and should, if existing at all, be only in the hands of the medical profession': a fairly clear slap at Stopes's Mothers' Clinic in Upper Holloway, in which women were seen by trained nurses, and a woman doctor only consulted for particular health problems.
[21] Statement by the Inspectors appointed in the High Court, Reginald E. Crosse, W. M. Abbot-Anderson, 8 Mar. 1916, BL Add Ms 586647.
[22] Hanne Blank (2007) *Virgin: the untouched history* (New York: Bloomsbury), pp. 32–41.
[23] Alfred Swaine Taylor (1910) *The Principles and Practice of Medical Jurisprudence*, 6th edn (London: JA Churchill), pp. 29–33; J. Dixon Mann & William A. Brend (1914) *Forensic Medicine and Toxicology* (London: Charles Griffin), pp. 107–108; John Glaister (1915) *A Text-Book of Medical Jurisprudence and Toxicology* (Edinburgh: E & S Livingstone), pp. 483–486; W. G. Aitchison Robertson (1916) *Manual of Medical Jurisprudence and Toxicology and Public Health* (London: A & C Black), pp. 255–256.
[24] Proceedings in the High Court Divorce Division, Gates orse [sic; i.e., 'otherwise'] Stopes against Gates, before Mr Justice Shearman, 9 May 1916, BL Add Ms 586647.
[25] Letter to Stopes from Braby and Waller, 20 Nov. 1916, BL Add Ms 586647.
[26] See, for example, Shani D'Cruze (1998) *Crimes of Outrage: sex, violence and Victorian working women* (London: Routledge); Ginger Frost (1995) *Promises Broken: courtship, class and gender in Victorian England* (Charlottesville, VA: University of Virginia Press).
[27] Report of the proceedings in court, 9 May 1916, Mr Willis for the petitioner, BL Add Ms 586647.
[28] Stopes (1922) *A New Gospel to All Peoples. (A revelation of God, uniting physiology and the religions of man)* (London: AL Humphreys).
[29] *Queen's Hall Meeting on Constructive Birth Control. Speeches and impressions* (London: GP Putnam's Sons, 1922).
[30] Sutherland, *Birth Control*, pp. 88–93.
[31] Ibid., pp. 101–102. On the Bradlaugh case, see S. Chandrasekhar (1981) *"A dirty filthy book": the writings of Charles Knowlton and Annie Besant on reproductive physiology and birth control and an account of the Bradlaugh-Besant trial with the definitive

texts of *Fruits of philosophy*, by Charles Knowlton, *The law of population*, by Annie Besant, *Theosophy and the law of population*, by Annie Besant (Berkeley: University of California Press).

[32] Writ in the case of *Stopes v Sutherland*, 11 May 1922, BL Add Ms 586647.
[33] June Rose, *Marie Stopes*, p. 162, and Ruth Hall (1977) *Marie Stopes: a biography* (London: Andre Deutsch), pp. 210–211; both mention this, on the basis of a rough draft letter to the DPP among Stopes's papers. Surprisingly little work has been done on the Aldred/Witcop case, which was a significant moment in the development of the British birth control movement: it is not even mentioned in most biographies of Margaret Sanger. There are brief references in Audrey Leathard (1980) *The Fight for Family Planning* (London: Macmillan), p. 26, and in R. A. Soloway (1982) *Birth Control and the Population Question in England, 1870–1930* (Chapel Hill: University of North Carolina Press), p. 230, and alluded to in biographies of individuals involved in the defence: Jane Tolerton (1992) *Ettie: A life of Ettie Rout* (Auckland: Penguin Books (NZ)), pp. 218–221; Lesley A. Hall (2011) *The Life and Times of Stella Browne, Feminist and Free Spirit* (London: IB Tauris), pp. 111–112
[34] F. W. Stella Browne to Havelock Ellis, 25 Dec. 1922, BL Add Ms 70539.
[35] F. W. Stella Browne to The Editor of the *Birth Control News*, 14 Sep. 1922; Marie Stopes to Stella Browne, 19 Sep. 1922, Marie Stopes papers, Wellcome Library, PP/MCS/A.42.
[36] Marie Stopes to Braby, 7 Jan. 1923, BL Add Ms 586647.
[37] Contemporary attitudes cited in Szreter & Fisher, *Sex before the Sexual Revolution*, p. 260, included 'very naughty', ' She was a fallen woman doing all that', 'a really filthy book'.
[38] See above, n33.
[39] Box, *The Trial of Marie Stopes*, pp. 46, 29.
[40] Ibid., p. 45.
[41] Ibid., p. 80.
[42] Rose, *Marie Stopes*, p. 167.
[43] Box, *The Trial of Marie Stopes*, p. 364.
[44] Ibid., p. 29.
[45] Rose, *Marie Stopes*, pp. 172–173.
[46] Ibid., pp. 174–175.
[47] George Bernard Shaw to Marie Stopes, 2 Dec. 1924, cited in Rose, *Marie Stopes*, p. 175.
[48] See above, notes 4 and 5.
[49] C. V. Drysdale to Margaret Sanger, 26 Mar. 1923, Margaret Sanger papers in the Library of Congress, Washington DC, Volume 21.
[50] F. W. Stella Browne to Havelock Ellis, 25 Aug. 1923, BL Add Ms 70539.
[51] Norman Himes to A. Pillay, 28 Apr 1937, Norman Himes papers in the Countway Library, Boston MA, BMS C77 Box 59 Marriage Hygiene 660.
[52] Rose, *Marie Stopes*, p. 188.
[53] Among books from Stopes's own collection now held in the Wellcome Library, Michael Fielding (1947) *Parenthood: Design or Accident? A manual of birth control 5th edition* (London: Williams and Norgate, first published 1928) includes among the more legible scrawls in her hand 'a lie' '*Bad*' '*Utterly* unreliable if alone'; and J. P. Gair (n.d. c.1920s) *Sexual Science as Applied to The Control of Motherhood* (London: Anglo-Eastern) has numerous underlinings, marginal question marks and exclamation points, and scrawled comments such as 'Cribbed from ML' [*Married Love*].
[54] Chandrasekhar, '*A dirty filthy book*'.
[55] Marie Stopes (1918) *'Gold in the Wood' and 'The Race.' Two new plays of life* (London: AC Fifield).

[56] Stopes, *A Banned Play*.
[57] Marie C. Stopes (1923) *Our Ostriches. A play ... in three acts* (London: GP Putnam's Sons).
[58] A much more detailed study of Stopes's dramatic oeuvre is in preparation by Christina Hauck; some material from this was presented in her paper 'A Baby of Her Own: maternal desire and English polity in the plays of Marie Stopes', at the conference 'The Birth of the Birth Control Clinic', Institute of Historical Research, University of London, 11 March 2011.
[59] Box, *The Trial of Marie Stopes*, pp. 77–78.
[60] Ibid., pp. 90–107.
[61] Ibid., p. 117–118.
[62] Ibid., p. 140.
[63] Ibid., p. 119.
[64] Ibid., p. 356.
[65] Ibid., p. 377.
[66] Ibid., pp. 90–107.

Body and Self: learning to be modern in 1920s–1930s Britain

Charlotte Macdonald

Observing the divergent tracks taken by historians of the 'modern self' and those of the 'modern body' the article focuses on health and fitness movements in Britain, c.1920s–1930s. Asking whether there is a place for the body in the history of women performing 'the self' in this context, the article suggests a way in which contemporaries found a way to have a 'self' in the body. Contemporary notions of the body emphasised its interdependence with 'the mind', health and happiness being functions of each other. In the language of health and beauty was a language of inner vitality and outer radiance, a modern formulation of the individual as a 'self' equipped to embrace the exciting but uncertain possibilities of the 'modern world'. Popular print culture on 'healthy living', reports by the BMA and the National Fitness Council are considered along with more extensive discussion of the Women's League for Health and Beauty founded in 1930 by Mollie Bagot Stack and inherited by her daughter, Prunella, 'Britain's Perfect Girl', in 1935.

When a new edition of the Boston Women's Health Book Collective's original manifesto was published as *Our Bodies, Our Selves* in 1971, it captured, and in turn propelled, a central creed of late twentieth-century feminism. A catalysing text of the movement, the work has continued to evolve, sustaining health action at a global level. *Our Bodies, Our Selves* signalled feminist women's demand to reclaim their bodies, and a desire to declare autonomy in them, the title making the link between bodily control and autonomous selves. As 'our' rather than 'my', the title signified both the work of a collective, and the political rather than individual focus of the content and its objectives.[1] A generation earlier, in the 1920s–1930s, women were more concerned with claiming a place for themselves and their bodies in public life. While that might appear, at first glance, an unexceptional observation, looking at recent histories of the making of the 'modern self', against those of the 'modern woman', provokes some intriguing questions. What is the place of the body in the history of women performing the self? Are there different answers to be offered for the period 1920s–1930s, for 1960s–1980s, or other times? Is 'the body' encountered in the archive—not so much lying, but leaping, walking, marching, dancing and singing—a record of a written 'self', or a deliberate performance for posterity?[2]

The question of how to link the history of the body with the history of the modern self has arisen in the course of a larger project on bodies, state and modernity in Britain, New Zealand, Australia and Canada in the 1920s–1940s.[3] And in particular, from the observation, admittedly at a general level, that historical imaginings of 'modern girls' and 'modern women' of this period have tended to follow two rather distinct tracks. The first emphasises the body, featuring female figures sporting short shingled or bobbed hair, wearing trousers or rayon dresses, smoking cigarettes, getting about in cars and even, occasionally, aeroplanes, or taking up the fad for what Christopher Wilk has called 'healthy body culture'.[4] The other focuses on the period as one in which a distinctive concept and language of 'inner life', the production of individuality, gained popular currency: to be a 'modern girl' or a 'modern woman' denoted some consciousness of self, in time and place. In what can only be a brief excursion, the discussion here suggests that body and self were more connected in contemporary discourse and popular movements of the interwar period than has been recognised, and that the connection might be considered an historically specific way in which women found a way to 'have' a self in the body.

Recent accounts of the emergence of a 'modern self' have emphasised three broad features: its historical contingency; the centrality of the notion of an internalised, psychologised, totalised inner self as core to unique identity testified through biography; and the burgeoning of what becomes 'a therapeutic state' in the maintenance of such a self, especially in the post-Second World War era. Nikolas Rose, in his *Inventing Our Selves. Psychology, power, and personhood*, (1998) and earlier *Governing the Soul: the shaping of the private self* (1990), Carolyn Steedman, in *Landscape for a Good Woman* (1986), and much of her subsequent work, and Becky Conekin, Frank Mort and Chris Waters' collection, *Moments of Modernity* (1999) are among those who have proposed an historicised 'self' along these lines.[5] While there are varieties of emphasis and approach, Anthony Giddens' argument of self-identity as the defining problem of modernity, and Foucault's notion of individuality produced by modern technologies of power, have been influential in accounts of the emergence of a language and practice of an individualised, interior self by the middle decades of the twentieth century. These are, in turn, part of discussions seeking to answer the wider historical question of when 'a new conception of the "self" signalled a modern age characterized by fixed ideas of personal identity, especially gender identity'.[6] Even more broadly, some describe the 'self' as part of a longer history of personal identity. In her keynote address to the 2010 Women's History Network Conference, Carolyn Steedman pointed to the prominence of these concerns in suggesting we might be confronting 'the selfish turn' in historical enquiry, the next in a cavalcade of 'turns' following the 'linguistic', 'cultural', 'material' and others of recent years.[7]

Taking Giddens' lead in emphasising an acceleration of 'self-reflexivity' in the phase of 'late modernity', Conekin, Mort and Waters emphasise the proliferation and fracturing of mechanisms 'for constructing and experiencing the self' in mid-twentieth-century Britain. The ways in which 'social selfhood' was manifest expanded and were constantly in transformation. Their richly innovative collection contains a range of studies of 'self-making', yet the focus of most remains beyond the realm of the active body.[8] Defining the 'problem' of the Western conception of the person, Rose observed that 'the person is construed as a self, a naturally unique and discrete entity, the boundaries of the body enclosing, as if by definition, an inner life of the psyche, in which are inscribed the experiences of an individual biography'.[9] Here 'the body' features as a container for the 'self', a kind of perimeter within which the individual resides. The notion of the self as bounded lies at the heart of arguments about writing, and especially letter-writing, in signifying the advent of the modern subject.[10] The bounded self is one that creates and represents itself through 'private' exchanges, such as letter writing, and in modern literary forms.

In the popular body movements of the interwar decades, and in surrounding discourses as to what constituted healthy and whole living, lies another realm of self-making; one of considerable significance to contemporaries and one which provided a distinctive mechanism, and space, in which it was possible for women to perform modern selves. Keep-fit exercises and outdoor pursuits (camping, hiking, cycling) were among the most conspicuous forms of interwar modernity. Part of a wider explosion in leisure, they went along with the growth of mass spectator sports, of huge crowds at Wembley, with the popularity of night-time dog racing at tracks around London, an increasingly glamorous profile for Wimbledon tennis stars, and the popularity of all kinds of sports played in suburban courts, local halls and sportsgrounds, the last the focus of the highly successful National Playing Fields Association founded in 1925. For young women, dancing in local halls or the sophisticated night clubs of London was a major new form of entertainment. Martin Pugh's recent revisionist history of the period emphasises the centrality of dancing through adopting the title of Barbara Cartland's memoir of her years as a young woman in 1920s London, *We Danced All Night*.[11] Leisure as a motif of the era has long been recognised, from Robert Graves and Alan Hodge's contemporary portrait *The Long Week-End* (1940) to John Stevenson's *British Society, 1914–45*, the cover featuring a painting of three 1930s women ramblers, clad in shorts, standing at a stile consulting a map.[12] The *New Survey of London Life and Labour* led by H. Llewellyn Smith, conducted in 1928 and published in a series of volumes from 1930, devoted a substantial section to Londoners' access to, and uses of, leisure, as did Rowntree's 1936 study of York.[13] Women's involvement in leisure, especially physical recreation and sport, was particularly noted—in social surveys and in contemporary iconography, the active female body appearing as a prime signifier of modernity, a marker of the disjuncture of this period from what had gone before.

New forms of life in the body marked the post-World War 1 world as unmistakably and irreversibly different.[14] Contemporary consciousness of novelty was part of interwar modernity, giving rise to a lively discourse on the body and how to look after it. Confidence in medical science meant health was increasingly framed as an individual achievement rather than a consequence of fate. Writing in a small handbook of 1934 entitled *The Body and How to Keep Fit*, Sabra Milligan noted the wide interest in her subject: 'Many are those who are keenly interested in their health and bodily development and who have the desire to improve their physique and activities.'[15] Milligan could speak with authority: she had won over fifty prizes and certificates for swimming, including being selected as the Birmingham University representative at the 1930 intervarsity competition, and a number of other awards for all round 'Physical Perfection'. Her handbook provided brief explanations of the human body's structure and functioning, followed by sets of exercises to maximise a state of health and fitness. Summarising her approach, in terms highly characteristic of this period, Milligan declared: 'Life is change, and change is brought about by movement. This, therefore, implies that one should lead an active life and never be idle and incapable of vigorous movement.'[16]

Milligan's book was just one in an impressive print output directed to the cultivation of the fit body. Pitmans published a series of books on the theme, including John F. Lucy's 1937 work *Keep Fit & Cheerful*.[17] Odhams, publishers in Long Acre, produced their own series around the same time. Left-wing doctor Harry Roberts' *The Practical Way to Keep Fit* was one in the series.[18] Dorothy M. Cooke's *'Keep Fit' Work for Women* and *The Keep Fit Magazine* (later renamed *Health of Britain*) were among those directed specifically to women, sitting alongside the more formal productions emanating from Phyllis Colson's Central Council for Recreative Physical Training (1935), and from other graduates of Bedford College (the prestigious provider of higher education qualifications to women in physical education).[19] Bengamin Gayelord Hauser's *Eat and Grow Beautiful* was published by Faber and Faber in 1939, the first in what proved a long run of titles.[20]

The sense of novelty of Sabra Milligan's manifesto of, or rather *for* the body, should not be underestimated. It runs through all these popular works, as well as pervading government, medical and commercial discourses of the period. The notion of the active body, of a constant condition of change—the impermanence and ephemerality of modernity, of the necessity of continuing to *use* the body to maintain its fitness and health, felt new. It was of particular salience to women and to thinking about the female body. The shift from nineteenth-century notions of a finite or closed body energy system and the danger of exertion to potential fertility and maternity, to the modern notion that an active body was now a necessity of health, was profound.[21] Having said this, competitive sport and 'over indulgence' in the pleasure of dancing was going too far for some contemporaries. Women's physical activity was conventionally regarded as still appropriately contained within the bounds of moderate exertion.

It was not simply an active body that was now embraced as the 'modern way'. Milligan, Roberts, Lucy, Cooke and other promoters of modern health and fitness were at pains to emphasise the connectedness of body and mind. Harry Roberts brought his handbook of healthy living to a close with a fervent call:

> Today in Britain, as probably in every other country, there is a real, though often unexpressed, enthusiasm for physical fitness ...
> To hear some people talk, one would think that a man's [sic] muscles were something as remote from his nerves and his intelligence as beans from the bag which holds them. But in reality, the relation between them is so intimate that scarcely a thought can flutter across our mind, or the tiniest emotion ruffle our peace, without muscle-fibres contracting. Nor, on the other hand, can one of our muscles move without elaborate nervous telegraphing to and fro, like Lloyd's at its busiest, without, also, mental occurrences, doubtless accompanied—as we may one day be able to recognize—by organic changes in the structure of our brain.
> To put it simply, there is no such thing as exercise of the body alone, or of the mind alone: and good, sensible exercise is that which leads to and fosters the harmonious, that is, the healthy, development of mind and body alike.[22]

The benefits of activity to health, and of the inter-dependence of mind and body, was not a product of a zealous fringe, it was equally articulated by the medical establishment. The British Medical Association opened its highly influential 1936 report on Physical Education declaring: 'The mind and body are so essentially one that the divorce between them in what is commonly called education appears as unscientific as it is pronounced.'[23] Fundamental to the report's recommendations was the argument that:

> An educated body is a balanced body, just as an educated mind in the true sense is a balanced mind. Balance of body, mind, and soul should go together and reinforce each other; and perfection of balance, physical, mental and spiritual, can be the only true and scientific aim of education.[24]

The Chamberlain government's January 1937 White Paper on Physical Training brought together a range of ideals and anxieties about the body, setting the direction from which the national fitness campaign (1937–1939) was launched with high hopes. Taking care to avoid the hint of compulsion or the unpopular physical drill, the government's purpose was described as:

> not to secure that between certain ages every boy and girl practises certain physical exercises or achieves a certain standard of physical development, but to inculcate a wider realisation that physical fitness has a vital part to play in promoting a healthy mind and human happiness. It is a way of life and an attitude of mind, the importance of which is continuous and not limited to certain years

in early youth. The ultimate aim of the campaign is 'a healthy mind and human happiness': the immediate aim is to convince all who need to be convinced that in the achievement of health and happiness physical fitness has 'a vital part to play'.[25]

In a further definition of what was at stake and why fitness might be a priority, the National Fitness Council explained:

> Physical fitness is not an end in itself but one of the means to a fuller life. It is not achieved by exercise alone—hygiene, nutrition and the avoidance of disease must play their part; but the training and exercise of physical powers are as necessary as the training of mind and character if the most is to be made of life. The steps indicated below would open for many, of all ages, the way to new opportunities for health and happiness.[26]

While the government's national fitness initiative was based, in part, on anxiety about Britain's lack of fitness, it was also attempting to catch the momentum of the fad for fitness, especially amongst women. Nowhere was this enthusiasm more apparent than in the high-profile and hugely popular Women's League for Health and Beauty, founded in 1930. By 1934, the League was staging its fourth annual monster demonstrations in which hundreds of women performed before live audiences and moving cameras at London's Hyde Park and the Royal Albert Hall. In elaborately choreographed exercise, dance, and rhythmical movement performed to music, with women dressed in sleeveless white shirts and black satin shorts or velvet skirts, the display was spectacular. The League's promise, in its title, and its motto, 'movement is life', was appealing. It caught the contemporary imagination. Founder Mollie (Mary) Bagot Stack, and her daughter, twenty-year-old Prunella, the world's 'perfect girl' attracted devotion.[27] Weekly exercise classes in local halls for a modest membership fee and sixpence a session, the sociable companionship of other women, the exciting prospect of performing in one of the big demonstrations or their local offshoots, and a charismatic leadership, all proved a winning combination. By 1937, the League boasted a membership of 120,000 in 220 branches throughout the British Isles. 'Dominion centres' existed in Canada and Australia, and, from 1938, also in New Zealand.[28] Six thousand women were said to take part in the 12 June 1937 demonstration at Wembley Stadium.[29] On this scale the League dwarfed all other women's sport, movement and recreation organisations.[30]

For all its contemporary prominence and endurance (surviving to the present as the Fitness League), the WLHB has been accorded relatively little historical significance.[31] What attention has been given has struggled to place the Bagot Stack-inspired phenomenon within the context of women's organisational activism and the left-right polarities of interwar politics and culture. Jill Julius Matthews' important 1987–1990 work acknowledges the interpretive dilemma surrounding the League's relationship to feminism, and the ambiguity of its stated goal of 'racial progress'. But Samantha Clements' passing mention of the League in a recent study of feminism, citizenship and social activity in local women's organisations, 1918–1969, is more typical of the League's marginal location in discussions of interwar gender politics.[32] Very recently Ina Zweiniger-Bargielowska has considered the League as part of an argument suggesting the 'ultimately conservative' nature of interwar fitness movements.[33] Obituaries following Prunella Stack's death at age ninety-six on 30 December 2010 focused on the proof of its healthy promise in its founding figure's longevity.[34]

'Movement is Life' encapsulated the League's aim and described its principal activity.[35] On the street, in parks, halls and on the screen, the League held out the belief, and promise, that activity, health and beauty (and health *as* beauty) were within every woman's grasp. Outward beauty was the radiance of inner health. The message captured the zeitgeist of modernity—speed, pace, mobility, vigour. Like Flora Poste, the fast moving, fashionable, young urban protagonist of Stella Gibbons' *Cold Comfort Farm* (1932), the League embraced the world of motor car and aeroplane, the freshness of modern dress and thrill of vitality.[36] While not advocating that women should become motorists, or pilots, or take up a 'modern' faith or political stance, it provided an appealing place to *be* modern, to have fun in the company of other women; to enjoy what it was to be modern, but not daring, to be drawn into the promise of excitement without endangering condemnation as 'fast'. Most of all, it gave women a sense of being in the stream of modern life.[37] They might not themselves be motorists or aviatrixes, or stars of the screen, but they belonged to a world in which such things were possible. That their leaders—Mollie and most supremely, Prunella, did live such lives—only reinforced such perceptions. When Prunella married boxer, flying hero and Highland aristocrat, Lord David Douglas-Hamilton, at Glasgow Cathedral in October 1938, a special train carried hundreds of League members from London to join the celebrations. They were among the huge crowds cheering the couple on the day.[38]

The annual mass demonstrations were highlights in the League calendar. Making performance from fitness and health was the secret to the League's success.[39] Mollie Bagot Stack was a highly talented producer of drama on the big scale. She was also a supremely talented publicist, understanding how to craft an appealing, eye-catching and authentic message, and then how to convey it to the widest possible audience through skilled use of the press, cinema, and influential endorsement. Taking the League's weekly local sessions and turning them into public extravaganzas transformed a fitness movement into a public space for modern femininity, one framed by the League's diffuse ideals of 'racial health' and 'peace'. Never elaborated into specific policies or programmes, they remained broad notions that signalled progress, optimism and linked individuals and the League with the causes of the contemporary world. To belong to the League was to serve a wider good. Preceded by marches down Oxford Street and church services at All Souls, the annual demonstrations drawing hundreds and then thousands of League members to London, were, themselves, occasions inspiring in their solidarity and exciting for those who participated. Designed to do more than simply showcase well-executed movements, the demonstrations included pageant-style sequences. The finale first performed at the 1933 Royal Albert Hall, and popularly repeated and adapted thereafter, enacted the League's commitment to 'Peace'. After a bugle call, the '"Long Long Trail" was played, and a slow trail of girls with heads and hands hanging came in and formed a line'. As blue lights faded to mauve another line of girls holding short swords at arm's length entered, followed by others coming in 'two and two bandaged, one carrying a wounded "man" on her back, one blind ... Then the bugle called louder and the faint singing of "Marching Feet" [the League song] was heard outside the scenes, the light grew stronger and hundreds of girls in uniforms' surrounded the stage, the tribute to fallen soldiers passing into hope for the future.[40] Mollie Bagot Stack's description of the performance in a letter to her sister was included in the 1937 'history' of the movement, a work that underlined the founder's status as martyr to the wider cause. Mollie Bagot Stack died of thyroid cancer in January 1935, the leadership passing to Prunella.[41]

Spectacles such as those staged by the League were hugely attractive both to members and to the contemporary press, cinema and radio. For members, the 'shop assistants, secretaries, typists, telephonists, etc.', the prospect of health and beauty also carried the prospect of elevation to the most prominent public stage—if only for one or two days in the year.[42] For the press, the novelty and scale of the visual spectacle offered by the League was irresistible. Mollie Bagot Stack, and successive leaders, welcomed the cameras of British Pathé, the newspaper and magazine reporters and photographers, and even the early experimenters with television. They were careful in shaping their own image, releasing well shot still photographs and publishing them in their own magazine *Mother and Daughter*. An attractive but always respectable, purposeful and healthily vigorous demeanour was portrayed. The all-female organisation, and especially the mother-daughter attachment modelled by Mollie and Prunella, was encouraged amongst members and deflected any sensation from what were remarkably revealing costumes and unguarded exhibitionism. At a time when newsreel, radio and illustrated press were reaching audiences on an unprecedented scale, a good story, such as that offered by the League, was a powerful thing.[43] That power came from the vast expansion in the reach of modern technologies of communication, but also in the nature of its newly visual and animated forms. Much of what gave moderns a sense of their self-conscious difference was the experience of living in a world rich with the wonders of visual culture in film and image, enlivened by the 'talking pictures' of sound movies and 'sound pictures' of radio. International networks, whether of the BBC Empire Service or the exploding commerical world of Hollywood, produced audiences on previously unimaginable scales and within them, a sense of common connection.

To watch surviving film footage of the League is to be reminded of the scale of their performances, the skillful orchestration of large groups of people, and the evident delight of those taking part.[44] If we accept that the 'self' might be something made through action and in visual forms, as well as in writing or in language derived from sciences of the mind, is it not possible to consider these events as places where many women found a way to have a 'self' in the body? To suggest that League members were enacting a modern self in such participation may not be possible to prove in any categorical way, but may be useful to lay alongside other claims of 'self-making' in mid-twentieth-century Britain. Performing as members of the League, whether in the big demonstrations or in weekly classes, went beyond the temporary contrivance of the stage. Women were engaged in a deliberate and active display of themselves as people, modern in form and action. A sense of self was created by such participation, from the embodied action and sense of active being by those performing. It was also created by recognition of the highly conspicuous image of what it was to be modern that the League brought to the contemporary visual lexicon. The 'modern self' was brought into being by action and image, rather than something unseen 'within' only mirrored on the 'outside'. Whether in the uniformed, unisoned collective enterprise of the all-women League with its wider purpose, or the mixed environment of the dance hall, where individuality and self-expression was to the fore, modern women had new ways to forge embodied selves. Such possibilities were not mutually exclusive.

The interwar language of health and beauty was itself a language of the self. In offering a way to describe the relationship between inner and outer 'person'—outward appearance and inner functioning, body and mind—the physical and that 'other' self were brought together. Whether in the League's promise of health and beauty leading to 'racial health' (interpreted by Matthews as a synonym for 'maternal', 'a non-specific concern with the health of future generations'),[45] or in other popular formulations of healthy living in these years, the emphasis on health of body and mind, outer radiance and inner zest, the interdependence of 'health and happiness', were all ways of linking an inner 'being' with a newly conscious sense of a healthy and active body. These were also recipes for how to live in the modern world. They provided guidance for how to approach living day-to-day, from morning exercises to nightly wash, from daily rush to weekly routine, discerning affordable purchases from false lures; taking up the fast-moving excitement while staying aware of the underlying threat and uncertainty. Health *as* beauty conveyed the popular notion of vitality, but could also serve a critical or reassuring purpose. Beauty could be found within and was not reliant on the outer adoption of commercially bought cosmetics or fashionable clothing.

In light of what has been suggested of how health and fitness movements operated in the interwar years, how might we revise Rose's definition of the modern self? Is it possible to add to existing understandings of mid-twentieth century 'self making' or 'social selfhood' something that goes beyond conceptions in which the body serves merely as the boundaries, or limits, to the core of an individual—a container of the uniquely identified, 'inner self'? There is something characteristically contradictory in noting that the period that is often identified as one in which an internalised, reflexive self came into existence is one that is also marked by an active, but historically neglected, body. Marshall Berman's classic evocation of modernity as a 'maelstrom', a storm of rival forces, would embrace such a notion.[46] I want to suggest that there is something to be added to our understanding of the self by paying heed to the interwar popularity of organisations such as the Women's League of Health and Beauty, and the popular discourses that linked what was variously described as mental and physiological aspects of the human whole. Such ideas go beyond the self-fashioning that has been usefully explored in this same period, particularly by historians of material culture and dress.[47] In the actual realm of performance such as the League's annual displays, or in the pervasive self consciousness of the era, there was a novel sense of expriencing life in ways that demanded a new vocabulary. The 'modern self' was its paramount product; something people enacted as they made sense of their world and something that became the subject for discussion as to the nature and limits of human capacities—physical, mental, technological. As historians, the task of writing an embodied history, a history 'life in the body' remains something worth wrestling with.

Acknowledgements

My thanks to Susan Foley and Megan Simpson for help in preparing this paper, and to the Faculty of Humanities and Social Sciences, Victoria University of Wellington for financial assistance in attending the Women's History Network Conference at the University of Warwick in September 2010.

Notes

[1] The first publication of the Boston Women's Health Book Collective's classic work appeared in 1970 under the title *Women and Their Bodies* (Boston: New England Free Press). In 1971 a new edition appeared as *Our Bodies, Ourselves* (New England Free Press). The first commercial edition, published by Simon & Schuster in 1973, appeared as *Our Bodies, Ourselves. A book by and for women*. See www.ourbodiesourselves.org/about, accessed 17 Aug. 2010. See also Ruth Rosen (2000) *The World Split Open: how the modern women's movement changed America* (New York: Viking); Sheila Rowbotham (1999) *A Century of Women: the history of women in Britain and the United States in the twentieth century* (New York: Penguin Books); Christine Dann (1985) *Up from Under: women and liberation in New Zealand, 1970–1985* (Wellington: Allen & Unwin); Marilyn Lake (1999) *Getting Equal: the history of Australian feminism* (St Leonards: Allen & Unwin).

[2] For further exploration of the archival question see Antoinette Burton (Ed.) (2005) *Archive Stories: facts, fictions and the writing of history* (Durham: Duke University Press).

[3] The larger project was published in 2011 as *Strong, Beautiful and Modern: national fitness in Britain, New Zealand, Australia and Canada, c.1935–1960* (Wellington and Vancouver: Bridget Williams Books/UBC Press).

[4] Christopher Wilk (Ed.) (2006) *Modernism: designing a new world, 1914–1939* (London: V&A); Sean O'Connell (2000) Gender and the car in interwar Britain, in Moira Donald & Linda Hurcombe (Eds) *Gender and Material Culture in Historical Perspective* (Basingstoke: St Martin's Press), pp. 175–191; Georgine Clarsen (2008) *Eat My Dust. Early women motorists* (Baltimore: Johns Hopkins University Press); Matthew Hilton (2000) *Smoking in British Popular Culture, 1800–2000. Perfect pleasures* (Manchester: Manchester University Press); Adrian Bingham (2004) 'An Era of Domesticity'? Histories of women and gender in interwar Britain, *Cultural and Social History Society*, 1(2), pp. 225–233; Ina Zweiniger-Bargielowska (2006) Building a British Superman: physical culture in interwar Britain, *Journal of Contemporary*

History, 41, pp. 595–610; (2011) The Making of a Modern Female Body: beauty, health and fitness in interwar Britain, *Women's History Review*, 20(2), pp. 299–317. While this discussion focuses on interwar Britain, similar trends are apparent across the wider 'British world', see, for example, Susie Johnston (2009) *Lighting Up: the social history of smoking in New Zealand, c.1920–62* (MA: Victoria University of Wellington); Jarrett Rudy (2005) *The Freedom to Smoke: tobacco consumption and identity* (Montreal: McGill-Queen's University Press); Charlotte Macdonald (2009) Marching Teams and Modern Girls: bodies and culture in interwar New Zealand, in Paula Birnbaum & Anna Novakov (Eds) *Essays on Women's Artistic and Cultural Contributions 1919–1939. Expanded social roles for the new woman following the first world war* (Lewiston: Edwin Mellen) pp. 23–36.

[5] Nikolas Rose (1998) *Inventing Our Selves. Psychology, power, and personhood* (Cambridge: Cambridge University Press); (1990) *Governing the Soul: the shaping of the private self* (London: Routledge); Carolyn Steedman (1986) *Landscape for a Good Woman: a story of two lives* (London: Virago); (1999) The Commercial Domain: advertising and the cultural management of demand, in Becky Conekin, Frank Mort & Chris Waters (Eds) *Moments of Modernity: reconstructing Britain 1945–1964* (London: Rivers Oram Press). See also discussion of Steedman's work in Geoff Eley (2005) *A Crooked Line: from cultural history to the history of society* (Ann Arbor: University of Michigan Press).

[6] Gregory S. Brown (2008) Am 'I' a 'Post-Revolutionary Self'? Historiography of the self in the age of the Enlightenment and Revolution, *History and Theory*, 47, p. 229. From a European perspective see also the important work of Jan Goldstein (2005) *The Post-Revolutionary Self. Politics and psyche in France, 1750–1850* (Cambridge, MA: Harvard University Press), and an earlier collection, Roy Porter (Ed.) (1997) *Rewriting the Self: histories from the Renaissance to the present* (London: Routledge).

[7] Carolyn Steedman (2010) On Not Writing About the Self. Frances Hamilton (1743–1802) of Bishops Lydeard, near Taunton, Somerset, paper presented at the *Conference of the Women's History Network* titled 'Performing the Self: women's lives in historical perspective', University of Warwick, 10–12 September 2010.

[8] Conekin, Mort & Waters, *Moments of Modernity*, p. 11.

[9] Rose, *Inventing Ourselves*, p. 22.

[10] Roger Chartier, Alain Boureau & Cécile Dauphin (1997) *Correspondence: models of letter-writing from the Middle Ages to the nineteenth century* (Princeton: Princeton University Press).

[11] Martin Pugh (2008) *'We Danced All Night'. A social history of Britain between the wars* (London: The Bodley Head).

[12] Robert Graves & Alan Hodge (1940) *The Long Weekend: a social history of Great Britain 1918–1939* (London: Faber); John Stevenson (1984) *British Society 1914–45. The Pelican social history of Britain* (London: Allen Lane).

[13] London School of Economics and Political Science (1930–35) *The New Survey of London Life & Labour* (London: PS King); Sally Alexander (2007) A New Civilization? London surveyed 1928–1940s, *History Workshop Journal*, 64, pp. 296–320; Ian Gazeley (2005) *Poverty in Britain, 1900–1965* (Basingstoke: Palgrave Macmillan), ch. 3.

[14] An argument made in Ana Carden-Coyne's recent *Reconstructing the Body* in discussion of classicism and modernism in Britain, Australia and the United States. Ana Carden Coyne (2009) *Reconstructing the Body: classicism, modernism, and the First World War* (Oxford: Oxford University Press).

[15] Sabra Milligan (1934) *The Body and How to Keep Fit* (Brighouse: Premier).

[16] Ibid., p. 5.

[17] John F. Lucy (1937) *Keep Fit & Cheerful for Young and Old of Both Sexes* (London: Talbot Press).

[18] Harry Roberts (1939) *The Practical Way to Keep Fit* (London: Odhams); (1940) *Keep Fit in War-Time* (London: Watts & Co) and other works.
[19] Dorothy M. Cooke (1937) *'Keep Fit' Work for Women* (London: Pitman). Sheila Fletcher (1984) *Women First: the female tradition in English physical education, 1880–1980* (London: Athlone Press).
[20] Bengamin Gayelord Hauser (1936) *Eat and Grow Beautiful* (London: Faber). First published Tempo Books, New York, 1936.
[21] Patricia Vertinsky (1994) *The Eternally Wounded Woman: women, doctors, and exercise in the late nineteenth century* (Urbana: University of Illinois Press); Lesley Hall (2000) *Sex, Gender and Social Change in Britain since 1880* (Basingstoke: Macmillan); W. F. Bynum & Roy Porter (Eds) (1993) *Companion Encyclopaedia of the History of Medicine* (London and New York: Routledge).
[22] Roberts, *The Practical Way to Keep Fit*, p. 289.
[23] British Medical Association (1936) *Report of the Physical Education Committee* (London: British Medical Association), p. 1.
[24] Ibid.
[25] National Fitness Council (1939) *The National Fitness Campaign* (London: National Fitness Council for England and Wales), p. 4.
[26] Ibid., p. 5.
[27] Prunella was dubbed 'the most physically perfect girl in the world' by the *Daily Mail* in 1933. She was widely referred to as 'Britain's Perfect Girl', Jill Julius Matthews (1990) 'They had such a lot of fun.' The Women's League of Health and Beauty between the wars, *History Workshop Journal*, 30(1), pp. 24, 33. See also Jill Julius Matthews (1987) Building the Body Beautiful, *Australian Feminist Studies*, 5, pp. 17–34, and Jill Julius Matthews (2004) Stack, Mary Meta Bagot (1883–1935) *Oxford Dictionary of National Biography* (Oxford: Oxford University Press), online edition, Jan. 2008.
[28] Millicent and Caroline Ward, proteges of Bagot Stack training in London travelled to New Zealand in 1937 setting up branches of the League in Auckland (1937) and Wellington (1938), *Evening Post* (Wellington), 31 July, 2 Aug., 17 Oct. 1938.
[29] Mrs A. J. Cruickshank & Prunella Stack (1937) *Movement is Life. The intimate history of the founder of the Women's League of Health and Beauty and of its origins, growth, achievements, and hopes for the future* (London: Bell), p. 229. The major historical work on the League has been done by Jill Julius Matthews, see her '"They had such a lot of fun"', 'Building the body beautiful', and 'Stack, Mary Meta Bagot'. The League may have exaggerated their numbers. The National Fitness Campaign gave their membership as 'something like 60,000 members' (1938–39), National Fitness Council, *The National Fitness Campaign*, p. 10.
[30] The next largest was the Amateur Gymnastic Association, noted as having 'around 7,000 members', National Fitness Council, *The National Fitness Campaign*, p. 10.
[31] The Fitness League, see www.thefitnessleague.com, existing most strongly in Britain but also in groups in New Zealand and possibly elsewhere.
[32] Samantha Clements (2008) *Feminism, Citizenship and Social Activity: the role and importance of local women's organisations, Nottingham, 1918–1969* (PhD, University of Nottingham), p. 78.
[33] Zweiniger-Bargielowska, The Making of a Modern Female Body, p. 313.
[34] *Guardian*, 2 Jan. 2011; *Daily Mail*, 31 Dec. 2010; 'Prunella Stack OBE 1914–2010', www.thefitnessleague.com/media-pr/prunella-stack-obe-1914-2010.
[35] The phrase was first made famous by Isadora Duncan in the 1920s. The widespread popularity of the idea can be found throughout the interwar period in books and organisations ranging from Annette Kellerman's (1918) *Physical Beauty and How to Keep It*, to the Margaret Morris Movement, and much beyond, see Matthews, 'Building the Body Beautiful'.

[36] Stella Gibbons (1932) *Cold Comfort Farm* (London: Longman).
[37] For further development of this theme see Wendy Parkins (2009) *Mobility and Modernity in Women's Novels, 1850s–1930s. Women moving dangerously* (Basingstoke: Palgrave Macmillan).
[38] Matthews, 'They Had Such a Lot of Fun', p. 36.
[39] Annual performances at Hyde Park began in 1930, indoor demonstrations followed at the Royal Albert Hall in 1931, moving to Olympia and later Wembley as the Hall proved too small.
[40] Mollie Bagot Stack to her sister Mrs Cruickshank quoted in Cruickshank and Stack, *Movement is Life*, p. 123.
[41] Matthews, Stack, Mary Meta Bagot (1883–1935), *Oxford Dictionary of National Biography*.
[42] As described on the title frame, '500 Business Girls' British Pathé, www.britishpathe.com.
[43] Adrian Bingham (2004), *Gender, Modernity and the Popular Press in Inter-War Britain* (Oxford: Clarendon Press).
[44] See, for example, '500 Business Girls', Women's League of Health and Beauty performs at Hyde Park 9 May 1932; 'Health and Beauty on Parade!', Hyde Park demonstration 22 May 1933; 'Women's League for Health and Beauty', n.d. silent footage; '"Miss Britain" Keeps Fit—to Music', 1950, all at www.britishpathe.com.
[45] Matthews, 'They Had Such a Lot of Fun', p. 25. Lucy Bland and Lesley Hall note the vagueness and diffusion of eugenic terms in Britain through the 1920s and 1930s, see Lucy Bland & Lesley Hall (2010) Eugenics in Britain: the view from the metropole, in Alison Bashford & Philippa Levine (Eds) *The Oxford Handbook of the History of Eugenics* (Oxford: Oxford University Press), ch. 11.
[46] Marshall Berman (1982) *All That is Solid Melts into Air: the experience of modernity* (New York: Simon & Schuster).
[47] Among them, Christine Boydell (2004) Review article. Refashioning Identities: gender, class and the self, *Journal of Contemporary History*, 39(1), pp. 137–146; Barbara Burman & Carole Turbin (2002) Material Strategies Engendered, *Gender and History*, 14(3), pp. 371–381; Christopher Breward & Caroline Evans (Eds) (2005) *Fashion and Modernity* (Oxford & New York: Berg); Bronwyn Labrum, Fiona McKergow & Stephanie Gibson (Eds) (2007) *Looking Flash. Clothing in Aotearoa New Zealand* (Auckland: Auckland University Press).

Performing the Political Self: a study of identity making and self representation in the autobiographies of India's first generation of parliamentary women

Annie Devenish

Although India boasts a number of prominent women politicians, there remains little critical scholarship on the agency and contribution of Indian women in politics post independence. Responding to this gap, this article explores how identity and agency is articulated in the autobiographies of three influential women who were part of India's first generation of women in post independence politics: Kamaladevi Chattopadhyay (1903–1988), Vijaya Lakshmi Pandit (1900–1990) and Renuka Ray (1904–1997). Using the framework of intersubjectivity—the notion of the construction of the self through a wider network of social relations and identities—this article analyses how these women performed the political self in their autobiographies by positioning their lives within a larger matrilineal lineage in their narratives. Situating themselves as the inheritors of their mothers' and grandmothers' struggle for social reform and education, who in their own lives take this legacy forward by their entry into political activism and statecraft, they emerge as pioneers in their public careers. Through their encouragement and criticism of their daughters' and granddaughters' generation, they both distinguish their specific generational contribution, but also put forward a challenge to this new generation to return to the Gandhian values and developmental strategies that shaped their political world view.

Over the past decade, a heated debate has been brewing in India's national Parliament around the introduction of a pioneering piece of legislation which, if passed, will dramatically change the landscape of parliamentary politics. The Women's Reservation Bill mandates 33% of seats in the Lok Sabha be reserved for women candidates. Supporters of the Bill argue that securing the presence of a critical mass of women within institutions of power is vital if women's interests are to be adequately addressed. Opponents emphasise that the Bill's agenda of empowerment is merely a front for upper class and caste interests.[1] The framing of this debate reflects an ongoing concern in Indian politics with the agency of women politicians, and the extent to which the political sphere offers women the scope to operate as subjects, rather than objects in the hands of other vested interests. India boasts a number of prominent women politicians from poetess Sarojini Naidu through to Indira Gandhi, the country's first female Prime Minister, and yet there remains little critical scholarship on Indian women in politics post independence. For example, were such women able to negotiate the nexus of class, caste, familial and religious identities to construct personas as political subjects? Did the political sphere offer them the possibility of liberation from the constraints of gender relations, or rather reproduce and reinforce these?

This article engages with some of these questions, by exploring the construction of the self in the autobiographies of three politically active Indian women: Kamaladevi Chattopadhyay, Vijaya Lakshmi Pandit and Renuka Ray. These women cut their political teeth in the Indian nationalist movement of the 1920s where they actively participated in the struggle against British colonial rule, then, after independence in 1947, moved into various public careers in politics, government and civil society. The eldest of this cohort, Vijaya Lakshmi Pandit (1900–1990), is best known as diplomat and sister to Jawaharlal Nehru, India's first Prime Minister (1947–1964), but she also pursued a successful political career which was well established by the time she entered the world of diplomacy. Between 1946 and 1962, she became an established figure on the international stage serving as Indian ambassador to Soviet Russia, the United States and Mexico, England, Ireland and Spain, and headed several Indian delegations to the UN, before returning to politics in 1962 as Governor of Maharashtra and a Member of Parliament. Kamaladevi Chattopadhyay's (1903–1988) career moves in a circle from an early interest in the arts, particularly theatre, into nationalist politics in the 1920s, and after independence returns to its original artistic orientation through her involvement in the co-operative movement and the development of Indian handicrafts. After committing herself passionately to the nationalist struggle as a teenager, Renuka Ray (1904–1997) was sent by her father to study Economics at LSE in the early 1920s. This was followed by her marriage to Satyen Ray, a civil servant whose job postings in rural India brought Ray into contact with village life and its problems. In the 1930s, she was able to apply this experience to the nationalist cause when Gandhiji asked her to volunteer in his village reconstruction programme, after which her career in social and constructive work took off. She continued to pursue her commitment to women's rights, rehabilitation and welfare after independence as a Member of Parliament and as a Cabinet Minister in West Bengal.

These women came of age at an important moment in India's anti-colonial struggle. By 1920 Mahatma Gandhi had emerged at the helm of the country's leading independence organisation, the Indian National Congress, and was transforming nationalist politics through Satyagraha, a form of peaceful civil disobedience against British rule that aimed to expose the moral bankruptcy of colonialism. Satyagraha took a variety of forms, including protests, courting imprisonment, boycotting British institutions and foreign products, and rural constructive work, and was a key strategy in the struggle for *Purna Swaraj*—the achievement of complete political, economic and moral independence. Gandhiji's first major Satyagraha campaign, the Non-Cooperation movement (1920–1922), opened up nationalist politics to middle-class Indian women for the first time. Ray, Pandit and Chattopadhyay were part of a generation of women who were able to pioneer political careers by entering the nationalist movement at this moment, and were able to deepen these initial gains through their participation in the later Civil Disobedience movement (1930–1931) and the Quit India campaign (1942–1944).

Another area in which this generation of women was able to break new ground in the 1920s and 1930s was in electoral and parliamentary politics. Although the franchise was only universally granted to Indian women under the Constitution in 1950, the colonial government devolved certain functions to educated Indians at provincial level. This devolution gave a small number of Indian women the right to vote and to be elected or nominated to provincial legislatures.[2] Pandit's political career began this way when she was elected to the municipal board of Allahabad city Council, and later in 1937 was made a state minister in the United Provinces government. Ray sat on the Central Assembly in 1943 while Chattopadhyay stood unsuccessfully as a candidate in the Provincial elections in Madras in 1927. Their credentials in the nationalist struggle, together with their early electoral and parliamentary experience, facilitated the entry of Pandit, Ray and Chattopadhyay into public life after independence, where they continued to break new ground, building and shaping India's nascent democracy.

Reflecting on their public careers the authors began to write and publish their autobiographies in the late 1970s and the first half of the 1980s, adding their voices to a growing body of Indian life writing. Autobiography as a form of postcolonial life writing provides a useful analytical tool for feminist scholars enabling the 'recovery' of women's voices from history.[3] Telling one's story requires a narrator; to have a voice one must have an identity as an individual. As Carolyn Steedman notes, one of the tacit assumptions accepted by scholars working with this genre is that writing is linked to subjectivities, the urge to tell the self is part of the process of self construction.[4] This self is not constructed in isolation but through the perspective of the 'self in society', inflecting the individual life through 'a wider network of relations and identities'.[5] The intersubjective or relational nature of identity construction has been identified as a feature of post-colonial and women's life writing by scholars such as Tess Cosslett, David Arnold, Stuart Blackburn and Bart Moore-Gilbert.[6] And it is precisely this intersubjectivity that makes these autobiographies useful tools for exploring how this generation of women negotiated within this nexus of social relations and historical forces to construct an identity for themselves as political subjects.

While the 'selves' in these autobiographies are remembering how their political careers were shaped by the social relations and historical forces of their time, this process of remembering takes place against the backdrop of a more recent period of Indian history, the 1970s and 1980s. The crafting of Pandit, Ray and Chattopadhyay's autobiographical characters in relation to this latter context transforms these texts into sites of self performance for their authors, providing a stage upon which the narrator consciously performs a 'public' version of themselves who engages with the 'present' context of their audience.

On Being Our Mothers' Daughters: pioneering a new identity from social reform to nationalist politics

The autobiographies of Ray, Chattopadhyay and Pandit display a number of characteristics conforming to the western canon of modern autobiography. They all present a chronological narrative, at the core of which is their political and social development as individuals. And yet these narratives are really about the nationalist story of India's struggle for freedom and its development as a country from their perspective as participants. The development of the autobiographical subject around the 'axis of the nation' where the political self develops in relation to a collective political consciousness defines these texts as typically postcolonial.[7] Ray, Chattopadhyay and Pandit's accounts offer detailed descriptions of various political personalities and events of their time, and are intertextual, weaving historical documents such as letters, speeches and photographs into their recollections, making these narratives mini historical archives.

One of the ways in which these women perform the self in relation to this larger historical account is through positioning themselves as part of a matrilineal lineage within their narratives.[8] Ray, Chattopadhyay and Pandit situate themselves as the inheritors of their mothers' and grandmothers' struggle for social reform and education for women. In their own lives, these women take this legacy forward expanding and re-orientating it by their entry into political activism and statecraft, while through their encouragement and criticism of their daughters' and granddaughters' generation, they both distinguish their specific generational contribution, but also put forward a challenge to this new generation to return to the Gandhian values that shaped their political world view.

It is within their family environments that these authors' political conscientisation first occurs and where their early sense of gender justice is ignited. The autobiographies of all three of these women begin with several chapters on their family background, emphasising both the politically and socially progressive nature of their home environments. Renuka Ray recalls growing up 'with nationalist slogans of "Bande Mataram" and "Swadeshi"' and 'longing for the liberty of our country' in her middle-class Bengali home in Calcutta.[9] Kamaladevi Chattopadhyay remembers her mother as a 'staunch nationalist' who 'had a lot of political literature lying around' the family home in Mangalore.[10] Pandit's political consciousness developed in her affluent family home in Allahabad where prominent nationalist characters were often invited to socialise.[11]

The close interlinking of nationalism with social reform is evident in the families of Ray, Chattopadhyay and Pandit, who supported both the freedom of Indian subjects from the British Raj, and the freedom of Indian women from the shackles of 'backwardness' and 'custom'. Launched by male reformers, such as Rammohun Roy and Pandit Vidyasagar, in the early nineteen century, the Indian social reform movement promoted the 'modernisation' of Indian women through education and social reform.[12] The work of historians such as Lata Mani, Uma Chakravarti, Partha Chatterjee and Tanika Sarkar has questioned the real motives behind this movement, arguing that Indian nationalists used the discourse of social reform to construct an identity for themselves as progressive citizens deserving of independence from British rule, and that consequently women became objects rather than subjects within this discourse.[13] This may indeed have been the case, but it does not preclude the possibility of women taking advantage of the new opportunities opened to them by social reform for their own development as individuals. Although the movement was initiated by male reformers, by the second half of the century pioneering women such as Pandita Ramabai, Anandibai Karve and Parvatibai Athavale, had also taken up this cause. These women were role models for Ray, Chattopadhyay and Pandit's mothers and grandmothers, offering a new example of how middle-class women could carve out a professional identity in the area of social work.

For the authors, in turn, the identity of their mothers and grandmothers provided inspiration for their own lives, and played a major role in the development of their nationalist consciousness and their sense of gender equality. In their autobiographies, the matrilineal inheritance of the narrators is deeply woven into their broader sense of family identity and inheritance. On the very first page of her autobiography, Renuka Ray describes her mother Chandra as 'an early feminist' who 'believed in equality of the sexes' and who had passed many of her ideals onto Ray and her siblings.[14] Kamaladevi describes her independent and well travelled maternal grandmother as 'a colossus who strode across my life'.[15] She recalls that many of her mother's heroines were contemporary freedom fighters such as Annie Besant and Pandita Ramabai, reminding her daughter that she too 'could become a crusader' like them.[16] In Pandit's life, her brother Jawaharlal Nehru and her father Motilal Nehru were the most influential figures both personally and politically; however, she too describes with pride a number of female relatives in the opening chapters of her autobiography. These included her remarkable grandmother, Indrani, who taught herself how to read and write in Hindi and her cousin's wife, Rameshwari Nehru, who 'was the only woman' invited by the British government to sit on a committee to fix the age of consent for girls.[17] Pandit begins her story by positioning her mother as traditional and orthodox, belonging to the old world of India, in contrast to her progressive and westernised father. In her narrative her parents represent the 'two Indias' of her generation, 'the young India of today and the ancient land of yesterday'.[18] As her life story progresses and the Nehru family become involved in the nationalist struggle, Pandit describes how her mother is invigorated when she is brought out of her limited world of home and family by participating in Gandhiji's Satyagraha campaigns.

In describing their matrilineal lineage in their autobiographies, these women tell the story of 'Indian woman', from ancient Vedic times through to her 'awakening' and participation in social reform and nationalism. This larger narrative is one of collective empowerment and agency, but it is told within the personal frame of the narrators' own lives and experiences. Take, for example, Renuka Ray's chapter entitled 'Women in India', which introduces this history as part of her own family narrative by describing her mother's reform activities among rural women in Bengal. These orthodox women adhered to the practice of Purdah, the seclusion of women in the home and outside world from the sight of men. To Ray they appeared 'totally alien' from the women she knew because their restrictive dress, behaviour and mobility represented a 'past world' in the context of her childhood family where the values of social reform had freed her mother to go out into the world to pursue a professional career.[19] In Pandit's autobiography, the artefacts of her family history become national history, as she tells us how her mother's 'bloodstained sari', worn during a Satyagraha protest where the police charged, was still preserved in a museum in Allahabad.[20]

By outlining their matrilineal inheritance, Ray, Chattopadhyay and Pandit set the scene for the entry of their characters into the public sphere. The watershed moment for Ray 'and for many of my generation' was the special Congress session in September 1920 in Calcutta where Gandhiji outlined his Satyagraha programme.[21] Ray, who was only sixteen at the time, recalls how she met Gandhiji for the first time and 'it changed my life'.[22] Pandit's first meeting with Gandhiji also took place at this crucial moment. She remembers being 'carried away' and donating her jewellery to the cause after Gandhiji called on volunteers to collect money to help the families of those arrested in his 1920 Satyagraha campaign.[23]

Kamaladevi first entered nationalist politics in 1923 when she was invited to become a volunteer in the *Seva Dal*, an organisation established to train satyagrahis. Shortly after this, she became involved in the Congress Youth movement. By the time of her participation in Gandhiji's 1930 Salt Satyagraha, a campaign against the British monopoly on the manufacture of Indian salt, she was beginning to show real leadership potential. Chattopadhyay's descriptions of this campaign, which ignited the Civil Disobedience movement, convey a sense of making history and breaking boundaries. In setting the scene, she writes that although India has had a long 'illustrious tradition of women warriors', that the Salt Satyagraha marked 'their first appearance in any modern militant political campaign'.[24] She goes on to recall that while signing her name on the campaign pledge, 'It seemed such a stupendous moment in my life, in the life of the women of my country. I felt I was tracing not the letters of my name but recording a historic event'.[25]

In the opening decades of the twentieth century, there were a few prominent women leaders in Indian politics, such as Sarojini Naidu and Annie Besant, but they were exceptions and, as Geraldine Forbes points out, their role within the political sphere was largely symbolic.[26] It was Gandhiji's entry into Indian nationalism in the 1920s and the non-violent nature of Satyagraha that facilitated the entry of women into politics as active participants.[27] Gandhiji argued that it was Indian women's moral purity and their capacity for self sacrifice and service that made them ideal nationalist workers. A highly gendered and class-based understanding of their role as wives and mothers both facilitated their participation in nationalist politics, but simultaneously defined and restricted the nature and scope of this participation.[28] What is significant about Gandhiji's political philosophy was the fact that he saw 'women not as objects of reform and humanitarianism but as self conscious subjects who could, if they chose, become arbiters of their own destiny'.[29] Their entry into the nationalist movement at this moment provided these authors with the opportunity to establish political careers for themselves as active participants and later leaders within this movement. By positioning themselves as pioneers in their matrilineal lineages, these women strove to carve out a role for themselves as autonomous subjects. In this way, their autobiographical characters emerge not as products of the social relations and political forces of their time, but rather as individuals who have negotiated a sense of political and personal identity within these relations and forces.

'An Asian victory': Vijaya Lakshmi Pandit and the politics of international diplomacy

Although Pandit held high-ranking representative positions as part of Congress government both before and after independence, reflecting on her public career in her autobiography she describes herself as belonging to the world of international diplomacy, rather than that of contemporary politics. On her ambassadorial career she comments, 'I have always felt equally at home in both worlds', the East and the West.[30] In contrast she describes herself as out of place 'In the political field after independence', stating 'I am not a politician. The ways of modern politics are not my metier'.[31] Pandit's identification as a diplomat by nature enables her to create a subject position for herself in her autobiography, which distinguishes her contribution to nation building from that of her family's role within the sphere of nationalist politics. This position also allows her to distance herself from the erosion of democracy associated with the leadership of her niece Indira Gandhi in the 1970s.

Pandit's heritage as a member of the Nehru family and her nationalist credentials gave her a legitimacy and profile on the international stage, while her Western-orientated upbringing familiarised her with the social etiquette and cultural milieu of the United Nations. This familiarity allowed her to socialise and negotiate with these representatives—a vital skill for a delegation leader.

Combined with her diplomatic aptitude, these abilities helped establish her popularity in this arena, where she was elected the first women President of the General Assembly in 1953, a major achievement in the masculine and Western dominated field of diplomacy.

In her role as an international diplomat, Pandit successfully manages to draw on her family identity as sister of India's first Prime Minister, and her collective identity as the embodiment of 'Indian womanhood', but she does not allow these two identities to subsume her in this role; she uses them strategically and stamps her own personality and vision onto the job. She performs her diplomatic career as being self-made through a process of learning, growing and developing. So when Gandhiji first persuades her to lead a diplomatic mission in 1946, she says that she was 'horrified' feeling completely unqualified for such a role.[32] Later on, while talking about her time at the UN, she states that she does not think that any ambassador was 'on the mat' as often as she was during her career with all the new the terms and ideas.[33] But she soon found her feet and later reflected that she 'taught herself a great deal by reading' and that at the end of the day 'I feel that my record was not wholly undistinguished'.[34]

Moving and thriving in what was at that time a highly masculine world, Pandit's career as an international diplomat offered her the opportunity to challenge gender stereotypes. She confesses how she enjoyed the ongoing surprise she created in the 1946 UN session where many people struggled to reconcile her presence with 'their firmly established view of an Indian woman—a clinging vine subservient to all manner of caste restrictions'.[35] On another occasion, she reminisces about how the question of whether she should be treated as a man or woman at formal dinners agitated the UN chief of Protocol. Pandit always insisted as firmly as possible that she would 'join the men for cognac and cigars'.[36]

During her time as leader of the Indian delegation in United Nations, and later in 1953 as its President, Pandit captured the world's imagination by drawing on the symbolic power that Indian women represented in the public sphere to promote the principles at the heart of India's foreign policy, such as independence for colonial territories in Asia and Africa. As an empowered woman who was able to engage with the world's political players on her own terms, she conveyed India as a new nation state grounded on the principles of equality, freedom and empowerment. It is quite possible that Gandhiji aimed to take advantage of this symbolism in choosing Pandit to lead the first Indian delegation to the UN in 1946. The Mahatma had been monitoring the deteriorating situation of Indian subjects in South Africa, and was especially alarmed when the government passed the Asiatic Land Tenure and Indian Representation Act of 1946, which restricted the property ownership and land rights of Indians living in the province of Natal. Gandhiji tasked Pandit with ensuring that this issue was inscribed on the UN's agenda. In successfully bringing discrimination against Indians in South Africa to the World's attention, Pandit set a precedent for all colonised people, ensuring that violations of their rights would no longer be accepted silently. In her autobiography she describes this success as 'An Asian victory'.[37] It was not only a personal or even national triumph, but became a symbol of the right to freedom for all Asian peoples around the world.

'No category of women as appendages to their husbands': Renuka Ray and the politics of outspokenness

In the final chapter of her autobiography, Renuka Ray reflects on her life, stating that she cannot claim to have been a pioneer in social and educational work, as her mother and grandmother had paved the way before her, but that the one area where she had been a 'proud pioneer' was that 'without breaking up married life I established the right of wives of those in public service to follow their own independent career'.[38] This, she states, set a precedent for future generations of women, in that it 'establishes that no category of women can be treated as appendages to their husbands'.[39] Ray's achievement is significant especially considering her husband, Satyen Ray, was a prominent civil servant (Chief Secretary to the Minister) in West Bengal. Prior to independence, this placed the couple in opposing camps with Satyen working for a British-ruled India, while Ray was challenging this India through her nationalist activities.

Ray was a pioneer not only in her ability to balance an independent public career with a family life, but also within her political career. She was the first woman to hold a state cabinet post as Minister of Relief and Rehabilitation in West Bengal (1952–1957) and was a long-standing Member of Parliament (1947–1952 and 1957–1967), during which time she was an outspoken advocate for the reform of social laws relating to women. She also held strategic influence within the Congress Party as a member of its executive committee. Ray's autonomy, her ability to 'be her own person', within the networks of her personal relations extended into the professional networks of her political career as well. She tells us that 'Since the time of Mahatma Gandhi I had always been able to express my viewpoint even when I differed with the party and sometimes won my point also'.[40] This became one of the defining features of her political personality post independence where her vocal criticism of Congress policy at certain moments enabled her to maintain a sense of autonomy, and a sense of a distinct and individual political orientation, rather than being defined merely as a Congress politician. In her autobiography, she describes how she was part of 'a small minority' who opposed Nehru and Congress over the degree of protection accorded to private property in the Indian Constitution.[41] Ray was chosen by this group to move their proposed amendment calling for changes to the property rights clause and she appendixes an extract from the speech she gave in support of it in her autobiography. This outspokenness surfaces again in her parliamentary career when she joined the Socialist Study group in Parliament which 'did not endear me to the party bosses' who felt she had moved too far to the left.[42]

Ray defines herself as a pioneer in her matrilineal narrative because of her success in separating her public and private worlds, thereby ensuring that her political persona remained removed from her identity as 'Mrs Satyen Ray'. The framing of her autobiography however reinforces the interdependence of the public and private. Ray was only able to develop a successful public career because of the support of her husband, 'whose deep understanding' as she states in her dedication of her autobiography, 'made it possible for me to pursue public activities without jeopardizing family life'.[43] Ray's public career, indeed the performance of her very life story, was only made possible by the existence of this overarching narrative relationship, which introduces her autobiography to the reader.

The rebel artist: Kamaladevi Chattopadhyay and the politics of self expression

While Gandhiji's Satyagraha campaigns enabled women to take up active roles in independence politics, they still demanded that women adhere to a certain moral and social code of behaviour. Just as the performance of Ray's political career was made possible by the support of her husband, so Kamaladevi Chattopadhyay's performance is constrained by the absence of a supportive husband and stable family life. First married as a child bride in 1917 and widowed two years later, Chattopadhyay defied Hindu tradition by remarrying Harindranath Chattopadhyay, the younger brother of Sarojini Naidu, at the age of twenty. This was a love match with both young people sharing a passion for amateur theatre and creative writing. But Chattopadhyay was unprepared to tolerate her husband's aggressive temperament and so defied tradition once again to divorce in 1933. With divorce being a taboo in India during this period, her respectability was likely to have been tarnished by the breakup of her family life and this could have negatively affected her career prospects in party politics.

Chattopadhyay describes her withdrawal from political affairs as a decision prompted by the changing nature of politics with the coming of independence: 'As Freedom came, service was replaced by struggle for positions of power... To me the beacon lay elsewhere, in the side lanes of creative and constructive work'.[44] Within her autobiography, however, there is a tension between her statements which dismiss an interest in a political career, and her actions as a political figure. Her active participation within the nationalist movement and her involvement as a founding member of the Congress Socialist Party defined her as someone who was intensely interested in the political sphere and was trying to carve out a space as a political actor.[45]

The events in Chattopadhyay's personal life might help us to better understand her disavowal of politics. Reena Nanda, one of her more recent biographers, argues that Chattopadhyay's political prospects in the Congress party were indeed impeded by her personal life, and that this marginalisation began in 1936 when Gandhiji, concerned that her divorce made her unsuitable moral role model, was influential in blocking her appointment to the Executive of the Congress.[46] Chattopadhyay mentions none of this in her autobiography. As her title, *Inner Recesses, Outer Spaces*, suggests, her narrative separates the story of her public career, the outer self which intersects with the world, from the private self lodged within inner recesses of her relationships and emotions. This right is claimed in the opening paragraphs of her story when she says that regardless of the recent trend towards the personal in autobiographical writing that she did not feel required 'to lower the barriers of the discreet reticence which govern our everyday life'.[47] In telling her life story, Chattopadhyay would have been caught between what Arnold and Blackburn describe as the 'desire to tell the truth and an equally intense desire to regulate it'.[48] The silence in her narrative offers a way to resolve these conflicting aspirations by removing her personal life from her autobiographical performance, providing a form of self protection from the public gaze.

Chattopadhyay disentangles her professional and personal narratives, writing the latter out of the script of her life story. Her life experience, however, like that of Ray, illustrates the interdependence of the public and the private spheres. Her career in party politics shows how the patriarchal power relations of the family—that define notions of social respectability—infiltrate the political sphere, constraining the freedom and choices available to individuals who rebel against such conventions. On one level Chattopadhyay's life trajectory can be interpreted as one defined by external constraints. Yet she emerges as an agent within this trajectory through her ability to negotiate determinedly and creatively around these restrictions. Like Pandit and Ray, her career in arts and handicrafts development emerges as a professional path that is self made, marked by her own personality, creativity and political orientation. With party political avenues narrowing, local economic development and refugee rehabilitation through arts and crafts provided an alternative path which allowed Chattopadhyay to reconcile her political and creative selves: 'Training, planning and the active fight for freedom exhilarated me, though politics was not my medium of expression'.[49]

Chattopadhyay's focus on the revival of village handicrafts as a means of sustainable livelihoods illustrates the way in which she combined the Gandhian philosophy of village regeneration and self sufficiency, her own socialist belief in cooperative development and decentralised power, and her love of traditional Indian arts and crafts. She diverged from a more traditionalist and romantic Gandhian approach to village revival, however, by being a pragmatist who realised the need to adapt crafts to make them marketable and desirable for a modern audience.[50] Chattopadhyay used her career in the development of rural arts and crafts for an explicitly political purpose. She was not just concerned with the preservation of craft forms for their aesthetic value, but also with how crafts and cottage industries could create livelihoods to ensure the survival of communities: 'At the core of the artist was a socialist politician whose interaction with peasants and workers had given her an insight into poverty and problems of rural artisans'.[51] Her career therefore provides not only an interesting case study of the way in which this generation of women interpreted, developed and implemented Gandhian philosophy, but also challenges conventional understandings of the boundaries of the political.

As Our Daughters' Mothers: engaging with the second wave women's movement

These autobiographies were written to tell the past, but they are equally concerned with shaping the future. Ray, Chattopadhyay and Pandit wrote and published their stories during the Prime Ministership of Indira Gandhi (1966–1977 and 1980–1984), a time of political and social upheaval in India. Responding to this turbulent climate, a new wave of social movements began to emerge, including a second wave women's movement, which articulated a very different culture and political ethos compared to the movement in which the authors' feminist consciousness had matured. One of the influential developments igniting this movement was the publication of the *Towards Equality Report* in 1974, which revealed that constitutional equality and legal reforms had not improved the quality of life for the majority of Indian women; in fact their quality of life had actually deteriorated. This research raised many questions about the legacy of the first wave movement.

These women's autobiographies attempt to engage with the politics of this emerging second wave in several ways. Firstly their stories are concerned with enabling this younger generation to understand the events of their time, as Ray puts it in her preface 'through the eyes of my generation'.[52] Situating their public careers as ground-breaking performances within a longer matrilineal narrative functioned to ensure that their pioneering contributions to women's empowerment and nation building would be acknowledged, and not overlooked or misinterpreted with the writing of a revisionist nationalist history. A message which is clearly articulated in the closing of Pandit's narrative when she pays 'heartfelt tribute' to her colleagues in the women's movement who she emphasises 'built the road' upon which the next generation of women 'can walk forward today'.[53]

While Pandit, Ray and Chattopadhyay's generation tended to distance themselves from their gendered identity in the public sphere, claiming the right to participate in this sphere on the basis of merit and citizenship, the second wave women's movement was deeply concerned with notions of difference and how these shaped power relations in the public sphere, not only differences between men and women but also differences of class and caste. This movement criticised their predecessors for their middle-class orientation which they argued ignored the needs of peasant and working class women. Ray, Pandit and Chattopadhyay, in turn, offer a response to this criticism warning of the dangers of an identity politics founded on difference. Pandit stresses in her autobiography that India had never needed a suffragette movement because 'there was no antagonism between the sexes'.[54] While Chattopadhyay laments the 'great tragedy' of contemporary women 'isolating themselves from a cohesive society'.[55] Rejecting difference enabled this generation of women to articulate an identity for the Indian women's movement which was distinct in approach and character from that of the women's movement in the west, and allowed the authors to claim equal citizenship and empowerment through merit, rather than through special treatment. Her generation, Chattopadhyay reminds her readers 'never sought reservations for women in any sphere. Nor nominations on bodies as *women* but because they qualified as citizens'.[56] Pandit, Ray and Chattopadhyay's disapproval of identity politics also needs to be understood within the political context of their time. During the nationalist struggle and the early years of independence when a fragile new nation consisting of many interests groups had to be held together, difference often acted as a divisive force—as the painful partition of the subcontinent demonstrated. Ultimately however the inability of the authors to acknowledge difference limited the type of freedom that they were able to envision for women in the public sphere, and in so doing marginalised the voices of other classes and castes of women in their autobiographies.

Conclusion

Pandit, Ray and Chattopadhyay's careful crafting of their autobiographical characters reminds us as readers of the 'artful, interpersonally negotiated and politicized construction of life stories'.[57] This cohort of women articulates a unique subject position for themselves in their autobiographies by situating their characters as pioneers within a longer matrilineal narrative and, in turn, within the larger story of India's birth and development as a nation. Their life stories allow the scholar to analyse not only their performance as autobiographical subjects, but also the refashioning of the authors as political subjects. Pandit, Ray and Chattopadhyay worked hard to develop public careers that were self-made; careers marked by their personalities, political orientations and creativity, which defined them not as the products of the social relations and political contexts of their time, but as subjects who were able to negotiate an individual identity for themselves within this context. But the possibilities for refashioning themselves as political subjects were also limited by the gender relations of their day, as the trajectory of Chattopadhyay's public career suggests, and their historical context, which blinded them from the very real divisions amongst Indian women. Although they warn their daughters and granddaughters of the danger of creating disunity through the politics of difference, it is precisely such a politics that enables this next generation to take the legacy of Ray, Chattopadhyay and Pandit forward. By using difference to reveal and challenge the way that power operates within Indian politics, this next generation of women follow in the pioneering footsteps of these authors, opening up the public sphere to new categories of Indian women.

Notes

[1] N. Menon (2000) Elusive 'Woman': feminism and the Women's Reservation Bill, *Economic and Political Weekly*, 35(43/44), pp. 3837–3838.
[2] See V. Agnew (1979) *Elite Women in Politics* (New Delhi: Vikas), pp. 110–112 and Geraldine Forbes (2009) *Women in Modern India* (Cambridge: Cambridge University Press), pp. 106, 124.
[3] Liz Stanley (2000) From 'Self-made Women' to 'Women's Made-selves'? Audit selves, simulation and surveillance in the rise of the public woman, in Tess Cosslett, Celia Lury & Penny Summerfield (Eds) *Feminism and Autobiography: texts, theories and methods* (London & New York: Routledge), p. 41.
[4] Carolyn Steedman (2000) Enforced Narratives: stories of another self, in Cosslett et al., *Feminism and Autobiography*, pp. 25–26.
[5] David Arnold & Stuart Blackburn (2004) Introduction: life histories in India, in David Arnold & Stuart Blackburn (Eds) *Telling Lives in India: biography, autobiography and life history* (Delhi: Permanent Black), pp. 19, 21.

[6] Ibid., pp. 19, 21.
[7] Bart Moore-Gilbert (2009) *Postcolonial Life-Writing: culture, politics and self representation* (London & New York: Routledge), p. 25.
[8] Drawing on elements of matrilineal identity within life histories as a way through which to frame and construct the self has been identified by several scholars working in the area of postcolonial life writing. See, for example, Sara Scott & Sue Scott (2000) Our Mother's Daughters: autobiographical inheritance through stories of gender and class; Tess Cosslett (2000) Matrilineal Narratives Revisited, both in Cosslett et al., *Feminism and Autobiography*, pp. 128–140 & 141–153; and Kirin Narayan (2004) 'Honour is Honour After All': silence and speech in the life stories of women in Kangra, North-West India, in Arnold & Blackburn, *Telling Lives in India*, pp. 227–251.
[9] Renuka Ray (1982) *My Reminiscences: social development during the Gandhian Era and after* (New Delhi: Allied), p. 5.
[10] Kamala Chattopadhyay (1986) *Inner Recesses Outer Spaces: memoirs* (New Delhi: Navrang), pp. 18, 23.
[11] Vijaya Lakshmi Pandit (1979) *The Scope of Happiness: a personal memoir* (New York: Crown), p. 64.
[12] These laws, such as The Hindu Widow Remarriage Act of 1856, were concerned with removing customs such as sati and child marriage.
[13] See, for example, L. Mani (1998) *Contentious Traditions: the debate on Sati in colonial India* (Berkeley: University of California Press); Uma Chakravarti (1999) Whatever Happened to the Vedic Dasi? Orientalism, nationalism, and a script for the past, in Kumkum Sangari & Sudesh Vaid (Eds) *Recasting Women: essays in colonial history*, pp. 88–126 & 27–87 (New Brunswick, NJ: Rugters University Press); Partha Chatterjee (2001) The Nationalist Resolution of the Women's Question, in Gregory Castle (Ed.) *Postcolonial Discourses: an anthology*, pp. 151–166 (Oxford: Blackwell); Tanika Sarkar (2001) *Hindu wife, Hindu Nation: community, religion and cultural nationalism* (London: Hurst & Co).
[14] Ray, *My Reminiscences*, p. 1.
[15] Chattopadhyay, *Inner Recesses Outer Spaces*, p. 15.
[16] Ibid., p. 18.
[17] Pandit, *The Scope of Happiness*, pp. 27, 31.
[18] Ibid., pp. 34–39, 24.
[19] Ray, *My Reminiscences*, p. 73
[20] Pandit, *The Scope of Happiness*, p. 144.
[21] Ray, *My Reminiscences*, p. 15.
[22] Ibid., p. 15.
[23] Pandit, *The Scope of Happiness*, p. 86.
[24] Ibid., pp. 152–153.
[25] Ibid.
[26] Forbes, *Women in Modern India*, pp. 122–123.
[27] Madhu Kishwar (1986) *Gandhiji and Women* (Delhi: Manushi Prakashan), p. 22.
[28] See, for example, Forbes (1998) *Women in Modern India*; Jayawardena Kumari (1994) *Feminism and Nationalism in the Third World* (London: Atlantic Heights); Gail Minault (Ed.) (1981) *The Extended Family: women and political participation in India* (Delhi: Chanakya).
[29] Kishwar, *Women and Gandhiji*, p. 1.
[30] Pandit, *The Scope of Happiness*, p. 318.
[31] Ibid., p. 319.
[32] Ibid., p. 205.
[33] Ibid., p. 214.
[34] Ibid., p. 318.

[35] Ibid., p. 214.
[36] Ibid., p. 251.
[37] Pandit, *The Scope of Happiness*, p. 208.
[38] Ray, *My Reminiscences*, p. 265.
[39] Ibid., pp. 265–266.
[40] Ibid., p. 227.
[41] Ibid., p. 52.
[42] Ibid., p. 51.
[43] Ibid., Dedication.
[44] Chattopadhyay, *Inner Recesses Outer Spaces*, p. 385.
[45] Reena Nanda (2002) *Kamaladevi Chattopadhyay: a biography* (Oxford: Oxford University Press), p. 34.
[46] Chattopadhyay, *Inner Recesses Outer Spaces*, pp. 78, 82–84.
[47] Ibid., p. 2.
[48] Arnold and Blackburn, Introduction, p. 17.
[49] Chattopadhyay, *Inner Recesses Outer Spaces*, p. 385.
[50] Nanda, *Kamaladevi Chattopadhyay*, p. 155.
[51] Ibid., p. 138.
[52] Ray, *My Reminiscences*, Preface.
[53] Pandit, *The Scope of Happiness*, pp. 312–313.
[54] Ibid., p. 313.
[55] Chattopadhyay, *Inner Recesses Outer Spaces*, pp. 123–124.
[56] Ibid.
[57] Narayan, 'Honour is Honour After All', p. 249.

Eve Drewelowe: feminist identity in American art

Lindsay E. Shannon

Eve Drewelowe (1899–1988) was an American artist who attended the University of Iowa, where she received a BA in Graphic and Plastic Arts in 1923. During these early years when university art programs were being established, Drewelowe became the first person to receive an MA in art from the University of Iowa; one of the first people to receive such a degree in the United States. Drewelowe reinvented herself throughout her life and her artwork reflects a current knowledge of modern styles that emerged in the twentieth century. Drewelowe exhibited under the name Eve Drewelowe Van Ek shortly after her marriage in 1924 until the early 1950s, when she chose to resume using only her own surname. During the three intervening decades, her signature varies from one artwork to the next. In some instances, the artist later rubbed out or painted over the 'Van Ek' with little attempt to conceal the change, leaving a visual indicator of the artist's identity struggles. Her personal papers also reflect the challenges she faced reconciling public expectations of her role as the wife of a university dean with her profession as an artist. This essay considers the ways Drewelowe performed her identity as an artist in order to maintain her personal autonomy against the backdrop of the male dominated social and artistic world.

'It is an exceedingly strange business—this being an artist', Eve Drewelowe wrote late in her life.[1] A lifetime of struggling with how to 'be' an artist produced this rather modest statement. Despite the fact that art training provided an increasingly popular career path for women in the early twentieth century, many continued to encounter challenges in their decision to pursue a professional career as an artist. Although circumstances varied widely, these women all faced forging a new identity for themselves as they interacted with colleagues and personal acquaintances that were unfamiliar with, and frequently unsupportive of, the role of a serious (woman) artist. Eve Drewelowe (1899–1988) (Figure 1) attended the University of Iowa where she completed a Bachelor of Arts degree in Graphic and Plastic Arts in 1923. As art departments were being established in liberal arts colleges and universities across the United States, Drewelowe became one of a new generation of artists trained domestically, with no European experience. To further her instruction, she petitioned the University to create a graduate-level course of study. In 1924, she became the first person to receive an MA in art from the University of Iowa; one of the first people to receive such a degree in the nation.[2] For the rest of her career, Drewelowe defined herself by such experiences—ahead of her time, unique, and independent. This attitude influenced the way Drewelowe performed her role as a professional artist, often eschewing public expectations of her other 'career' as a wife.

Just one generation earlier, women were forging a place for themselves to study art. The late nineteenth century brought increasing opportunities in art schools and studios in the United States, United Kingdom, and Europe. By the turn of the twentieth century, conditions had altered enough that women were allowed equal access to nude models for study, which had previously been a major obstacle in the development of technical drawing skills on a par with male colleagues. But as female art students became more integrated into mainstream training, critics from the 1890s onward were simultaneously beginning to shift the aesthetic foundations of the art world. The sudden alteration in critical rhetoric to emphasize active, masculine characteristics and individual expression above professional training and skill was detrimental to the careers of both male and female artists who had built careers on the concept of professionalism in the arts. According to art historian Kristen Swinth:

> In the 1890s... Successes by women artists and anxieties about masculinity that were sweeping the country called the alliance between technique and refinement into question and triggered a revision of art criticism's language and tone. Rejecting refinement as too 'feminine' and technique as too mechanical, critics called for greater individuality and virility in American art.[3]

Thus, the idea of the artist as individual genius, which began to dominate rhetoric in the late nineteenth century, became fully developed in the early twentieth century, just as Drewelowe was coming of age as an artist. As academic training began to succumb to modernist expressionism, training credentials and technical skill were no longer the definition of a serious artist. Instead, individual expression—characterized by an original formal style—became the measure of

Figure 1 Eve Drewelowe, ca. 1924.
Source: Eve Drewelowe Digital Collection, Iowa Digital Library, drewe12-01, courtesy The University of Iowa Libraries and School of Art and Art History.

the modern artistic genius. This setback significantly affected women artists, just after their full acceptance into art academies, and continued to shape their relationship to the art world throughout the twentieth century. The recent, and largely tentative, acceptance of women as professional artists meant that their work was often less valued and patronage more difficult to obtain. The aesthetic risks necessary to join the ranks of the modernists were therefore even riskier for a woman artist, who could not count on admiring patrons or critics to overcome a decided bias that women were incapable of producing 'virile', individualistic art. Meanwhile, relatively steady, albeit pithy, commissions could be gotten for those who continued to paint in the populist academic tradition.

This generation of women was seeking to move beyond equal education and use the gains it promised to pursue professional careers. Although the evolution from education to productive work would seem a logical path, there was widespread resistance to women entering the workplace. Lucy Lippard commented on the first generation of feminist artists who came of age in this environment, writing:

> A simultaneous pride in uniqueness and an underlying fear of inferiority seemed then to affect the ranks of women artists... tales of maltreatment and inhumanity emerged... from art-school students whose professors classically discouraged them by historical and sexual denigration. This treatment was even handed out by well-meaning men so conditioned that it never occurred to them that they were making it impossible for many women to continue working.[4]

While Drewelowe's personal writings reflect a positive and indeed optimistic attitude towards her art training, she nonetheless encountered such attitudes as a student. She recounted that her painting professor, Charles A. Cumming, despaired of her talents being applied to a serious career as an artist when she married in 1923 while still completing her graduate degree:

> He said that marriage would finish me as an artist, that the act of it would end my career. I'm sure I must have viewed his disapproval partly as a challenge, and I resolved then and there that I would never sacrifice my creative existence to the accepted structure of wifely duties.[5]

Marriage (for women) was still widely considered to be an insurmountable obstacle to a professional career, and Drewelowe astutely acknowledged the expectations placed on women to perform household work as a primary source of the problem. Despite her determination to circumvent this 'accepted structure', it must have been psychologically painful for Drewelowe to have her mentor, previously so supportive, balk at her future potential. What must have been most frustrating was that his concern stemmed not from a lack of talent or commitment, but a personal lifestyle choice which was perfectly acceptable (if not useful) for her male colleagues. Although her professors and the University administration supported her desire to obtain an advanced degree and encouraged her to pursue a career in art, Drewelowe experienced lingering discrimination as a married woman which would affect her attitude towards her work for the rest of her life.

The challenges Drewelowe faced in the transition from promising student to serious artist caused her to see herself first and foremost as a professional, dedicated to her work. Late in her life she continued to insist on the importance of serious art training for students, when she compared her training to late twentieth-century university art programmes. Drewelowe felt that technical achievement was being sacrificed in favour of expression, and observed an increase in the number of students who were choosing art as an 'easy' course of study, rather than the ambition to become great artists.[6] As art training in the late twentieth century became increasingly influenced by modernist concerns with abstraction, less emphasis was placed on mastering the technical drawing skills which had been instrumental to Drewelowe's early training and sense of personal achievement. Her commitment to professionalism and technical skill as requisites to a serious career demonstrates a continuation of the strategy which had been so effective for the previous generation of female artists who were fighting for a place in the art world.

Despite her continued dedication to professional skill, Drewelowe also made no secret of her individualism. After marrying in 1923, Drewelowe continued to sign her paintings and student papers with her maiden name; however, after leaving school in 1924 she began to vary her signature from one artwork to the next. Between this date and the early 1950s, several different signatures were applied to her work. Although she apparently continued to use the stylized 'Drewelowe' signature from her student years, many works bear her married name 'Eve Van Ek' or even 'Eve Drewelowe Van Ek'.[7] Drewelowe exhibited publicly under both of the latter names during this period, although *never* as Mrs., which was common for many of her co-exhibitors. However, her personal preferences did not always prevent the conventions of the time from taking precedence. In her personal papers, a Boulder, Colorado, newspaper clipping from 1941 lists Drewelowe's participation in an exhibition as 'Mrs. Van Ek'.[8] She inserted 'EVE' in clear, bold lettering over 'Mrs.' Her correction affords her a first name as an artist for posterity, if only in her personal records on this occasion.

In the late 1920s, her husband, Jacob Van Ek, was promoted to the position of dean at the University of Colorado, Boulder. Drewelowe was wholly unprepared for the impact that the change in his career would have on her own identity and, subsequently, on her career. Although he supported her work as an artist throughout her career, Drewelowe was surprised to find that the university community expected her to fulfill numerous duties as the dean's wife without pay or recognition. Drewelowe recorded in detail the rigors and expectations of her new 'position' in her journals, memoirs, and oral interviews. A strong belief in her individuality and distaste for housework were strengthened considerably due to a gastrointestinal illness that plagued her throughout her early career, and she believed it to have been induced by the hostess duties laid out for her as the dean's wife.[9] Her illness culminated in a 1940 surgery, followed by a lengthy period of recovery which eventually solidified her decision to reject this role and rededicate herself to her art. She marked this event by permanently returning to her 'Drewelowe' signature as a statement of her artistic identity.

Contemporaries who also retained their maiden names and struggled with establishing an individual identity separate from that of a prominent husband are Georgia O'Keefe and Lee Krasner. For both artists, issues of feminine aesthetics and the role of a woman artist as counterpart to a more famous artist-husband have dominated discussions of their work. Both artists fought against misinterpretations of their work by critics and challenged the tendency for the press to characterise them as either a woman *or* an artist. Often, this entailed limiting discussions of their work to formalism in order to untangle their artistic identity from public perceptions of feminine identity. According to Ann M. Wagner, Krasner's:

> refusal to produce a self in painting ... was quite simply an answer in paint—hard won, intellectually rigorous—to the most problematic issue she faced: establishing an otherness to [Jackson] Pollock that would not be seen as the otherness of Woman. Its urgency was only heightened by social circumstance—by being a wife.[10]

Equally as important, both of these artists played with gender stereotypes in their public presentations of their persons. Krasner most notably masculinised her name to Lee and even adopted the neutral artistic signature 'L.K.' for her artwork. Both artists adopted no-nonsense clothing that was modern, professional, and evocatively masculine all at the same time. But unlike O'Keefe and Krasner, Drewelowe was not married to an artist. She did not live, nor did she regularly circulate in, the New York art world. Instead, Drewelowe was rather isolated as an artist in a university community with a husband whose own career was financially secure, sympathetic to, and not in direct competition with her own. These factors are important to reading the strategies adopted by Drewelowe to establish herself as a serious artist in her community and among colleagues nationally.

By the early 1950s, Drewelowe had not only reclaimed her maiden name as a sign of her artistic identity, but she retroactively altered her earlier works to reflect (and emphasise) her contemporary attitude. In some cases Drewelowe rubbed out or painted over 'Van Ek' on her works with little attempt to conceal the change, leaving a visual indicator of the artist's identity struggles. An incident described by Drewelowe in relation to the issue of legal surnames is very revealing in this context. Around 1945, she sought the advice of a friend, Supreme Court Judge Wiley B. Rutledge, who supported her assertion that women were under no legal obligation to change their names at marriage or to be addressed as 'Mrs'. She indicated that she was then 'sorting things out' and 'with that sort of endorsement, I knew I was right'.[11] During the same period Drewelowe was also writing letters to local newspapers on the issue. Her ongoing interest in feminist issues is also apparent in the writings found in her personal papers. In 1924, she had written an essay as part of her MA degree on women's dress in classical Greece, based on depictions from classical Greek vase painting. When the paper was returned to her in an envelope mislabelled with the title 'A Study of Greek Dress during the Greek Classical Period', Drewelowe used a red marking pen to vigorously cross out the first 'Greek' in favour of the insertion 'Women's Dress' to emphasise her annoyance at the mistake.[12] Later, a 1935 visit to the USSR resulted in a series of writings, many of which focus on her interest in the status of women as independent workers and salary earners. She wrote:

> They have their own income—a definite and regular salary—separate from that of their husbands ... A wife therefore does not have to depend on her husband or a daughter on her father for subsistence as the women of Russia did before 1917. A great deal of emphasis is placed, by the Soviet [g]overnment, on the contrast of the position of women ... to the German and Italian women. Hitler and Mussolini have made women of these countries more and more subservient ... Hitler has even taken away from them educational advantages which women formerly had in Germany.[13]

The emphasis placed on productive careers and equal access to education in this passage confirm Drewelowe's belief that the two were mutually connected—and that women had yet to take full advantage of both. Ironically, due to Drewelowe's propensity to write on any available scrap of paper, these observations were drafted on the back of her husband's blank correspondence forms. Her independent nature which led her to challenge social conventions was equally unafraid to assert itself in the art world—even when it meant confronting her closest mentors.

Art historian Erika Doss has suggested that 'One major area of inquiry should lead to accounting for the various styles and subjects selected by women artists in the Rocky Mountain region from the beginnings of Western suffrage through the advent of abstract art'.[14] Her observation of the variety of stylistic choices made by women artists of this region, including Drewelowe, resonates with the output of many others in the twentieth century. Drewelowe never adopted or settled on a single style for long, and never seemed to consider it a necessary part of artistic output, as the idea of style or consistency is never broached in any of her writings or interviews. In fact, Drewelowe never 'named' any of her working methods, referring only to the subject matter that her work was engaged in at the time. The issue of why stylistic consistency has not been as widespread of a trend in the work of women artists in the twentieth century is often commented upon, but rarely examined in relation to individual artists. Drewelowe's formal style changed several times throughout her career, diverging from her university training in impressionistic academic 'realism' almost immediately into experimentation with more abstract and stylized imagery. She recalled a visit from Professor Cumming to her studio in Boulder after leaving school. 'He thought "Eve's gone completely crazy," I think, by what I was doing. You see, I'd rejected everything.'[15] Cumming had not approved of exposure to outside artistic influences during her training. Although the standard components of art history studies with classicist Charles Weller and a study trip to view the collection at the Art Institute of Chicago were part of her degree requirements, more radical forms of contemporary art were not embraced by academic art instructors. As an academic portraitist, Cumming was known to be quite vocal in his disapproval of modern art styles of the early twentieth century, particularly Cubism.[16] A paper Drewelowe wrote on Cubism as a student reflects this attitude to a certain degree, although she later went to the trouble to revise the paper in a more positive tone, more accurately revealing her own interest in abstraction. The very fact that she chose to write the paper despite her professor's disapproval of modern art shows that Drewelowe was probably very aware and curious about emerging styles at an early point in her career. In the opening paragraph she highlighted the passage, 'Art has not escaped this spirit of alteration and experiment. Nor should we regret this situation for if there is to be development there must be change.'[17] Although Drewelowe never recalled making a conscious decision to alter her style after leaving school, it is evident that her investment in academic training by no means led her to limit the exploration of other stylistic influences in her work. This experimentation in her work is significant as a backdrop against the changes in her signature, signalling a liminality displayed by both formal style and text. The fact that Drewelowe made numerous changes to both her writings and her artistic signature, even some that no one else would likely ever see, suggests that public expectations did not often allow her the personal freedom to express herself.

In none of her personal papers does Drewelowe directly discuss particular artists or stylistic movements which may have influenced her own work, to the extent that she did not even comment on exchanges with other living artists with whom she was in contact. There is ample evidence to conclude that she was not only knowledgeable about, but actually experimenting with, contemporary styles of modern art. For example, the formal elements characteristic of the Blue Rider group are discernable in the stylized clouds and vegetation of her early pen and ink drawings, and in the 1930s she began experimenting with styles and subject matter evocative of Regionalism.[18] Her experimentation with the Blue Rider mode has been attributed to her broader exposure to modern European art during her extensive travels abroad beginning in 1928. It is also probable that Drewelowe's 'Regionalism' was inspired in part by exposure to Social Realist art during her 1935 trip to the Soviet Union (Figure 2). Her artistic output during this period is not merely a reflection of the contemporary movement in the US, but rather suited her preoccupation at that time with painting the regional landscape and people around her. Drewelowe's reluctance to associate her own work with outside influences may be a vestige of training with Cumming, but more likely her own individualism precluded close associations between her own experimentation and the work of other artists. In order to negotiate her own choices in subject and style, and to assert herself as an individual on equal terms with male colleagues, Drewelowe probably chose deliberately not to commit herself to discussions of style which may have appeared derivative. This demonstrates a distinct departure in strategy from artists who regularly circulated in the urban art centres of New York or Paris, who regularly conversed with their peers on topics of aesthetics, influence, and were expected to demonstrate their knowledge of the contemporary art scene. Instead, Drewelowe identified herself as an artist in her community by becoming a charter member of the Boulder Artists' Guild, giving public presentations about her work, and furthering exhibition opportunities for her work in the region in addition to participating in national venues. Associating with a much smaller and more diverse group of local artists,

Figure 2 St. Sophia's, Kiev, Russia, 1935.
Source: Eve Drewelowe Digital Collection, Iowa Digital Library, 34MP, courtesy The University of Iowa Libraries and School of Art and Art History.

brought together by a common interest in art rather than common aesthetic practices or acquaintances, subject became the common vocabulary of the Boulder Artists' Guild members.[19] It would have certainly been the most useful device for Drewelowe when describing her art to a general audience attending her area lectures and exhibitions.

In response to the popularity of her 'Regionalist' works of the 1930s and 1940s, Drewelowe commented, 'I think that's nice, if people like my old things—I like that, but I don't think it's the end ... I can paint some of the old landscapes ... but they'd be different'.[20] In fact, Drewelowe continued to revisit some of her 'old landscapes' throughout her life, but they were indeed 'different'. Drewelowe described her re-examination of this earlier work in 1981, stating 'Now when I look back on my earlier Findings and [reflect] on the erosion that has ensued, I am dismayed and appalled at the deprivation called "progress"'.[21] Drewelowe's active observation of the land dominates her discussion of these works, not the changing techniques used to depict it, although her formal approach to the subject certainly did change over time. These later paintings demonstrate an increased human presence in the landscape and its visual impact on the land, as well as her longing to return to a more spiritual connection with nature. Her careful study of the changes taking place around her acts as a metaphor for the stylistic evolution of her art works, always careful to maintain relevance and freshness over stability.

One subject that would be expected of Drewelowe, given her preoccupation with individuality, is relatively rare in comparison to her overall output—self-portraits. Drewelowe's early self-portraits reflect the methodical, realistic life-drawing exercises from her student days. As her work evolved into more stylized and symbolic images, her self-portraiture began to represent important events in her contemporary life, such as *Self-Portrait (Reincarnation)* from 1939. In 1975, Drewelowe explored the theme in an entirely abstract form, coinciding with abstract geometric work in her broader output. Her final self-portrait, *Maverick* (1984), blends the realism of her earlier work with abstraction, producing an interesting synthesis of tension and harmony.

Self-Portrait (Reincarnation) (Figure 3) represents this initial shift away from pure representation and towards introspection. The viewer has a bird's eye view of Drewelowe's bedroom, looking down on the unmade, quilt-covered bed. The bed bisects the picture plane diagonally, focusing the viewer's attention on the surrounding objects: furnishings and textiles designed by Drewelowe and one of her pen and ink drawings on the wall. Smaller objects on either side of the central horizontal can be identified as books, a radio, and what appear to be pill boxes and a medicine bottle. It is then that the central figure is most apparent at the intersection between the horizontal and vertical axes; the back of a small, crumpled figure is just visible beneath the bed quilt. Although the watercolour employs the stylised realism characteristic of her work during the 1930s, this self-portrait is more symbolic than representative. Drewelowe's figure takes on an abstract form, barely noticeable to the casual viewer, while her bedroom surroundings become a metaphor for her physical illness and emotional recovery process. At the end of her life, Drewelowe employed a reverse strategy in *Maverick* (1984) (Figure 4). Her figure is dominant in this image, executed in the impressionistic realism of her student days, but the tools of her trade which surround her, palette, brushes, and an

Figure 3 Self-portrait (Reincarnation), 1939.
Source: Eve Drewelowe Digital Collection, Iowa Digital Library, 62.30P, courtesy The University of Iowa Libraries and School of Art and Art History.

in-progress canvas, are rendered in more abstract forms. The contrast between these areas, most apparent at the top third of the canvas, becomes less pronounced near the bottom where the artist's enlarged hand and the unravelling stripes on her dress almost merge with the abstract forms around her. It is here, on the fringes, that Drewelowe the woman merges with Drewelowe the artist. These two paintings

Figure 4 Maverick, 1984.
Source: Eve Drewelowe Digital Collection, Iowa Digital Library, 5.80C, courtesy The University of Iowa Libraries and School of Art and Art History.

are arguably among Drewelowe's most successful works, and certainly the most successful of her self-portraits. The combination of her proficiency in traditional representational techniques and contemporary abstraction is not just a technical achievement for her work. The merging of representation and abstraction in her self-portraits seems to mirror her personal journey as an artist, constantly navigating between the roles of professional artist and finding her own voice as an individual. In these paintings, Drewelowe seems to reveal her persona as an artist as a performance, one which she discovered would allow her to act out her individuality on a very public stage—the university community.

Drewelowe's interest in both name-identity and stylistic exploration clearly reveal a consciousness of her relationship to the art world as a 'woman artist', a dual entity. Her choice to belong to and actively exhibit with the National Association of Women Artists during her 'reawakening' period in the 1940s makes this evident.[22] Serious artists (including O'Keefe and Krasner) were often ambiguous about the impact that identifying as a 'woman artist' would have on their professional reputation, as opposed to the challenges of navigating the broader art world as an individual who was nonetheless classed as a woman artist. Achieving recognition through mainstream institutions in the art world gave the appearance of equality, even though many female artists did not have the same access to colleagues, patrons, and critics that their male colleagues could command. Drewelowe seems to have straddled this divide; she worked alone in her studio and early in her career exhibited either alone or in group shows that included top-name artists. At the same time, she continued to insist on the tradition of artistic professionalism and participated in local exhibitions, especially after the 1950s, which were frequently denigrated as amateur by critics and urban art circles. This suggests that creating a strong identity as an artist within her own community in Boulder was a more effective strategy for Drewelowe than cultivating a reputation among urban art circles by exhibiting in New York or other national venues.

Unlike many of her contemporaries, Drewelowe did not base the authentication of her art practice exclusively on her individuality as defined by formal expression, but rather on her professionalism. This may appear strange, because she departed so quickly from her training in academic techniques and placed a great deal of emphasis on her position as an individual in her writings. However, Drewelowe seems to have established her *identity* as an artist as the grounds for being treated as an autonomous individual, creating a distinct persona separate from her husband and his work, while simultaneously maintaining her proficiency in technique as the basis for her *status* as a professional artist. Drewelowe's performance-based strategy acts as a parallel to the urban art scene, where artists often used dress to establish identities outside of the mainstream—or even within their own artistic circles. As Susan Fillin-Yeh points out:

> In a climate in which women's images and actions as independent artists were without precedent, they made themselves up as they went along, defining themselves in new—and shifting—contexts. Thus women's dandy's images took on meanings which were empowering. They framed a challenge to the dominant mode of male discourse by using its own symbols against it.[23]

A university community in the western US would have harboured a number of formerly urban, perhaps East Coast, professors and administrators who cultivated their own public image of being cultured, reasonably open-minded, and sophisticated. Drewelowe seems to have taken advantage of this cultural climate to transform expectations of her own position in the community. While 'wives' were still expected to take on the role of an unpaid hostess to assist their husband's careers, an *artist* was something else altogether and it would have appeared decidedly unsophisticated to interfere in the work of another intellectual professional. Establishing a firm identity as an artist created social advantages which allowed Drewelowe to live as an individual, rather than the departmental help-mate.

While it is evident that Drewelowe struggled at times with her own dual status as a woman artist and valued the distinction of a reputation in urban art circles, she used the situation she defined for herself as both an individual and an artist to negotiate an unstable social position in her daily life. Drewelowe recognised that by performing her work as an artist on the local scene, rather than in the more rarefied atmosphere of New York, she could reclaim a space to be 'Eve' instead of always being identified as 'Mrs. Van Ek', the dean's wife. By attaching her personal identity to her professional work, Drewelowe was able to maintain her autonomy within her own community. Concurrently, because artists were viewed as being independent by nature, it was her profession which allowed her to openly perform that individuality in the community with little criticism, at a time when married women encountered resistance both to maintaining professional careers and their own independence. It was indeed a 'strange business', but Drewelowe managed to create, and re-create, her role as an artist to navigate challenges to her individuality.

Notes

[1] Eve Drewelowe (1988) *Eve Drewelowe* (Iowa City: University of Iowa School of Art and Art History), p. x.
[2] Drewelowe benefited from the University's pioneering decision to accept creative work in lieu of theses for graduate degrees beginning in 1922.
[3] Kirsten Swinth (2001) *Painting Professionals: women artists & the development of modern American art, 1870–1930* (Chapel Hill: University of North Carolina Press), pp. 131–132.
[4] Lucy Lippard (1976) *From the Center: feminist essays on women's art* (New York: Dutton Press), p. 44.
[5] Drewelowe, *Eve Drewelowe*, p. vi.
[6] AC 1332, Eve Drewelowe papers, Iowa Women's Archives, University of Iowa Libraries, Iowa City.
[7] Drewelowe always signed finished works, and the existence of unaltered 'Drewelowe' signatures from works of this period suggests that she continued to use this name along with the other signatures.
[8] Boulder Subjects Predominate in Artists' Guild Show; Techniques are Widely Varied, unidentified newspaper (Boulder, Colorado, 28 Apr. 1941). Box 9, Eve Drewelowe papers.
[9] Monica DeMott (1996) *Eve Drewelowe: transformations within her life and work* (MA, University of Iowa).
[10] Anne M. Wagner (1989) Lee Krasner as L.K., *Representations*, 25, pp. 42–57.
[11] AC 1332, Eve Drewelowe papers.
[12] Box 3, Eve Drewelowe papers. Full paper is located in the Special Collections & University Archives, University of Iowa Libraries.
[13] Box 4, Eve Drewelowe papers.
[14] Erica Doss (1995) 'I must paint': women artists of the Rocky Mountain region, in *Independent Spirits: women painters of the American West, 1890–1945* (Berkeley, CA: Autry Museum of Western Heritage), p. 112.
[15] AC 1332, Eve Drewelowe papers. After moving to Boulder, Colorado, in late 1924, Drewelowe and Van Ek embarked on their first travels abroad in 1928–1929. Charles A. Cumming spent a year of sabbatical in California in 1926 and died in

1932. It seems probable that Cumming stopped in Boulder during his travels in 1926. Charles A. Cumming papers, Special Collections & University Archives, University of Iowa Libraries.
[16] AC 1332, Eve Drewelowe papers.
[17] Box 3, Eve Drewelowe papers.
[18] Anon. (1989) Five Artists of the 1930s and 1940s, *Art News*, 88(4), p. 211.
[19] The Boulder Artists' Guild (1925–1989) held regular exhibitions of its members' work. Featured artists in exhibition brochures, including Drewelowe, discuss professional credentials and primary subject matter of the artist, rather than an artist's statement. Box 5, Eve Drewelowe papers.
[20] AC 1332, Eve Drewelowe papers.
[21] Drewelowe, *Eve Drewelowe*, p. xiii.
[22] Drewelowe was a member of the National Association of Women Artists (formerly the National Association of Women Painters and Sculptors) and participated in its annual exhibitions 1939–1948. She had been personally invited to submit her work to the jury for membership in 1938. In 1940 and 1941she had solo exhibitions at the organization's Argent Galleries in New York. From the 1950s onward Drewelowe favored participation in local and regional art associations, including the Boulder chapter of the Artists' Equity Association. Boxes 2–5, Eve Drewelowe papers.
[23] Susan Fillin-Yeh (1995) Dandies, Marginality and Modernism: Georgia O'Keeffe, Marcel Duchamp and other cross-dressers, *Oxford Art Journal*, 18(2), p. 36.

Women Activists: rewriting Greenham's history

Elaine Titcombe

The Greenham Common Women's Peace Camp protest of the 1980s and 1990s has become synonymous with radical feminism. Given that many of the challenges raised and discourses employed were similar, it might appear as a relatively uncomplicated progression from Women's Liberation. From this perspective, the threat of nuclear war could be viewed as a stark indication of the persistence of male violence enabled by an unremittingly patriarchal world. The women's protest was therefore often described by those who took part as a direct challenge to the status quo, intended to bring about the cultural revolution required to overthrow it. This article examines two histories of the event published in the 'post-feminist' era of the mid 2000s. It will demonstrate how a shift in discourses since the end of the protest has enabled these emergent texts to challenge the previously dominant version of the Greenham peace camp. It will go on to suggest that this shift was necessary in order to communicate a new contemporary political message: a message that gains its authority by drawing on other 'silent' discourses from Greenham. It will compare this development to the post-suffrage period as observed by other historians. In so doing, it will once again reveal how closely the 'present' influences the reflections of the 'past', and how this affects the performances of participants in their autobiographical accounts.

In 1981, a march began from South Wales to the United States Air Force (USAF) base at Greenham Common, to protest against the positioning there of ninety-six nuclear Cruise missiles. Upon arrival at the Berkshire military base, four women from the group that called itself 'Women for Life on Earth: Women's Action for Disarmament' decided to chain themselves to the perimeter fence to publicise their protest.[1] This action gave rise to the formation of a spontaneous peace camp. Within a few months, it began to attract worldwide attention and by 1982 it had evolved into several (distinct) camps around the military base.[2] A decision had also been taken to make the protest a women-only campaign and male residents were asked to leave the site.[3] On several days during the existence of the camps, supporters arrived en masse at the base and it was claimed that between 30,000 and 50,000 were present.[4] Over time, the various camps fluctuated in size, and the mass protest days reduced in terms of numbers involved and in frequency. In 1987, the Intermediate-Range Nuclear Forces Treaty (INF) was signed by President Reagan and General Secretary Gorbachev; consequently, the last nuclear weapons left Greenham in 1991. The closure of the last protest camp, however, at the main entrance (also known as Yellow Gate), took place several years later, on the anniversary of the arrival of the original march on 5 September 2000.

Competing Histories

This article will focus upon two accounts of the protest: Sarah Hipperson's (2005), *Greenham: Non-Violent Women v The Crown Prerogative*; and Ann Pettitt's (2006), *Walking to Greenham: how the peace camp began and the Cold War ended*.[5] Pettitt, a trained teacher, was the founder member of the original march to Greenham. At the time she was living with her partner in rural Wales with their two young children. She spent only short periods at Greenham (up until 1984) due to her family commitments. Hipperson, also a mother but of five adult children, joined the Greenham peace camp in March 1983, following the first attempted evictions of the protestors by the local authorities, and made Yellow Gate her home until 2000.[6] A trained nurse and midwife in the 1940s, she had also worked as a magistrate for a short time before moving to Greenham. She had been mildly involved with the Campaign for Nuclear Disarmament (CND) in the 1960s, and had formed the Catholic Peace Action group in the early 1980s.

From the outset the protest was led by women, but ideologically it was not necessarily feminist. The campaign was often portrayed by the women participants as a desire to prevent nuclear war in order to save their children: 'The presence of nuclear weapons on our soil is causing serious mental harm. Women are afraid of having more children. I personally would like to be at home with my family ... but if we lose this case we stand to lose our children'.[7] Many of the women also drew explicitly from their traditional positions as mothers and carers in an appeal to redistribute resources away from weapons:

> The government spent more on 'defence' last year than on either health or education, and ... housing ... There are now fewer places in hospitals or day-care

centres for the elderly and the sick, which means that they will have to be looked after at home, invariably by women.[8]

Neither of these positions was specifically feminist and attracted criticism from some involved with Women's Liberation because the peace movement was perceived to be diverting women's attention away from the fight to liberate women from patriarchy.[9] From this perspective, it was argued that the maternal position served to perpetuate the sex-role stereotyping that women had been fighting against through Women's Liberation.[10] Whilst fighting for peace, women were charged with 'seeing their own oppression as subsidiary or secondary'.[11]

In answer to this, others have argued that Greenham enabled women who had not engaged with Women's Liberation in the 1970s to develop a feminist identity. Sasha Roseneil, who stayed at the camp for ten months in 1982–83, asserted that the position of 'campaigning on the basis of a mother's moral and practical duty to protect life' was the 'earliest external face presented by the camp'.[12] Referring to Jill Liddington's history of women's peace campaigns, she maintained that historically in the absence of a 'visible feminist movement, women's commitment to peace work tended to be framed entirely in terms of women's maternal role'.[13] This was how women were 'permitted' to work politically without threatening the separate spheres necessary to maintain a patriarchal society. However, particularly after 1982, when men were not allowed to stay at the camps, the space created at Greenham enabled women to explore their 'consciousness' and consequently the discourse began to shift and become increasingly feminist and radical in outlook. This was, she maintained, because there was a feminist discourse available (i.e. from Women's Liberation), and not in spite of it.

In this analysis, Roseneil implied that many women went through a form of re-education and transformation at Greenham. They were able to undergo a shift from their 'female' understanding of the world gained from their 'socially constructed' lived experience as mothers and carers, to a 'feminist' one where the root cause in the growth of militarism was identified as the persistence of male power through patriarchy. This was due directly to the nature of the space at Greenham which allowed women to explore themselves outside the confines of patriarchy. Indeed, there is testimony that some women did experience this. As one unidentified woman said when interviewed at the camp, 'You get so trapped into this way that you've got to be, values that you're supposed to have. Your values change here, and you're bound to take that back with you.'[14]

As time progressed a shift in the discourse did occur in the pamphlets, slogans, letters and personal testimonies of Greenham.[15] Initially, the literature from the camp addressed an imagined like-minded female audience on the outside of the cause, in the context of her involvement in traditional roles. For the Rainbow Dragon protest in June 1983, women were invited to 'contain the nuclear fire that threatens all life on this planet'. By building and containing small fires around the base but to 'use them for a life giving purpose—the cooking and sharing of food and warmth', they were invited to bring their 'recipes for peace'. Men were asked to support by 'organising children's fire dragon feasts and crèches in local areas—leaving mothers free to come on their own'.[16] Other leaflets from this period also contained photographs from the site that attempted to influence women into supporting the cause by identifying with their maternal role by featuring mothers with young children.[17]

However, by the mid 1980s, the language and imagery had begun to change and consequently the emphasis shifted. It was often argued, for instance, that war was a particularly male act and that the violence of war had parallels with the violence that many women suffered at the hands of men in their everyday lives: 'Nuclear missiles [are] the ultimate destructive expression of patriarchy... the masculist values of warfare is the same mentality that creates pornography... [the] rape of women goes hand in hand with ecological destruction of the earth and imperialism'.[18] The solution to these problems was expressed as a need to overthrow the power systems that were in operation and to initiate a feminist revolution: 'Imagine the possibilities of so many women... coming together to plan... To heal the world we have... Together we can celebrate the future that one day will truly be ours... We can make the world we want!'[19]

In the attempt to effect this change, the campaign outwardly became more resistant in nature to all forms of authority. In addition, as had first been discussed within the Women's Liberation movement, the Greenham discourse began to challenge the dominance of the heterosexual woman as the ideal for women. Many participants perceived this to be the tool by which men ultimately maintained their patriarchal power. The result was an increasingly separatist philosophy and a growing hostility between many of the Greenham women. As Roseneil also pointed out, the camps increasingly attracted women who desired a 'female' space.[20] This also affected the interaction of the Peace women with the State and its agents, as well as the press and other (mixed) peace organisations such as CND.[21]

The relationship between Greenham and feminism was complex and the emergence of a revised Greenham identity was problematic. In this way Greenham was similar to other women's movements. As June Hannam notes: 'There has always been debate about what it means to be a feminist, which goals should be pursued and which tactics should be used... the many differences between women are bound to lead to a variety of feminisms... [it] has never been a monolithic movement'.[22] A passionate debate about the nature and direction of the protest was clearly evident in the texts from Greenham and other peace 'organisations' of the time, particularly after men were evicted from the camp:

> Many women become involved because of their children... most expect motherhood to be important for women in the future... Others reject motherhood as an option and certainly as women's destiny. Still others do not want personal relationships with men. These different perspectives give rise to differences of opinion and emphasis, and to continuing, sometimes bitter, discussion.[23]

Therefore, the change in emphasis can be interpreted as the outcome of an internal battle to control the discursive nature of the Greenham protest as the demographic of the women involved in the camps changed over time, as well as the shift of attitude of individuals concerned.

As historians we are tasked with exposing the master signifiers and analysing the 'labour to exclude certain forms of knowledge'.[24] Given the intensity of the debate prevalent in the contemporary texts and the strong feelings still held by many involved in the early part of the campaign, it is evident that a dominant collective public identity did emerge. Alternative identities opposed to this became excluded, giving rise to the 'silent' other. It was this choice of discourse that ultimately led to Greenham being predominately classed as a radical feminist moment by librarians, archivists and historians, to the exclusion of 'other', equally tenable, versions.

In adopting the discourse of radical feminism to represent the Greenham protest, the activists purposefully put in place the framework in which their characters could perform and their opposition to nuclear weapons be coherently articulated. Individuals were empowered by aligning their actions, words and written texts with this, gaining support from others within the movement. However, it has been widely contended that individuals are a complex mix of thoughts, actions and ideas resulting in a hybridity of identity and plurality of voices.[25] As a result, the collective identity of any political movement and any subsequent linear history is known to be highly problematic and unstable. Therefore, there is a recognition that the work of controlling the dominant discourse(s) persists long after, impacting on the subsequent memories and stories told of the event.[26]

This article will argue that Hipperson and Pettitt offer a challenge to the dominance of the radical feminist discourse. It will demonstrate that the established collective identity was not an option for either of these two women in the creation of their activist 'self', particularly in the post (second wave) feminist era. Indicating that the subsequent historical narration of events by participants can be equally revealing about the time in which they are written as they are about the nature of the power/truth systems in operation at the time of the event, it will suggest that whilst both women positioned their created autobiographical 'self' apart from the figure of the radical feminist, they are compelled by its dominance to continue to draw upon this identity. It is a necessary reference point in their attempts to shift the discourse of the historic event to one which better supports their current political message. In spite of this shared objective, however, they do not present us with new versions of the event, which indicates further that there is a multiplicity of other voices and identities that have been hitherto excluded from the Greenham history.

Sarah Hipperson

In her autobiographical account of the years 1995–2000, Sarah Hipperson describes the final years of the main gate camp at Greenham. The book gives an account of how the women continued to promote the philosophy of Peace and to press for an end to nuclear weapons worldwide. They also launched appeals through the courts to prove the British Government had acted illegally when it had allowed Greenham Common to become home to the USAF missiles. The book closes with the return of the land to the people of Newbury (which Hipperson attributes to the women of Yellow Gate) and the subsequent campaign to erect a permanent memorial to the women on the site of the main gate protest.

In the opening passages of the book, Hipperson urged the reader to view her book as the final in a trilogy of texts that gave 'a true and lasting historical record'.[27] Her trilogy refers to Harford and Hopkins, *Women at the Wire*; and B. Junor, *Greenham Common Women's Peace Camp: a history of non-violent resistance 1984–1995*, with her book as the conclusion. Her alignment with these selected texts was intended to point to the existence of a single authoritative narrative of the protest. Quoting Beth Junor, she emphasised that 'at last we've been able to tell our own story and project our own image of ourselves'.[28] The assertion of the collective 'our', which appears to encompass all, encouraged the view that her version was representative and therefore valid. The emphasis on the trilogy enabled the Greenham story to appear coherent and unified from start to finish, which in turn also added weight to Hipperson's assertion that her account was reliable. However, by proclaiming the legitimacy of these texts, she also emphasised that other conflicting narratives were in existence. Indeed she acknowledged that she could not speak for all women at Greenham. But in the action of establishing a trilogy, she effectively undermined all other versions by ensuring they would be considered peripheral to the main narrative. From the outset, therefore, Hipperson was concerned with 'writing out' other versions.

This intention was evident before the publication of her book. The final action by the women of Yellow Gate (of which Hipperson was a principal figure), to deliberately choose a symbolic date to end the protest in 2000, was calculated to secure the attention of historians. Drawing a direct line between themselves and the original marchers and forming a neat conclusion to the protest, the women embarked upon the process of creating the (new) Greenham story. They had set the scene and they subsequently proceeded to fill in the inner chapters of the narrative by collating their memories and placing their (selected) documents in the Women's Library archives.[29] Their voices were also recorded and deposited as oral histories.[30] They further legitimised themselves by securing the permanent commemorative garden/memorial on the site of the Yellow Gate camp. All this served to reinforce the suggestion that what had taken place was of historical and moral importance deserving of recognition. These actions were deliberate and also demonstrated their awareness of the history writing which would subsequently occur. (As historians we are aware that all histories are bound by the signs and discursive texts that participants and other agencies record.)

This was nothing new, as Hilda Kean has pointed out in a review of first-wave feminists: 'British militant suffrage feminists had a strong sense of their role in history ... [and can] be remembered both because of the nature of their campaigns, but also through the histories they helped to construct themselves ... The suffragettes contributed to their own historical survival'.[31] However, it is

Hipperson's preoccupation with ensuring the historical status of Yellow Gate that is central to an understanding of her attempt to close out other versions of the story.

Initially, when the first women arrived at Greenham in 1981, they set up camp outside the main entrance. As more women arrived and the work began at the base to build the missile silos and facilities to house the USAF troops, several other camps were established from 1983 at the other gate entrances to the site. Each gate soon became known as a colour of the rainbow and emphasised a particular taste and/or community of women.[32] Women did occasionally move between the gates, often due to fluctuating numbers of women on site (decreasing during the winter and increasing during warmer months). However, as the protest progressed, allegiances and differences between the groups at each of the gates began to emerge, making the interchange between them, in some instances, impossible.

It was publicly reported in 1987 that a split occurred between the women of Yellow Gate and the other camps.[33] There are different accounts of what caused this split. Some women attributed it to racism, whilst other testimonies explained it as an attempt by an external group to control Greenham and impose a structure of command that was not acceptable to the majority of the camps at Greenham.[34] Hipperson's book specifically deals with a period several years after this episode, but it is nevertheless present in her text, which draws our attention to it. It is made all the more conspicuous because her reference to it is cryptic:

> There was the unstinting practical support... given to us by the Wages for Housework Campaign,... whose very name offended 'feminist' careerists within the women's peace movement, including as it does the word 'housework'. There were those who struggled with the political direction [of] Yellow Gate... [which insisted] on a commitment to non-violent direct action rather than lifestyle politics... The women [of Yellow Gate]... were far too focused on our work against the Cruise Missile.... The events of 1987 that were attributed to the 'split' in some ways were a convenient hook for some women to hang their personal 'time to move on' decisions.[35]

Her language is telling. The description of the fallout from the split indicates how acrimonious it was and also how the bitterness had not subsided by the time of publication in 2005. To an outsider without any knowledge, there is no real explanation of the rift; to those who were aware, it appears as another stinging attack. The pursuit of what she termed 'lifestyle politics' appears frivolous in comparison with the threat posed by nuclear weapons. She also dismissed the form of feminism that many radicals within the Women's Liberation movement had called for: a complete overhaul of the role of women in society. She accepted that women continued to work within a domestic sphere. This deliberate positioning apart from the radical feminists (to a position more aligned to the original politics of the campaign) in direct reference to the split at Greenham had the effect of inferring that those with that agenda were resident at the other gates. Consequently the conclusion could only be that the women of Yellow Gate were motivated much less by a feminist agenda.

It is clear throughout that Hipperson's aim was to ensure that the Yellow Gate Camp was distinguished from all others by her reader. In this version of the history, it was irrelevant what charges the 'others' brought because the Yellow Gate focus was always on the 'real' reason for being there—to remove nuclear weapons. Thus, those with 'hidden agendas' were portrayed as any who questioned (then or now) the authority of Yellow Gate to speak on behalf of Greenham.[36] On several other occasions, she referred to Yellow Gate as the original peace camp and the only one to have been constantly occupied throughout the nineteen years of protest.[37] This too elevated Yellow Gate (and by implication its occupants) to the top of the hierarchy. The 'others' in Hipperson's history were held in less esteem because they could not maintain a permanent presence; therefore their resolve and political basis could not have been as secure as those at the main gate.[38] This is interesting given that in this construction of the Greenham protest, Hipperson presented a history that directly conflicted with the literature produced during the early years of the protest. This consistently emphasised the leaderless nature of Greenham and the high levels of respect that the women had for each other's opinions at the camps. It was this, many argued, that made it necessary for the camp to be 'women only' as it was in this space that women could 'find' their voice.[39] What appears apparent, therefore, is that Hipperson, after the event (and in particular the 1987 split), was determined to 'write out' other versions in order to legitimise and propel her own to the fore, even if that meant betraying the original outward ethos of the protest.

It is striking that Hipperson disregarded the radical feminism of the campaign in her text. With reference to the Women's Liberation movement she stated that 'Greenham's quarrel was not with the man next door and his "privileged" life within the hierarchy/patriarchy'.[40] Women who saw it in that way, she claimed, were missing the true point of Greenham. In the Hipperson version, the importance of Greenham was in the power of the individual to bear witness to the immoral actions of the State: 'Greenham challenged the State at its highest level. It struck at the heart of Her Majesty's Government, at the politicians, the military, bureaucrats, the law, courts and prison systems. Women were prepared to take these on ... in defence of life itself'.[41]

In Hipperson's writings and oral testimonies, the projection of 'self' was consistently defined by a discourse of morality and righteousness. Quoted in the camp newsletter in May 1983, Hipperson declared: 'We should uphold the law of God not man. I symbolically cut the fence on loyalty to our Redeemer who suffered so that we could be free to follow Him. Not to be enslaved by the laws of the world but offered the freedom of His Kingdom'.[42] Though she did not always exude such religious reasoning, she was the founder of Catholic Peace Action and much of her language does evoke these concepts. On the basis of the concepts of righteousness, morality, self-sacrifice and bearing witness, she links her campaign to the civil rights movement led by Martin Luther King Jr, using quotations and inferences from him in her text.[43] She traces her declared belief in the effectiveness of non-violent direct action to movements such as Mahatma Gandhi's campaign for Indian independence.[44] Indeed, many of the protests and tactics the Yellow Gate women engaged with (as described in the trilogy) are carefully written to force the reader to make the direct link to Gandhi. For example, they not only engage in non-violent direct action, but also practise fasting and non-cooperation when arrested and/or imprisoned. Both Martin Luther King Jr and Gandhi also had strong religious ethics as the basis of their actions.

Thus, Hipperson proclaimed the virtue of the Yellow Gate women. In her version, they were working for all of humankind (not just womankind), in exposing an unjust and immoral State (which is not necessarily defined as overtly male). They acted as the moral conscience and as upholders of the concept of law within a fair and just society, and this was the legacy she intended to project:

> The non-violent resistance paradigm practiced on Greenham Common could now open up new paths of connection with others seeking a better world for all people of this earth. Greenham need no longer be confined to a 'women only' agenda, but could seek to take the work and the history to a wider arena.[45]

In order to confirm the perception of the Yellow Gate women as righteous, a considerable amount of Hipperson's time at the camp was used in attempts to challenge the legality of state action through the Courts. As a former magistrate, Hipperson was quick to confront the authorities on their own terms. She already had experience of legal discourse and therefore understood how it could be subverted to act against the agencies of state. In the latter years, she worked to prove that the Ministry of Defence had acquired the land at Greenham Common illegally. In so doing, she sought publicly to record that all arrests and subsequent imprisonments for causing criminal damage were also illegal. Hipperson's determination to effectively clear protesters' names in the official record was a blatant attempt to rewrite history. Success would ensure that they were no longer viewed as criminals. Such a reversal of the state judgement would also render all that they did as justifiable and morally sound. To add weight to this moral role, Hipperson made direct reference to the teachings of Jesus Christ by quoting from the book of Matthew. She describes the story of Christ challenging the legal profession not to apply the rule of a law, if that law is shown to be unjust or immoral.[46]

By acting as guardians of society's morality and by taking the lead from Christ himself, Hipperson was performing a particular version of the self to ensure she (and the other Yellow Gate women) had a legitimate voice in the future. This allowed them a place in the battle against militarism post-Greenham. In this interpretation, Hipperson was using her account of Greenham to gain the authority to speak out against any future government acting without the explicit consent of the people, as it had done in 1979 when it agreed to the placement of American missiles in the UK. Hipperson's publication contained a clear indication of this in relation to the Afghan–Iraq wars following 9/11: 'I believe ... we need to challenge the immunity the State allots to itself when it undemocratically declares war without the consent of its people'.[47] She went on to challenge the response of the State to the threat of terrorism: 'The Home Secretary requires only "reasonable belief" that those detained are a threat to national security ... It calls into question the very existence of an ancient liberty... freedom from arbitrary arrest and detention'.[48]

The emphasis on morality was clearly a principal point for Hipperson throughout the life she presents in her book, but significantly she draws upon it heavily in relation to Yellow Gate. In her text, the reader is continually led to see all the Yellow Gate women as Hipperson. She defines them by the language of her own identity and in turn allows their words to also define her own character in the book. There are occasions where it is difficult to determine which woman is speaking in the text as everything is coherently focused on the arguments against the State/Law. The impact upon the reader is the image of a unified single identity shared by all the Yellow Gate women, driven by morality and righteousness. Because her text was explicitly about the Yellow Gate women, she actively excluded the radical feminists from this new/revised identity. Her text placed the radicals at the other gates of Greenham, and by emphasising the morality of the Yellow Gate women, she placed this motivation above the aims and aspirations of feminism.

By the time of publication in 2005, the radical second-wave feminism of Women's Liberation and Greenham had declined to the extent that no active, high-profile campaign operated. In this environment a new declaration of radical feminism by a former activist was unlikely to attract much attention. By considering Hipperson's account against this backdrop, it is clear that she was carving out a different direction for herself in the historical record. Her text was suggestive that acting as the moral conscience of society was an identity which she felt remained relevant post Greenham. Indeed, she made reference to organisations such as the Fellowship of Reconciliation and Pax Christi which continue to work for peace from a religious basis (perhaps also a pointer for her reader to get involved).[49] Significantly, this clear alignment allowed her to maintain her integrity as it did not divorce her from her work and identity at Greenham.

Hipperson emphasised at length how 'authentic' her account was, but this in itself raised questions about why she felt this necessary at all. Instead, it indicated that she was engaged in a process of historical construction and an attempt to cover up that process. She devised a plot, defined characters and created roles for them to perform in order to exclude what she perceived as the undesirable aspects of the campaign. The women in her text only carried out the actions that served to support her (revised) version of the story. They performed according to a pre-defined script or were quickly dismissed as those with lesser agendas. In particular, versions written by perceived 'outsiders' were rejected with disdain as misrepresentations: 'so much... has been centred on social issues and hype, ignoring the political content of the protest'.[50] She encouraged her audience to view them as exaggerated distractions. To avoid the charge that the revised collective identity depicted in her text was an extension of her own constructed 'self', she drew upon other authors to support her 'version' of events. Significantly however, in doing this, she drew attention to her endeavours to shut out the conflicting accounts.

Ann Pettitt

Ann Pettitt, the founder member of the original march to Greenham, significantly did not align herself with the work of the camps in the Hipperson model. There is no suggestion of any continuity between her action and that of the final Greenham residents. Indeed Pettitt makes no distinctions between any of the women at Greenham in her account, but there are some important similarities in her depiction to that of Hipperson, particularly in relation to the portrayal of feminism.

The title of Pettitt's book, *Walking to Greenham: how the peace-camp began and the Cold War ended*, was revealing as its emphasis was upon the beginning and the end of the event rather than the time in between. In this way, she immediately differed from the other versions whose task appeared to be to enlighten their readers of the intervening years. Pettitt used this approach for two reasons: firstly, from a practical point as she was not a permanent resident at the Peace Camps and in fact went there for the last time in 1984; and secondly, because she was inviting a new reading of the event.

She was also keen to re-emphasise the 'real' purpose of the protest: the antinuclear message. In doing so she made the same attempt as Hipperson to marginalise the principal alternative: the radical feminist version. Pettitt recognised this rendering took the meaning of Greenham to a different place, where the 'emphasis moved further towards preparing and politicising women' to overthrow patriarchy.[51] Her tactic was not, like Hipperson, to dismiss and largely ignore these women; instead she designed her text to undermine them:

> Many of the women becoming involved either were to begin with, or became lesbian ... the emphasis inevitably began to shift away from opposing 'Cruise' and towards the idea that what mattered was to create a space where women, by living together, proclaimed female values. When CND, in the autumn of 1983, wanted to hold a demonstration ... the majority of women actually living at the Peace camp refused to countenance this, as it wouldn't be women-only. We—by 'we' I mean people actively involved in the peace movement—became bitterly divided over this issue, and the rights and wrongs of women-only protests seemed to overshadow the gathering pace of the arms race, which for some of the women now permanently at Greenham, had evidently dwindled in importance.... With apparently sensible people descending into serious discussion over the spelling of the word 'women'—should it be 'wimmin', 'womyn' or 'wombyn'?[52]

Pettitt differentiated herself from the women who joined Greenham later and declared it as their own. The constructed identity she created for them and claimed they inhabited is substantially different from that which she created for herself. There are obvious statements such as:

> Karmen and I were on the 'wrong' side as were some of the other 'originals', in supporting the idea of a mixed demonstration. We didn't see that anybody could own demonstration rights over a patch of land.[53]

Again she emphasised that her (created) vision of the peace protest, the one dreamt up in South Wales, was not the dominant discourse at Greenham.[54] In her version, it was not necessary to exclude men entirely, though it was important that women controlled the event. Thus, she is defined as something 'other than' the Greenham woman as she did not need a specifically female space in which to operate, thereby challenging the whole notion that the site had to be a completely female place at all. By describing the protest in these terms, she demonstrated that there was (and is still) an alternative possibility for political women.

It is apparent that she was just as keen to emphasise what she 'is not' as much as she was keen to state what she 'is' (or rather what the reader is to think of her as). She was not lesbian; she was not interested in intellectual concepts such as women's space or an overthrowing of patriarchy; she was not a feminist. In fact, she created an image of herself as primarily a mother, a partner, and a daughter. She referred to herself (and those she aligned herself with) on several occasions as 'normal' or 'ordinary'. This repetition was intentional in order to separate her from what became the popular image in the media of the Greenham woman. She placed emphasis on her responsibilities in those (traditional) roles, and used these to justify her decision to initiate the march as much as her decision not to stay on at Greenham. In the persona that Pettitt created, there is as much of a gap between the 'Greenham' women and herself, as there was between them and the perceived disengaged general public:

> One woman in particular had a reputation as the most 'hard-line' of the anti-men tendency. She was American, and with her near-shaven head, militaristic style of dressing, an emaciated body and an expression of intense severity, she seemed to embody everything scary the public had come to stick in between the two words 'Greenham' and 'women'... Her massively off-putting, ridiculously aggressive style was one which was increasingly shared by quite a few of the other women at the camp.... The image that to this day causes many people to be more frightened than they are inspired by the words 'Greenham Women'.[55]

Pettitt therefore created an identity for herself. It was designed to enable an alignment to take place between the implied author (the 'self' created by Pettitt) and her imagined audience. Throughout the text, her choice of signifiers, and by implication her rejection of others, enabled the creation of an identity aligned with traditional feminine characteristics and with an idea of plain common sense without 'confusing' intellectual or abstract imagery. From this, it is possible to surmise who Pettitt's imagined readers are. They are not those exclusively from academia and they are not those who had any significant involvement with radical feminism. Indeed, her assertion that men could play a part in the demand to rid the world of weapons meant her audience need not be female either. Instead, they appear to be those who have some knowledge of the campaign (otherwise there would be no need to attack the overtly feminist image of the protest), but with no previous affinity to it. Pettitt suggested that by the time the camp was only a few years into its existence in the mid 1980s, the point had been lost and the message was diluted. Consequently, she placed doubt on any possible claim that the Greenham camps could have affected the end of the Cold War, despite claims to the contrary.

Her alternative version was that those who moved on from Greenham had played a much greater role than has hitherto been acknowledged. From Pettitt's version, the historian is led to conclude that the march and the early phases of the peace camp were important in gaining attention from both the public and international governments. However, it was the role that Pettitt and others like her played in taking the anti-nuclear message to the Soviet Union that precipitated the moves necessary to enable the INF treaty in 1987. This charge subtly undermined other accounts of Greenham and encouraged the reader to reach the conclusion that perhaps the persistent militancy of the Greenham women was less significant than others have led people to believe.

Again, this tactic was not new. It was reminiscent of the conflict, described by Hilda Kean, between former militant suffragettes and constitutional suffragists after the partial enfranchisement of women in 1918. In order to redress the imbalance she perceived in the Greenham historical record, Pettitt was redeploying a strategy used by those in opposition to the Women's Social and Political Union (WSPU) and Women's Freedom League (WFL) to dispute the significance of the militants. In fact, Pettitt's language on occasion was distinctly similar in its derision:

> A lot of the more daring 'Actions' were now undertaken by big groups of very confident young and young-ish lesbians, who had huge fun and didn't give a damn what anyone thought of them or their behaviour.[56]

Ray Strachey in 1928 wrote of the militants:

> 'Deeds not words' was the motto of the organisation, and its deliberate policy was to seek sensational achievement rather than anything else. Its leaders did not scruple to brush aside the ordinary niceties of procedure, and they did not care whom they shocked and antagonised.[57]

Pettitt was not innocently drawing these parallels. The question of whether the militant suffragettes were as successful as they claimed is now relatively well known. Her aim, therefore, was to persuade the reader to look beyond the romance and imagery of the militants, and see the 'constitutionalists' at work. So not only was there a historical story being paralleled here, but an academic discourse was also being redeployed to appeal to a wider audience.

This works because the Greenham women themselves intentionally painted the suffragettes into the picture of the movement they created (a connection which Pettitt also included without coincidence). As Laura Nym Mayhall has pointed out, identification with the suffrage campaign was a tactic deployed by second-wave feminists involved in the Women's Liberation Movement.[58] This factor made the transference of the same language and imagery to the Greenham campaign more likely. Many Greenham women's accounts refer to them having a suffragette ancestor. This is an indication that they often were working to portray their movement as the continuation of a longer struggle for women's voices to be heard.[59] This gave an air of legitimacy to their proceedings and it is therefore not surprising that so much effort was put into this imagined sisterhood. The romance of the suffragettes and their sacrifice was consumed eagerly by many women. There are few testimonies that do not make comparisons or refer to the painting of banners in the colours of the militant suffragettes; the wearing of the symbolic colours as well as actions that mimic those of the Edwardian militants. The Greenham women chained themselves to fences, committed damage to property, were arrested, went to prison, adopted a non-compliant attitude and also overtly adopted the suffragette language and their methods of communication (i.e. songs, pamphlets, banners etc.).

Motivations

There was a distinct difference between Pettitt's and Hipperson's motivations. Pettitt was engaged in writing herself into the history (although to do so she had to undermine the militant actions of all the Greenham women, including Hipperson). By contrast, Hipperson was concerned with writing others out (Pettitt also being one of these 'others' on the basis that she was not there to bear witness throughout the campaign). Hipperson's alignment with the original marchers was simply to serve the purpose of establishing the length and persistence of the Yellow Gate camp and thus to award her authority to speak for Greenham.

Both Hipperson and Pettitt distanced themselves from the radical feminism they point to as the lasting popular image of Greenham, but there are differences between each account. Hippperson was already a part of the history of Greenham and consequently her narrative was primarily concerned with overriding the versions that did not project her particular politics of the event. Pettitt, on the other hand, has been awarded only a peripheral role in the Greenham story, and for this reason her tale is more concerned with 'reclaiming' the event, and placing herself in a pivotal role in that history. Pettitt therefore excluded the other versions, not to debate what took place at Greenham, but rather to redefine where the historical emphasis should focus. In Pettitt's narrative, Greenham was just the beginning of the story, whose place was to set the scene for what was truly relevant in bringing about the end of the Cold War; it was not the full story in itself. In this reading, being a central part of that beginning was therefore of vital importance.

However, Pettitt may have taken up her pen upon her realisation that she had become an anonymous player in the history of the event she instigated. From that standpoint any claim of hers to a wider, more important role in the history of the end of the Cold War would be difficult. She wrote:

> For many years I held on to this story ... It sat, maturing, in the compost-heap that is my life. Then one day I went on a walking holiday with a group of women, ... the talk ... turned to their experiences of Greenham Common (it seemed they had all been involved in some way or other) and they asked if I had been there, I said nothing. I didn't know where to begin, and anyway it was late.[60]

Like the compost heap, her exclusion festered following the realisation that she was no longer a recognisable figure of Greenham. By drawing attention to the fact that she was forced into being reflective because twenty-five years had passed, she highlighted her understanding that it is impossible to recover the past as it happened or was experienced. As Raphael Samuel and Paul Thompson pointed out, history is an 'active relationship between past and present'.[61] What is now known, that was not known then, automatically invades the text and directly influences the 'I' being created and projected and thus the memories or story being told.[62] Therefore, Pettitt's admission that her version was not 'fresh' implied that it was not without retrospect and self-criticism. In doing this, she awarded herself the authority to speak. Her account was not written in the heat of the moment, but with perspective and maturity. Interestingly, she also indicated that she recognised the potential to refocus the debate through a re-writing of the event, but her aim was to convince the reader that she had done this in a balanced way in order to maintain the legitimacy of her narrative.

That the desire to re-enter the Greenham history had a purpose for Pettitt appears in the final few pages of her text as a postscript (creating the illusion of an after-thought). It has its basis firmly rooted in 2006:

> Now the US reigns alone, waging its impossible war on 'global terrorism' ... Patriotism blocks the mouths of critics almost as efficiently as fear did in the old USSR, and a nation eating itself to death believes its way of life is the best for everyone, and any means are justified to ensure the delivery of that enlightenment to a world where most people still don't own a car or a television or a telephone, but do still grow some food and sit down to eat it together.[63]

> We are left, still, with the problem of what to do about the nuclear weapons, the only real weapons of mass destruction. They, the weapons and the technology needed to make them, still threaten us, and it is still the case that the majority of people deciding on our behalf to hang on to these relics of a bygone age are woolly-minded male politicians unable to reach a sensible agreement about how to get rid of them.[64]

It is for this that Pettitt goes into battle with Greenham. Like Hipperson, in order to make these contemporary political statements, she had to create an identity that bestowed the voice of authority to the reader. Pettitt wanted to be viewed as being informed in her subject, yet as a reasoned, rounded individual. She determined that she must establish her credentials through a re-analysis of her past in order to gain respect, and ultimately power, in the world that she inhabits now. To do this, she must rid herself of the undesirable image of the popularised Greenham Woman of the 1980s and 1990s, by carrying out a deconstruction of that image. It is both interesting and disturbing to see that she relied on traditional feminine characteristics to do this. Arguably, this tells us just as much about the space we inhabit today.[65]

If, as this reading of Pettitt suggests, one must reject much of Greenham in order to be heard in the post-Greenham era, then we should also consider why Hipperson's attack of 'lifestyle' feminist politics was confined to only a few pages of her book. To Hipperson such ideologies can be largely ignored, because the discourse she associated with her 'experience' of Greenham did not contain their language.

As Hipperson's struggle was not to refocus attention away from Greenham after 1984, but rather to emphasise the importance attached both practically and symbolically to its end in 2000, continuing with the same discourse used during the campaign was vital. Hipperson, in contrast to Pettitt, claimed her authority to speak by the fact that she lived at the site for almost eighteen years. Pettitt had to claim her entitlement in spite of never having lived at the camp.

Conclusion

Language is understood to be separate from the 'real' that it refers to; a signifier of the object or action (signified) rather than that object or action itself.[66] In the same way, the 'author', presented to us through carefully chosen language in an autobiographical text, cannot be taken to be the same as the 'real' person. She is but a projection of the living being whose name is attributed to the text and who took part in the historical events described. Her 'voice' is the constructed version of the author's 'self' that the story requires in order to convince the (implied) audience (being written to) that the version of events is plausible. This 'second self' has the ability to be the precise person that the author wishes or needs her to be in order to write the desired history of the event to the 'imagined' audience.[67] By allowing this 'self' to employ language or adopt personas in a particular way, a new political perspective can be made to fit with the actions that her character undertook as part of the campaign. In this way, therefore, the constructed 'self' is made to perform in a particular fashion that ultimately contributes to a sense of authenticity for the rewritten version of events. This enables the reader to be convinced by the whole, irrespective of whether or not it is representative of the past as it happened or was experienced.

> That which makes for probability also makes for aesthetic coherence and harmony. A probable action ... is not only an action which convinces an audience that it possesses a general truthfulness, but also an action which fits convincingly into a chain of actions (a plot) and contributes to a unified ... whole.[68]

It is evident from the texts examined in this article that both authors were seeking to give authority back to themselves and/or their movement. To do this they constructed the Greenham set and populated it with a diverse range of characters (heroines and villains). They subsequently allowed them to perform roles and interact with one another in ways which were defined in terms of the developing 'plot' and 'sub-plots'. Tensions between individuals or groups of women were described in order to steer the story (and the readers) in specific directions. Events were presented in a logical and sequential way and words were spoken as if in the moment. As a consequence, the reader could be drawn willingly into the illusion that the world being staged for them was a genuine reflection of the 'real'. This literary tactic should not take us by surprise, as Greenham was a highly political and public debate. Participants became intensely aware of the power of language and the adoption of personas to inspire supporters and ridicule opponents as the movement grew.

In both texts, there was a constructed narrator 'self' overseeing and passing comment on all. The narrator in both instances was coherent and inhabited a largely singular identity in so far as there was little contradiction/multiplicity or significant self-reproach evident in her 'voice'. This reveals how 'she' was carefully written into the text to represent both the author and the activist (both of whom she is separate from) in a specific way. Her primary role was to justify the (sometimes naïve) 'self' who participated in the campaign, and to merge her with a new but informed persona (which in neither Pettitt nor Hipperson's case was overtly feminist). The aim was ultimately to appeal to a new audience.

As activists, these women were operating within the public domain and as such were immediately open to criticism for their beliefs and actions. In order to limit any loss of political ground at the time of the protest, the construction of a coherent 'public self' would have been vital, especially in view of the lack of a defined set of principles (which arguably binds official political parties or organisations together and offers some protection from attack). In their subsequent autobiographical accounts, the need to establish a new 'public self' continued so that they could draw from the political power of their past.

This article has demonstrated how these two participant historians made attempts to realign the Greenham protest and shift the balance of power between the various discourses. Their attempt was not to disprove the radical feminist account or to claim that it did not exist, but rather to shift the emphasis to other less prominent (silent) versions in order to draw upon the power that the movement undoubtedly had to politicise vast numbers of women.

This illustrates the complex nature of writing history and that different versions of any story are always possible. As historians, we are powerless to assert the validity of one over another. We are reminded clearly that we can never regain access to the past and can neither prove nor disprove any version we are presented with. All we can aim to do is to 'discover how [the] choice of truth, inside which we are caught but which we ceaselessly renew, was made—but also how it was repeated, renewed and displaced'.[69] It is precisely because of this recognition that we are able to see that the battle to control the political space at Greenham was not concluded before the end of the camps and has carried on through the collection, preservation and display of its history. If feminism was not the answer to the problem of militarism, and if no feminist revolution has yet taken place to effect such a change, other discourses must be employed. To enable these, the history of Greenham must be rewritten.

Notes

[1] See A. Pettitt (2006) *Walking to Greenham: how the peace-camp began and the Cold War ended* (Aberystwyth: Honno); L. Jones (1983) On Common Ground: the women's peace camp at Greenham Common, in L. Jones (Ed.) *Keeping the Peace* (London: The Women's Press), pp. 79–97. For short oral histories refer to interviews with Ann Pettitt; Karmen Cutler; Thalia Campbell & Helen John, *Guardian* website 'Your Greenham', http://www.yourgreenham.co.uk/#march.

[2] A camp was established outside all seven entrance gates and at two other locations. These were referred to as colours of the rainbow. For a map see D. Fairhall (2006) *The Story of Greenham Common Ground* (London: I. B. Tauris).

[3] The camps became all female in February 1982. See Fairhall, *Common Ground*; Jones, *Keeping the Peace*; B. Harford & S. Hopkins (Eds) (1984) *Greenham Common: women at the wire* (London: Women's Press); S. Roseneil (1995) *Disarming Patriarchy: feminism and political action at Greenham* (Buckingham: Open University Press).

[4] S. Hipperson, (2005) *Greenham: Non-Violent Women v The Crown Prerogative* (London: Greenham Publications), p. 11 and p. 16. Reference to 'Embrace the Base', December 1982 and 'Reflect the Base', December 1983.

[5] Hipperson, *Greenham* and Pettitt, *Walking to Greenham*.

[6] Hipperson visited Greenham for protest days before deciding to live there from March 1983.

[7] Simone Wilkinson quoted in the *Women's Peace Camp Newsletter* (February 1983), p. 5.

[8] A. Cook & G. Kirk (1983) *Greenham Women Everywhere* (London: Pluto Press), p. 33.

[9] B. Whisker, J. Bishop, L. Mohin & T. Longdon (Eds) (1983) *Breaching the Peace: a collection of radical feminist papers* (London: Only Women Press).

[10] See Sue Copping's review of D. Thompson (Ed.) (1983) *Over our Dead Bodies: women against the bomb* (London: Virago) published in *Big Flame* (February–March 1983) (a magazine published by a 'revolutionary socialist feminist' organisation of the same name).

[11] J. Bishop (1983) Support These Women for their Children's Sake: a critical perspective, in Whisker *et al.* (Eds), *Breaching the Peace*, p. 32.

[12] S. Roseneil (1994) *Feminist Political Action: the case of the Greenham Common women's peace camp* (PhD thesis, London School of Economics and Political Science), p. 14.

[13] J. Liddington (1989) *The Long Road to Greenham: feminism and anti-militarism in Britain since 1820* (London: Virago); Roseneil, *Feminist Political Action*, p. 14.

[14] *Guardian* website, 'Your Greenham', http://www.yourgreenham.co.uk/#politics.

[15] Copious pamphlets and leaflets to advertise and celebrate actions were circulated. The letter was also a particularly important form of communication ranging from the use of chain letters to attract new women to the campaign, to personal letters of support for women in prison, and open letters to protest against government policy. M. Jolly (2003) Writing the Web: letters from the women's peace movement, *Online Journal*. http://www.feministseventies.net/Greenham.html.

[16] Anon. (1983) *Full Moon in June* (Greenham Women's Peace Camp leaflet).

[17] The Women's Peace Camp newsletter from February 1983 depicts a woman looking into the Base with a small child looking up at her and a banner attached to the fence, 'All living in Fear'. A 'Reflect the Base' protest advertising pamphlet from 1983 shows a woman holding a small child and a banner on the fence, 'We won't live with Cruise'.

[18] J. Freer (1984) *Raging Womyn: in reply to breaching the peace: a comment on the women's liberation movement and the common womyn's peace camp at Greenham* (London: Wymn's Land Fund), p. 12.

[19] Anon. (1984) *10 Million Women for 10 Days at Greenham* (Birmingham Peace Centre), Greenham leaflet.

[20] Roseneil, *Disarming Patriarchy*.

[21] Anon. (1983) *Anti-Nuclear Action: discussion magazine for socialists and feminists in CND*.

[22] J. Hannam (2007) *Feminism* (Harlow: Pearson Education), pp. 164 and 167.

[23] Cook & Kirk, *Greenham Women Everywhere*, p. 90.
[24] M. Foucault quoted in S. Mills (1997) *Discourse: the new critical idiom* (London: Routledge), p. 19. Drawing upon the linguist Saussure, and the concepts of signs and signified in language, the dominant discourse is that of the master signifiers. However, as Lacan noted, 'meaning' shifts over time and therefore the master signifiers can change.
[25] F. Lionett (1989) *Autobiographical Voices: race, gender, self-portraiture* (Ithaca: Cornell University Press).
[26] J. W. Scott (1991) The Evidence of Experience, *Critical Inquiry*, 17, pp. 773–797; L. Passerini (1990) Mythbiography in Oral History, in R. Samuel & P. Thompson (Eds) *The Myths We Live By* (London: Routledge), pp. 49–60; J. Sangster (1994) Telling Our Stories: feminist debates and the use of oral history, *Women's History Review*, 3(1), pp. 5–28. S. Smith (1987) *A Poetics of Women's Autobiography: Marginality and the Fictions of Self Representation* (Bloomington: Indiana University Press); S. Smith (1995) Performativity, Autobiographical Practice, Resistance, in S. Smith & J. Watson (Eds) *Women, Autobiography, Theory: a reader* (Wisconsin: University of Wisconsin Press), pp. 108–115. Also C. Steedman (1992) *Past Tenses: essays on writing, autobiography and history* (London: Rivers Oram Press); and L. Stanley (1992) *The Autobiographical I* (Manchester: Manchester University Press).
[27] Hipperson, *Greenham*, p. 1. The trilogy to which she refers also includes Harford & Hopkins, *Women at the Wire*; and B. Junor (1995) *Greenham Common Women's Peace Camp: a history of non-violent resistance 1984–1995* (London: Working Press).
[28] Hipperson, *Greenham*, p. 2.
[29] Yellow Gate archives held at The Women's Library, London (Collection reference 5GCW). Other archives include the Women's Archive of Wales, Glamorgan record Office (ref GB 0214 DWAW9) submitted in 1984. There are also records at Bradford University and the National Library of Wales.
[30] Imperial War Museum Sound Archive.
[31] H. Kean (2005) Public History and Popular Memory: issues in the commemoration of the British militant suffrage campaign, *Women's History Review*, 14(3 & 4), p. 581.
[32] Green Gate was a women-only camp at all times (men could visit the other camps during the day); Violet Gate was religiously focused; Red Gate was the artists' gate; Blue Gate had a new age focus; Orange Gate was music gate (it may also have been Welsh gate for a time).
[33] Reported in the socialist newspaper, *Morning Star* (29 September 1987); *Reading Weekly Post* (26 September 1987). Also F. Shand (1987) Greenham Rifts: as Cruise's future looks uncertain why are the women campers turning on each other?, *Marxism Today*, 31(11).
[34] See Junor, *Greenham Common Women's Peace Camp*; Roseneil, *Disarming Patriarchy* and Liddington, *Long Road to Greenham*.
[35] Hipperson, *Greenham*, p. 32.
[36] F. Shand, *Greenham Rifts* suggested that an implied superiority of the Yellow Gate women was partially to blame for the 1987 split.
[37] Hipperson, *Greenham*, pp. 1, 10, 152 and 157.
[38] For other examples of this inference see, Junor, *Greenham Common Women's Peace Camp*, pp. 96–100 in reference to Orange and Woad Gate closures in 1987.
[39] Cook & Kirk, *Greenham Women Everywhere*.
[40] Hipperson, *Greenham*, p. 23.
[41] Ibid.
[42] *Women's Peace Camp Newsletter* (May 1983), p. 5. The quotation is attributed to 'Sarah' and goes on to describe her intention to carry out a fast whilst on a three-week sentence in prison. It is believed this was Hipperson, as she refers to carrying

out a water-only fast whilst in prison in November 1983 in Junor, *Greenham Common Women's Peace Camp*, p. 15.
[43] Hipperson, *Greenham*, p. 39. Also echoes of Martin Luther King Jr words on p. 33.
[44] Ibid., p. 5.
[45] Ibid., p. 160.
[46] Ibid., p. 59. Quotation from Matthew 23.23–24
[47] Ibid., p. 52.
[48] Ibid., p. 52.
[49] Ibid., p. 161.
[50] Ibid., p. 2.
[51] Harford & Hopkins, *Women at the Wire*, p. 6.
[52] Pettitt, *Walking to Greenham*, pp. 272–273.
[53] Ibid., p. 273.
[54] See Roseneil, *Disarming Patriarchy* for a response to Ann Pettitt's complaint that Greenham had changed from her original vision.
[55] Pettitt, *Walking to Greenham*, pp. 286–287.
[56] Ibid., p. 285.
[57] R. Strachey, quoted in H. Kean (1994) Searching for the Past in Present Defeat: the construction of historical and political identity in British feminism in the 1920s and 1930s, *Women's History Review*, 3(1), p. 59.
[58] L. E. Nym Mayhall (1995) Creating the Suffragette Spirit: British feminism and the historical imagination, *Women's History Review*, 4(3), pp. 319–338.
[59] Rebecca Johnson reiterated this at the Women's History Month pre-launch on 20 January 2011 at Portcullis House, London.
[60] Pettitt, *Walking to Greenham*, p. 2.
[61] R. Samuel & P. Thompson (1990) *The Myths We Live By* (London: Routledge), p. 5.
[62] N. King (2000) *Memory, Narrative, Identity: remembering the self* (Edinburgh: Edinburgh University Press), p. 8.
[63] Pettitt, *Walking to Greenham*, p. 303.
[64] Ibid., p. 309.
[65] For discussion of the decline in feminism and the persistence of the traditional woman refer to S. Faludi (1992) *Backlash: the undeclared war against women* (London: Chatto & Windus)
[66] Concepts of signs and signified in language refer to work of the linguist Saussure.
[67] W. C. Booth (1961) *The Rhetoric of Fiction*, extract in R. Seldon (Ed.) (1988) *The Theory of Criticism* (London: Longman), p. 339. Theory of implied authors and readers within texts.
[68] Seldon, *Theory of Criticism*, p. 41.
[69] M. Foucault quoted in Mills, *Discourse*, p. 19.

The Changing Face of Exhibiting Women's Wartime Work at the Imperial War Museum

Alyson Mercer

This article examines the performative narratives present in three historical exhibitions produced by the Imperial War Museum (IWM) on the topic of women's wartime work. The focus is in particular on the visual representation of women through the display of uniforms, as well as how methods of presenting this material culture have, at various points in the near century-long history of the institution, taken on different roles within exhibition spaces. The display techniques used in early exhibitions will be compared to more recent permanent and temporary spaces at two branches of the IWM located in London and Manchester, in order to determine whether the performative nature of early exhibitions has extended to recent developments.

In 2005, HM Queen Elizabeth II unveiled a monument as part of events celebrating the sixtieth anniversary of the end of the Second World War. A bronze cenotaph depicting seventeen different uniforms worn by women during this conflict stands proudly on the centre lane of Whitehall in London between the Ministry of Defence and the Cabinet Office (as seen in Figure 1). A photograph of a 1940s cloakroom at a dance hall was cited by sculptor John Mills as being the inspiration for his design, but the denotation of uniforms in disuse speaks volumes to those reading women's history as a literal hanging up of one's hat at the end of the conflict.[1] This visual construction of disuse also sparks another image, which is difficult for the passing gaze of the general public to ignore, the striking disembodiment of women from the wartime experiences to which they are inextricably linked. According to traditional narratives, upon the return of men from the front lines, women were forced to once again take up their previously unrecognized 'uniforms' of housewife, mother, and numerous other forms of employment hidden from public recognition through lack of formal accoutrements. This method of displaying a variety of uniforms is in stark contrast to the active and authoritative representation of servicewomen used in many museums across the country and the world. The bodiless uniforms seen here do not equate to a representative memorial of sacrifice, but rather a testament to those who performed a visible role in the conflict.

All over Britain, museums have dedicated their exhibition spaces to teaching the public about past conflicts which have shaped today's society. They assist in educating the population on subjects controversial in nature, and provide a visual context for the unimaginable evils of modern warfare. They also serve as informal memorials and perpetuate the memory of important battles that would otherwise live on for many people solely through the pages of history books or the stories of older generations. Although the Internet provides those actively seeking information on particular topics with a wealth of resources, museum exhibitions are still understood to be one of the more authoritative voices on matters of the

Figure 1 Photograph of The Women of World War Two memorial, Whitehall. Source: Author's own photograph, 20 February 2010.

past. The importance of displaying uniforms as a way of representing the past cannot be underestimated.

This essay aims to explore the performative nature of visitor/display interaction in relation to the exhibitions examined here in the form of case studies. Judith Butler defines performativity as 'that reiterative power of discourse to produce the phenomena that it regulates and constrains'.[1] In a museum context, curated exhibits 'perform' the displayed phenomenon, creating meaning through display. At a basic level, audiences may be viewed as passively observing the museum's performance, and the display can be understood as a unidirectional form of communicating knowledge and power. Yet, as Eilean Hooper-Greenhill suggests, roles within the gallery space are complicated by the interaction between social and museological narratives.[3] The experience of viewing displays is enhanced by preexisting knowledge of the subject matter, when there is familiarity with objects on display outside of the museum context. Therefore, those visiting early exhibitions hosted by the Imperial War Museum (IWM) would be confronted with objects from their day to day lives, while those visiting post-1945 exhibitions would experience a more reflective interaction through the recollection of positive nostalgic or painful negative memories associated with objects on display. Alternatively, the experience of complete unfamiliarity can cause a different type of recognition, through the learning of new information. As a result, the viewer also becomes implicated in the museum's performance, becoming part of the performance as they bring their own ideas and interpretations to their educational experience.

The first of the three case studies explored here identifies issues surrounding audience engagement when confronted by a costumed member of staff rather than simply viewing a mannequin as part of a static display. In this instance, an example of a uniformed volunteer waitress serving teas at an exhibition hosted by the Women's Work Sub-committee of the IWM (WWS) in 1918 is used. The analysis of this type of interaction will be followed with an exploration of how performative aspects of exhibition design were addressed during another temporary exhibition of the IWM: 'Women at War, 1914–18' in 1977. Finally, the shifting focus of display techniques will be examined using the example of the current 'Women and War' gallery at the Imperial War Museum North (IWM-N).

The identification of an audience-wide performance, where individuals interact with material on display, assists with the recognition process of the visitor's constructed knowledge through museum collections. This in turn built upon the construction of the collective 'national self' as it has evolved to meet the needs of the country throughout the past century of women's wartime work exhibitions at the Imperial War Museum.

Designing Patriotism

The first uniforms worn by women were viewed as somewhat of a curiosity.[4] They were modelled upon those worn in men's services and were generally an unattractive prospect forced upon those joining up. For the first uniform designs, a fine line was drawn between those worn by military men and women volunteers. Early Auxiliary Territorial Service uniforms, designed by Commander-in-Chief Helen Gwynne-Vaughan were considered to be particularly unflattering, consisting of 'a serge, khaki tunic, buttoning to the right in the male fashion, and mid-calf skirt, worn with thick, khaki stockings and low-heeled brown shoes'.[5] Those of the Women's Royal Naval Service and Women's Auxiliary Air Force were widely considered to be more attractive due to the flattering nature of their design.

The unfeminine nature of First World War military-style uniforms also caused problems because of their associations. Krisztina Robert has suggested that, 'owing to the common soldiers' reputation for licentiousness and heavy drinking, for women to mix with them was immoral'.[6] Women in uniform risked being viewed in similar ways. Nevertheless, Vining and Hacker argue that, 'the desire for uniforms belonged as much or more to the women who wore them as to the organization that employed them'.[7] This may have been because many women viewed uniforms as symbolic of their patriotism and duty.[8] This was encouraged by recruitment propaganda for the military services, which encouraged women to positively associate the uniform with the performance of duty to the state. Various popular histories that include interviews with women about their wartime memories cite that many women stated that the sole reason for joining up was that they thought the uniform was particularly attractive.[9] Numerous exhibitions that took place during the First World War encouraged women to enrol in services, not only because they would be helping their country, but so that they would stand apart from those women not serving due to wearing a uniform. Women were expected to wear their uniforms with pride, and as a result, both official and unofficial uniforms began to appear, taking the design lead from men's service uniforms. The garments displayed in exhibitions discussed in this essay represented a historical association with employment and patriotic duty.

Creating a National War Museum Fit for Britain

The First World War was well under way when the suggestion was made in 1917 to create a national war memorial to commemorate the conflict. The objective of the new national museum would be to collect ephemera, armaments, and munitions for posterity. In theory, the idea of a museum as a war memorial was a touching attempt by the government to honour the hard work of the British population, although in reality, the timing of the announcement of the new war museum was much more than a coincidence. The political atmosphere in England at the end of 1916 was that of uncertainty. Support for the war was wavering after several devastatingly hard fought campaigns that resulted in large losses of life.[10] The government had changed hands, with Liberal Prime Minister Asquith conceding victory to another Liberal, David Lloyd George, and fresh enthusiasm on the part of the new leader led to massive restructuring within the Cabinet. Despite being plagued by war-weariness, media censorship and manipulation, the majority of the British population still felt the cause worth fighting for. The new war museum was considered to be exactly what was needed to rejuvenate the British population's support. The propaganda work of the Department (later Ministry) of Information had paved the way for the public's desire for more details about what was happening to their loved ones abroad. The War Cabinet, on the other hand, sought to achieve a different objective, not necessarily to record and remember, but rather to stimulate a renewed enthusiasm for the war effort.

On 5 March 1917, the War Cabinet approved the creation of the National War Museum as 'a memorial, a record, and a place of study of the war in which the forces and civilian populations of the countries of the British Empire were then engaged'.[11] Shortly thereafter, a committee was formed to oversee the development of the museum. Representatives included Sir Alfred Mond as Chairman and Sir Martin Conway (father of Miss Agnes Ethel Conway of the Women's Work Sub-committee) as Director General. Members of the six-man committee each oversaw a sub-committee on specific subjects that were considered to cover each area of the current conflict.[12] During this time, the committee members were able to earmark for the museum many war-related items still in use. At the end of the Great War, these items were appreciatively donated and a deluge of material inundated the museum. Charles ffoulkes, Curator of the Tower Armouries commented in his autobiography, 'with the end of the war, exhibits began to pour in. Departments were closed down. Munitions works and women's organizations ceased to exist. Every government department was only too pleased to unload examples of their war activities'.[13] However, the War Cabinet thought that if everyone's contribution were included, the museum would turn out to be 'a vast heterogeneous collection of models and memorials, [...] of munitions workers, Boy Scouts and Girl Guides [that] would in a few years interest nobody and merely encumber space'.[14] Despite this sentiment, the Women's Work Sub-committee (WWS) was formed on 4 April 1917 under the direction of Sir Alfred Mond in order to fulfil the original remit set out for the museum of providing a representative sample of each area relating to the conflict. Just weeks after its inception, the WWS was set to work on preparing a room at the Royal Academy, Burlington House as part of one of the museum's publicity exhibitions to raise awareness of the project.

That women played an important part in the planning and shaping of the collection of artefacts at the Imperial War Museum (IWM) is undisputed. The WWS made it possible for future generations to appreciate relics from the Great War.[15] Members of the committee wanted to be certain that they were not perceived as outsiders looking in at the war effort. The six female members included devoted suffragette turned war worker, Lady Priscilla Norman as Chairman, and Voluntary Aid Detachment worker Miss Agnes Ethel Conway as Honorary Secretary. None of the committee were professionally trained in museums or exhibition design, but all were the wives (or daughters) of well-connected politicians, high-ranking military personnel, and other members of the elite classes, which inevitably facilitated their appointment to the project. Meeting minutes show that the Chairman was deeply involved with the activities of her committee, and she encouraged members to seek female practitioners when looking to employ painters, photographers, model makers, journalists, and others for their assignments. The hard work and determination to create a complete collection of items relating to women's wartime work has enabled an analysis of the tireless efforts of women across Britain. These acquisitions were drawn upon for contemporary exhibitions and continue to form a section of the material on display at the IWM.

This exhibition was of great importance to the sub-committee members who had only three months to prepare a section depicting every aspect of the conflict in which women were then engaged. The WWS worked tirelessly to ensure the production of high-quality records to represent women of all backgrounds from different areas of the country. Sub-committee meeting minutes detail a flurry of activity surrounding discussions not only of the subject matter for possible inclusion, but also of the visual requirements to create an area attractive to those visiting. One suggestion was a 'live' exhibit to honour the Army Corps depicting women performing their work. However, in discussion with Sir Martin Conway, it was realised that an exhibition featuring living women would be inappropriate, as the aim of the exhibition was simply to popularise the idea of a National War Museum.[16] In the end, scale models were used, in addition to three-dimensional artefacts (such as the first six inch and four inch shells made by women at the Cunard Company), photographs of various industries, and graphs showing the growth of women's employment in the first years of the War.[17] Despite the fact that visitors did not engage with actors, the exhibitions emotionally engaged the audience, in some cases evoking fierce national pride, demonstrated when a member of the Royal Academy tore down German flags on display, which had been purchased to hang over captured German guns in a separate section of the exhibition.[18]

A commonplace practice during the First World War was to include a recruiting element in public exhibitions.[19] The WWS section at Burlington House was no exception. Although the organisers did not permit the distribution of promotional material within their section of the gallery, targeted services for recruitment included the Aircraft Service, the Royal Naval Air Service and the Women's Auxiliary Army Corps.[20] According to several weekly periodicals, the women's section of the exhibition was well received and the area was described as rooms 'filled with war material exclusively the work of women—work of such excellence it evokes admiration'.[21] This recruitment element not only reinforced the need for participation among the larger female population, but also changed the dynamic of exhibitions from being spaces where members of the public visited for enlightenment, to places where content informed audience members of current events and asked for their participation in return.

Despite their failed attempt to integrate an interactive aspect into their assigned display space, the next WWS project afforded more creative freedom. Only a few months after the Burlington House exhibition, the WWS was back to work full-time after being offered the opportunity to produce a fully-funded temporary exhibition on women's work at Whitechapel Art Gallery in the east end of London, one of many locations hosting displays on wartime activities. By 25 April 1918 the committee had recorded their intention to include such examples as munitions work, female substitution in various industries, hospital, and canteen work. As with the Burlington House exhibition, the WWS members were keen to create displays that would be educational, but also enjoyable. They were given free rein over the creative aspects of this venture. Teaming up with the Home Office and the Ministry of Labour, the scope of exhibits was expanded to address aspects of 'the great industrial development of women during the war' and the ministry offered an array of objects for display.[22]

The WWS took full advantage of having creative control of the gallery. Whitechapel Art Gallery embraced the idea of having volunteer waitresses in uniform provide teas in the portion of the exhibit dedicated to canteens, such as those run by the YMCA, YWCA, Salvation Army, and Catholic Women's League.[23] The ground floor consisted of bays, complete with scale models and mannequins fitted in uniforms and badges worn by WAACS, Wrens, and munitions workers, showing the various forms of work in which women were engaged. Other sections on this floor included a bay by the Home Office showcasing a variety of industries, while the Ministry of Labour, whose bays were devoted to the various women's services, occupied the top floor of the exhibition. A *Times* correspondent noted surprise at a stuffed cow which reportedly required ten soldiers to carry it in, much to the amazement of the many children attending the exhibition.[24]

The use of both living women demonstrating their employment and static mannequins to represent other services (where it may not have been a viable option to have women present) in a present-day setting emphasises the performative function behind the curatorial process in exhibition design. The Whitechapel exhibition, created by the non-specialised and untrained WWS team provided a contrasting insight into the participatory nature of the early exhibitions. Museums today regularly employ costumed interpreters as part of their educational remit.[25] Although parallels may be drawn with modern exhibitions, it is important to contextualise interpretations within their respective time frames to understand how the performances are being used as tools. All may be considered entertaining, and even educational, but the Whitechapel exhibition possessed the added dimension of recruitment to services, which had particular resonance with the contemporary context of the war. The interactivity between subject and viewer that is realised in 'real life' situations in a museum setting performs a function of expanded learning. Women serving teas to raise awareness of their war work became a demonstration of their daily routine, while mannequins sporting uniforms had a new immediacy as visitors might exit the exhibition only to be confronted by women attired in the same garments on their way to work, thus blurring the lines between exhibition and the reality of everyday life. In this way, the museum's displays are normalised, reinforcing the power of their message in providing an explanatory narrative for people to apply to their own everyday experiences and understandings of the past. In so doing, it helped the wartime audience better imagine themselves as participants in the war in a manner controlled by the museum curators. The next section will examine how this interactive performativity was addressed in the decades immediately following the Second World War.

The Changing Face of Representing Women's Wartime Work

In 1972, the Imperial War Museum embarked on a major refurbishment project aimed at reorganising the public galleries into chronological and thematic sections. During this period, a number of major and minor temporary exhibitions were mounted, many of which incorporated the story of women's involvement in the services during the two World Wars. Exhibitions which took place during the period when the IWM was undergoing nearly three decades of refurbishment included: 'Women at War, 1914–18' (major exhibition, 1977), 'Mummy, what did you do in the Great War?' (minor exhibition, 1984), 'Women in Green: the WVS in Wartime' (minor exhibition, 1988), 'Forces Sweethearts' (major exhibition, 1993), and 'Fashion Forties and the New Look' (major exhibition, 1996).[26] In 1989, the new atrium was unveiled, along with the galleries for the Second World War and Inter-War Years and the Blitz Experience. The following year, the First World War gallery and the Trench Experience opened to the public.

Women were represented in two major temporary exhibitions at the London branch of the IWM in 1977 and 2003. Both exhibitions were given variations on the same title, but the themes for each focused on different aspects of women's lives. 'Women at War, 1914–18' ran for seven months in 1977 and 'Women and War', for six months in 2003 to 2004. Both exhibitions were occasions when the IWM chose to showcase an extremely important part of their collection that formed an integral part of the long history of the institution. The 1977 exhibition will be the focus of this section of the essay.

In addition to recognising their contributions, the 'Women and War, 1914–18' exhibition detailed the eventual mobilisation of all classes of women, while drawing attention to the achievements of heroic individuals. It was not the intention of the curators to focus on the sacrifices of these heroines, but rather to include them in the larger narrative celebrating the working lives of ordinary women all over the country through photographs, original films and manuscripts from the museum archives.[27] An article in *The Observer* quoted curator Christopher Dowling as saying that the exhibition 'should provide a welcome surprise to those who associate this museum with male chauvinist fascists going 'ack-ack' at one another and marveling at the size of the cannon-balls'.[28] This quote demonstrates that, at this period in the Museum's history, an attempt was being made to draw attention to social inclusion, and museums around the country were making an effort to draw in new groups of visitors.[29]

An undated press release compiled by Jean Liddiard in the Department of Education and Publications at the IWM, detailed the proposed scope of the Great War exhibition as having two main themes reflected in the displays.[30] The first was to show women's gradual awareness of their own abilities when challenged by the experiences of warfare, while the second highlighted recognition of official organisations, such as the Wrens, who were among the many women working as 'civilians in uniform'.[31]

From this remit, the theme of women in uniform was explored not only through the conceptual storyline, but also in the use of physical space. Although the models used to display uniforms were stationary, it is important to examine the way in which they were positioned in active poses that demonstrated the type of employment associated with their garment. The staging of a scene, as depicted in Figure 2, supported this. Visitors viewed the display as if they were looking through a factory window. They observed mannequins and received the educative message from a safe distance. As this exhibition was set up in 1977, it is conceivable some of those visiting during that period could have participated in the war effort and attended accompanied by their children or grandchildren. The interactive and performative aspects of this display could therefore become a dialogue between individuals visiting together, discussing 'how things used to be', as well as participating in a nostalgic observation of unnamed, uniformed mannequins through a window. Although this type of observation lacks physical interaction between visitor and display, the separation of standing on the other side of the display's windows looking in at the mannequins' acts as a type of peepshow into the past. This form of display stands in direct contrast to living displays, which are designed to help the people imagine themselves in a historical moment, thus emphasising the nostalgic element of this exhibition. This contrast between the early Whitechapel exhibition and this post-1945 reflection on a previous period, poses a dichotomy between the aims of each exhibition in their display of uniforms. The importance of the timing of this exhibition cannot be overlooked.

Figure 2 Photograph of 'Women at War, 1914–18' exhibition taken during the construction of the exhibition. It is a view of the services section of the exhibition. In this display, WAAC uniforms are hanging on the wall, while a mannequin demonstrates a task. Source: Exhibition file, IWM MH.23115.

This display not only marked the Silver Jubilee of Queen Elizabeth II, and the period when Margaret Thatcher entered her final years as Leader of the Opposition (and prepared to stand for election as the next prime minister). Thus women held an unusually prominent place in the public eye. It was the era of the second wave of the feminist movement, campaigning for nationally for women's rights. Female empowerment by means of displaying the heroic efforts of past women could certainly do no harm in encouraging the contemporary female population to do their part in the fight for equality. The next section will explore a third method of representation through the display of women's garments, in an effort to draw parallels between the performative nature of each space with regard to reflections of selfhood.

Contemporary Representation at the Imperial War Museum North

In July 2002, the Imperial War Museum expanded its scope to include a satellite location in the North of England. The remit of this new museum was to show how 'war shapes lives' and in particular, how it has affected those in that area of the country.[32] Nearly a decade in the making, this new venue today sits proudly on the Manchester Ship Canal. As visitors begin their chronological journey along the timeline located around the perimeter of the permanent gallery space, the second 'silo' display space they encounter is that belonging to the Women and War collection. The contents of this 'silo' may be arbitrarily divided into three sections to deconstruct the thematic elements housed in the enclosure. Fighting for change; personal accounts of war; and representation through clothing, make up the content of this space. This section focuses on the latter theme.

The uniform display in the Women and War gallery stretches the length of one wall of the silo (as seen in Figure 3). In this section, a line of uniforms on faceless mannequins creates an imposing arrangement that dominates the space. These uniforms are divided into several categories. From left to right, displayed clothing belongs to named personalities, including First World War civilian nurses, Mairi Chisholm and Elsie Knocker; World War Two Special Operations Executive Radio Operator Yvonne Comeau; BBC Correspondent Audrey Russell; and actress Marlene Dietrich. The next segment is divided into five parts, with uniforms belonging to unnamed military women, land workers, munitions workers, medical workers and unpaid workers. The final category, that of unpaid workers, includes voluntary work by women in organisations such as the Red Cross, as well as in an unofficial capacity, including tasks such as looking after children, growing food and making clothing.

The fixation on uniforms has not only translated through space, but also through time. The Women and War gallery at the IWM-N features a row of faceless mannequins wearing a variety of pristine uniforms and garments associated with the two World Wars. While observing this grouping, it is easy for visitors of both sexes to let their minds wander to the subject of what they would have done had they been alive at the time of these two great conflicts. While it is difficult

Figure 3 Photograph of the Women and War gallery, Imperial War Museum.
Source: Author's own photograph, 15 March 2009 at the Imperial War Museum North.

to interact with the garments beyond a passing gaze, it is fascinating to picture oneself faced with the prospect of donning such uniforms. Had the display at the IWM-N been placed slightly lower, it would have been possible for relatively tall adult visitors to catch sight of their own reflections looking back at them, with their own heads mounted on the body of the faceless mannequins behind the reflective glass case. In other respects, the uniforms and the performative nature of their associated stories remain protected and inaccessible behind the glass encasement, acting not only as a physical barrier, but one lacking profound emotional resonance as well. The display does not provide visitors with a connection with women of the past. Despite this unsentimental method of display, it coincides with the building's architecture, symbolic of a world torn apart by war, as well as the individual nature of the 'silo' display spaces found within. The design technique used in creating the IWM-N display echoes that which is apparent on the 'Women of World War Two' memorial on Whitehall. The former display of faceless floating garments and the latter of the bodiless discarded uniforms share many similarities: the denotation of disuse, the unsuitability of emotional interaction, and uncertainty of who and what the collective nature of garments displayed together actually represents. With previous exhibitions highlighted in this essay, garments placed in the context of their associated employment portrayed an easily absorbed message, while that exuded by the displays at the IWM-N and Whitehall is less direct and more open to interpretation. This disassociation of the bodily experience in the display of uniforms is therefore significant because it demonstrates a physical distancing from the experience of war that was so visible in previous exhibitions.

Conclusion

While the early displays curated by the WWS team, as well as the special 'Women and War, 1914–18' exhibition at the IWM in London were all temporary, the 'Women and War' silo at the IWM-North is part of a permanent gallery. This in turn relates back to the monument mentioned at the beginning of this essay. As has been highlighted, the recognition of women who have served their country in a uniformed capacity has been celebrated time and time again. The obvious problem faced by those attempting to immortalise a group by their uniforms is the issue of the longevity of different types of visual design. With reference to the monumental function of the cenotaph, for example, Jay Winter warns that:

> fading away is inevitable: all war memorials have a 'shelf-life,' a bounded period of time in which their meaning relates to the concerns of a particular group of people who created them or who use or appropriate them as ceremonial or reflective sites of memory.[33]

Permanent exhibitions in museums in this country are designed to last five years, with conservation being periodically monitored, while temporary exhibitions are aimed at a period of under a year. This essay has drawn parallels between the IWM-N exhibition and the cenotaph and it is relevant to draw comparisons between the expected longevity of each method of representation. Nearly two decades ago, Eric Hobsbawm referred to the plethora of monumental public statuary of heroic figures as, 'an open-air museum of national history as seen through great men'.[34] It may be argued that the 'Women of World War II' cenotaph could be viewed as the most permanent type of exhibition, intended to last in its current form for hundreds of years. It is therefore a fairly safe assumption that women's wartime work will continue to be represented through the display of uniforms for the foreseeable future. It is for this reason that it is vital to account not only for present methods of representing women's contributions, but also to reflect on how past exhibitions can assist in determining the best course of action for curators and exhibition designers looking to create spaces that not only educate, but perform an interactive function in serving to represent past contexts relating to the collective national self.

The history of women's involvement with the Imperial War Museum as highlighted through the early exhibitions not only represented the extent of WWS engagement in the collection of material and the production of exhibitions, but also a shift in the focus of these spaces. This ranged from an attempt to raise awareness and recruitment for the various women's forces at the Royal Academy in 1917, to giving the WWS women a chance to showcase their work, continue recruiting, and recognise their fallen sisters at Whitechapel as the war raged on in 1918, to a post-1945 celebration and commemorative effort present in later exhibitions, such as the retrospective examination of women's wartime contributions in the 1977 temporary exhibit at the IWM, or the current 'Women and War silo' at the IWM-N.

When exploring exhibitions past and present, it is often left to the audience make the most of their visiting experience. With the earliest WWS exhibitions, the curatorial team developed them with the intent of being educational, but also entertaining. Later exhibitions were less concerned with the entertainment aspect, but played more heavily on the nostalgic element with the 1977 'Women at War 1914–18' exhibition, and an attractive comparative garment display in the IWM-N gallery. While the way in which visitors interact with displays on a performative level changed over this ninety-four year period, it is vital for present-day examinations of the past to identify how, and in what context, these changes took place. Because the audience was very much a part of the early exhibitions taking place during the First World War, it was important to have an element of reality present in what people were actually experiencing, both within the walls of the gallery space, as well as outside of the windows and doors of the gallery. Playing on the patriotic feelings of the day, the WWS were able to use their exhibition spaces to teach, but also to lighten the mood of wartime Britain. The aspect of entering through the doors of the galleries away from the reality of war was an inherent addition to the content, making the audience actors in the exhibition itself.

The element of separation is therefore important in later exhibitions due to them being chronologically further from the events, with the audience's imagination coming into play much more in their interactions with the displays, rather than their earlier immersion within it. As the element of perceived reality through exhibition spaces continues to play a part in the design of gallery layout and content, curators of the future will be forced to contend with the reality of representing historical events in different ways. This may take the form of providing more explicit contextual information to situate important events within an overarching historical narrative to a more distanced audience, while also ensuring the objects on display play a vital role in performing the past, so as to bring history to life in the imaginations of the visiting public.

Acknowledgments

I would like to extend my thanks to Drs Sarah Richardson and Katie Barclay, as well as Prof. Pat Thane and Dr Suzannah Biernoff for their valuable and insightful suggestions for this essay.

Notes

[1] Interview with John Mills, *Daily Telegraph*, 9 July 2005.
[2] Judith Butler (1993) *Bodies that Matter: on the discursive limits of sex* (London: Routledge), p. 2.

[3] Eilean Hooper-Greenhill (2006) *Museums and the Interpretation of Visual Culture* (London: Routledge), p. 77.
[4] Laura Doan (2006) Topsy-Turvydom: gender inversion, Sapphism, and the Great War, *GLQ*, 12(4), p. 522.
[5] The National Archives (TNA), WO 32/4705, *ATS Uniform and Badges-Draft*, 14 Sep. 1938.
[6] Krisztina Robert (1997) Gender, Class, and Patriotism: women's paramilitary units in First World War Britain, *The International History Review*, 19(1), p. 54.
[7] Margaret Vining & Barton C. Hacker (2001) From Camp Follower to Lady in Uniform: women, social class and military institutions before 1920, *Contemporary European History*, 10(3), pp. 353–354.
[8] Lucy Noakes (2006) *Women in the British Army* (London: Routledge), p. 109.
[9] Anne De Courcy (2005) *Debs at War: how wartime changed their lives, 1939–1945* (London: Weidenfeld & Nicholson); Nigel Fountain (Ed.) (2005) *Women at War: voices from the twentieth century* (London: Imperial War Museum); Kate Adie (2003) *Corsets to Camouflage: women and war* (London: Imperial War Museum).
[10] Campaigns included the Battle of Jutland, 31 May 1916–1 June 1916, and the Battle of the Somme on 1 July 1916, among others.
[11] 'Imperial War Museum. Memorial and Record of Deeds in Two World Wars', *The Times*, 31 Jan. 1953, p. 7.
[12] Committees included: Art, Munitions, Admiralty, War Office, Library and at different periods, Red Cross, Women's Work, Air Services, Religious work, Medical work, Dominions and Loan Exhibitions.
[13] Charles ffoulkes (1939) *Arms and the Tower* (London: J. Murray), pp. 123–126.
[14] Gaynor Kavanagh (1988) Museum as Memorial: the origins of the Imperial War Museum, *Journal of Contemporary History*, 23(1), p. 88.
[15] Gaynor Kavanagh (1998) *Museums and the First World War: a social history* (London: Leicester University Press), p. 122.
[16] Minutes of Women's Work Subcommittee Meeting dated 22 Nov. 1917, from Imperial War Museum Central files, EN1/3/GEN10.
[17] Lady Muir Mackenzie, The Women's Section of the Imperial War Exhibition at Burlington House, *Ladies' Field*, 16 Feb. 1918, p. 403.
[18] Paul Cornish (2004) 'Sacred Relics', objects in the Imperial War Museum 1917–1939, in Nicholas J. Saunders (Ed.) *Matters of Conflict: material culture, memory and the First World War* (London: Routledge), pp. 40–41.
[19] Kavanagh, *Museums and the First World War*, pp. 65–70.
[20] 'Minutes of Women's Work Subcommittee Meeting' dated 26 Oct. 1917, from Imperial War Museum Central files, EN1/3/GEN10.
[21] Muir Mackenzie, The Women's Section of the Imperial War Exhibition, p. 403.
[22] A Museum of Women's War Work. Exhibition at Whitechapel Art Gallery, *Lady's Pictorial*, 19 Oct. 1918, p. 458.
[23] Minutes of Women's Work Subcommittee Meeting dated 18 July 1918, from Imperial War Museum Central files, EN1/3/GEN10.
[24] Women's War Museum, *The Times*, 8 Oct. 1918, p. 11.
[25] Such as at the Royal Armouries in Leeds where costumed performers tell lively stories about past events.
[26] Due to restructuring within the museum, files do not exist on exhibitions which took place in the 1980s. Major exhibitions included those which occupied between seventy-five and 1,500 square metres, many of those produced by the Department of Exhibitions also included a loan component. Minor exhibitions occupied less than seventy-five square metres.
[27] Jean Liddiard (1977) unpublished note in Women and War, 1914–18 exhibition file at Imperial War Museum.

[28] When Women Went to War, *Observer*, 27 Mar. 1977.
[29] Geoffrey Lewis (1989) *For Instruction and Recreation – a centenary history of the Museums Association* (London: Quiller Press), p. 54.
[30] Press release (1977) unpublished note in Women and War, 1914–18 exhibition file at Imperial War Museum.
[31] Women's Royal Naval Service (1917–1919) Information Sheet, The National Archives
[32] IWM North Newsletter, IWM archive. EN4/47/CF/S7/1 and meeting minute, May 1997, ENG/2/NOR/1/1997/2.
[33] Jay Winter (2006) *Remembering War: the Great War between memory and history in the twentieth century* (London: Yale University Press), p. 140.
[34] Eric Hobsbawm cited in draft of Brian S. Osborne (2001) *Landscapes, Memory, Monuments, and Commemoration: putting identity in its place*, commissioned by the Department of Canadian Heritage for the Ethnocultural, Racial, Religious, and Linguistic Diversity and Identity Seminar, Halifax, Nova Scotia, 1–2 November, 2001, p. 15.

Concluding Thoughts: performance, the self, and women's history

Penny Summerfield

These concluding reflections on the special edition 'Performing the Self: Women's Lives in Historical Perspective' highlight the significance for women's history of concepts such as audience, persona, composure and biography, review different theories concerning peformativity and subjectivity, and demonstrate how the articles in this edition are contributing to debates in this area.

'All the world's a stage, / And all the men and women merely players: / They have their exits and their entrances' declares the melancholy Jaques in 'As You Like It'.[1] Shakespeare uses the tension between experience and performance to question the value of life as it is lived. Since the 1960s the performance metaphor has been revived by historians with the opposite intention, namely to validate and interpret women's place in the past. The original tension remains, however, with implications for the use of the metaphor by historians. The papers in this collection, in different ways, address these issues.

Much work in women's history, especially in its early days, referred to women's 'roles'.[2] Women were seen as assuming roles in the family, at work, in voluntary organisations, in politics, and so on, which were distinct from men's roles (as breadwinners, skilled workers, political leaders, intellectuals, etc.) but no less worthy of study. The language of 'role' became so common that it is easy to forget that it is an analogy. It suggests adopting a persona, playing a part, speaking a script, occupying a space, wearing a costume, presenting a scene. It also suggests that life's roles are given: there is little to be done but play the part, even if the actors might endeavour to modify the roles over time.[3]

A neglected dimension of the performance metaphor in the era of 'role' history was the idea that parts were performed for the benefit of an audience. More recent historical work discards the idea of generalised 'roles' in favour of a focus on specific performances for particular audiences.[4] In doing so it makes more consistent use of the theatrical analogy. Thus Lesley Hall in this volume depicts Marie Stopes' court cases as 'dramas' in which Stopes performed the character of a reputable, albeit misunderstood, woman with a morally justified position, for audiences in and out of the courtroom. Stopes' immediate objectives were to gain the annulment of her first marriage in 1916 and damages for libel in 1923; her close secondary aim was to enhance her renown as a birth control campaigner and practitioner. Hall discusses Stopes' success as a self-dramatist as well as her limitations: in spite of numerous ambiguities she won her annulment, but in the large and complex 'theatre of the High Court' in 1923 the 'script' slipped away from her and she ultimately lost her libel case; nevertheless, argues Hall, she retained the support of, and possibly enlarged, her out-of-court audience.

The idea of 'audience' is a central part of sociological conceptions of 'the self' that use a performance metaphor. Social interactionist theory suggests that we create our own selfhoods: 'in making masks appropriate for the performance of our various roles we make ourselves'.[5] Audience reactions are crucial, since the fronts we present must convince others; hence their production is social or even co-operative. Jane Berney, in this volume, presents a case study of the importance of audience recognition of a constructed persona. In 1867 eighteen-year-old Tang-San-Ki appealed to the colonial authorities to be allowed to remain in a Hong Kong brothel rather than sent back to her former slave-owner in Canton. Berney shows that her success depended on the snug fit of the story she told with the laws and regulations that colonial officials were, at that time, seeking to uphold. The authorities did not return runaway (as opposed to abducted) slaves; they condoned (or even encouraged) prostitution in Hong Kong on condition that the women working as prostitutes attested that they were not acting under coercion and submitted to medical inspection. Tang got what she was recorded as wanting because she succeeded in presenting herself (through her statement) within a set of temporally and locationally specific ideas about the female colonial subject which accorded with those of the powerful men who constituted her audience. As Berney acknowledges, the status of Tang's (dictated and translated) statement as autobiography is unknowable for lack of other documentation of her life. But whether or not it represented a carefully crafted fabrication, it presented a persona with which the authorities were evidently familiar.

The mask analogy suggests that such a persona is a front which can be put on and taken off at will. It implies that there is someone behind the mask, a self which prepares for and chooses its performances. Judith Butler's theory of performativity, on which several of these papers draw, complicates this notion. Referring specifically to the idea of a gendered self, Butler argues that no-one has a core identity that their acts may express, but that identities are produced through performance. Gender identities do not pre-exist the performances that enact them. Gender is an 'act' whose meaning is constituted repeatedly by performances which take place within a set of socially established meanings about men and women, masculinity and femininity, shared by both the actors and the audience. In Butler's words, 'There is no gender identity behind the expressions of gender; that identity is performatively constituted by the very "expressions" that are said to be its results'.[6] The notion of 'a true gender identity', she argues, is part of a 'strategy' to conceal 'gender's performative character'.[7]

According to Butler, possibilities for change rest in subversions of the performance of gender, such as the failure to repeat the normative performance and, especially, the practice of parody. She argues that drag, cross-dressing, and disguises involving sexual stylization expose the baselessness of gender identity. Butler's contention is that the stylised acts that constitute gender identities are repeated so consistently that they seem 'natural', until parody reveals their unnaturalness. Cast in terms of the mask, the habitual wearing of the mask of gender renders it an invisible component of the identity it expresses. Parody, however, waves the mask provocatively in the face of the audience.

Butler's theories have inspired feminist scholarship in literary studies as well as history. Turner, in this volume, uses Butler's ideas to analyse cross dressing and disguise in fourteenth-century *chansons de geste*, or epic poems. She argues that in 'Tristan de Nanteuil' disguise unveils the constructedness not only of gender but also of racial identities. Thus a Christian noblewoman, Aye, disguises herself as a Saracen knight and successfully performs manly feats such as fighting in battles and tournaments. Eventually, however, the absence of socially expected signs of masculinity (such as a beard) give her away. Ganor, a Saracen knight, on the other hand, disguises himself as a Christian pilgrim, crossing boundaries of skin colour, religion and racial stereotypes without detection. Going beyond Butler's formulations (which are restricted to gender), Turner finds that there was an important difference between the constitution of racial and gender identities in the middle-ages. She argues that stories of disguise rested on the convention that racial otherness was itself unstable, suggesting that racial identities were relatively fluid in medieval societies. In contrast, gender identities were more rigid. Inabilities to conform to gendered expectations based on conventions of reproductive heterosexuality could not, ultimately, be disguised. Turner's findings should act as a stimulus to social and cultural historians to compare the representations in these epic poems with other types of documentation of the experience of racial difference in this period.[8]

In the case of the *chansons de geste* the term 'performance' describes both the oral presentation of the poems to the public and the deeds of characters whose identities are constituted performatively within the poems. 'Performance' likewise makes sense as a descriptor of documented activities that took place in the past in public spaces. Examples from these papers include courtroom interactions, public speaking, political activism, museum re-enactments and displays of bodily fitness. Charlotte Macdonald analyses a case of the latter: the spectacles and marches staged by members of the Women's League of Health and Beauty in Britain in the 1930s. Macdonald argues that the public performance of fitness and health offered many women a new way 'to have a "self"' in the inter-war years. The active, female, performing body fostered by the League was both a constituent and a signifier of the modern self. To use Butler's formulations, the League contributed to a shift in the terms of gender performativity in the mid-twentieth century without challenging the notion that such performances were underpinned by distinctive gender identities. A similar argument could be made about the use of women's wartime uniforms in exhibitions in twentieth-century museums, discussed by Mercer. Uniformed women performing war work represented new ways of being a woman. Such displays, in these two cases of the healthy female body and of women's wartime uniforms, are of interest to historians as signs of change in social and cultural understandings of what it was to be a woman. They indicate discursive shifts in dialogue with new types of performance; they mark changes in the ways in which gender has been performatively constituted.

Historians who have examined such performances on the part of particular women or men in order to understand the identities they comprise have followed the 'biographical turn' in history. That 'turn' as James Hinton puts it, directs 'attention to the moment in which individuals make their own history'.[9] In Michael Roper's words, 'a biographical perspective allows us to see the assimilation of cultural codes as a matter of negotiation involving an active subject'.[10] These are issues of abiding importance for women's history.

The biographical methodology, as Liz Stanley argues, involves reconstructing and interpreting protagonists' various personae from a range of different types of text.[11] In this volume, Lindy Moore's study of Isabella Fyvie Mayo, an Aberdeen poet, novelist and social reformer of the late-nineteenth and early-twentieth centuries, does so through an extensive archive consisting of Mayo's own memoir; letters by and about Mayo; newspaper articles; an obituary; and Mayo's fictional and other writing. In Lindsay Shannon's study of the American artist Eve Drewelowe, whose work spanned the 1920s to the 1980s, an important additional form of documentation is Drewelowe's paintings themselves, including a rare self-portrait which provides clues as to Drewelowe's troubled inner state at a crucial phase in her life. Analysis in both papers focuses on these women's struggles against social conventions that dictated that their 'feminine' identities should take precedence over their public identities, in Mayo's case as a Tolstoyan campaigner for social justice and in Drewelowe's as a professional artist. Neither Mayo nor Drewelowe appears to have engaged in parodies of gender, yet both challenged socially accepted versions of what it meant to be a woman in their social milieu, not least through name play. Mayo published morally-improving novels and onslaughts against racial prejudice under a male pseudonym. After a long illness following her husband's promotion to university dean and her wifely incorporation as hostess, Drewelowe pointedly dropped her married name from her artistic signature. In both cases the practice of alternative naming could be seen as equivalent to putting on and taking off a mask. Even if such performances did not expose the baselessness of gender identities, they did destabilise conventional gender configurations.

These examples of naming are indicative of the ways in which an author 'performs' through or in the text. Since she cannot be physically present, her textual performance is an effect of her narrative in the imaginations of her readers. Tang 'performed' in this way, as we have seen, to the colonial authorities in Hong Kong in 1867. Likewise the mid-twentieth-century Indian women politicians whose life writing Annie Devenish discusses, also in this volume, 'performed' their identities in their autobiographies. They presented themselves as nationalists, followers of Gandhi, social reformers, and the beneficiaries of matrilineal histories of struggle in the context of the anti-imperial upheavals of the 1920s to the 1940s. They omitted details of their personal lives that complicated or compromised the public stories about themselves that they wished to tell. They aimed their narratives at specific audiences: the younger Indian women of the 1970s and 1980s whose understanding of the politics of their feminist foremothers was, in the eyes of the autobiographers, at risk of misrepresentation in the changed circumstances of these decades. In a similar vein, Elaine Titcombe discusses the memoirs of two British women involved in the struggle against the location of nuclear weapons at Greenham Common by the United States Air Force in the 1980s and 1990s. Each of these activists created an autobiographical self, in the mid-2000s, that challenged alternative versions of the meaning of the Greenham protest. Both drew parallels with suffrage history to claim legitimacy for the protest and both claimed 'authenticity' for their very different accounts. As Titcombe argues, it is not the 'truth' of either account that we need to concern ourselves with, since there is never a single, objective historical truth, but the nature of the competing truth claims. Who is included, who excluded, and why? What present-day stories are at work in shaping these memories of the past?

Butler's central idea that identity is performative and not foundational occupies a theoretical position alongside Joan W. Scott's concept of the relationship between subjectivity, experience and history. Scott argues that subjectivity is constituted through experience, which is given expression in cultural forms, in particular through the codes and meanings invested in language. She has written 'it is not individuals who have experience, but subjects who are constituted through experience', and elaborating on this theme continues, 'subjects are constituted discursively and experience is a linguistic event [which] doesn't happen outside established meanings'.[12] Scott argues that historical agency cannot happen beyond the discursive frameworks within which actors operate and on which they draw to express themselves. These ideas have been immensely liberating for feminist scholars as well as hotly contested over the past two decades. They are potent reminders of what is knowable about people in the past, and how historians apprehend that knowledge. However, the problem of conceptualising the self or the subject remains. Michael Roper argues that we need to recognise the limits of the idea that subjectivity is constituted through cultural codes.

He argues that such codes, and other types of symbolic representation, do not determine but are in dialogue with lived experience. A historian may reasonably ask why any historical actor chose one strategy of (performative, linguistic) self-actualisation over another, and why they made such choices at one time rather than another. Without attention to motivation, emotion and 'psychological processes', argues Roper, 'we deny to history the rich depth of emotional experience that surely animates us in our own lives'.[13]

The concept of 'composure' developed by popular memory theorists and used by numerous historians helps with this task.[14] 'Composure' indicates the dual process of composing a story about a life and achieving personal composure or psychic equilibrium in so doing. Autobiographical writing is in both senses composed. Memoirs, diaries, and letters are constructed narratives, in which, as Sidonie Smith and Julia Watson argue, narrators perform a range of 'rhetorical acts' in the process of producing an understanding of the 'meaning of a life'.[15] Sarah Stoddart Hazlitt's journal, discussed in this volume by Beattie-Smith, is a case in point. Ostensibly a 'composed' narrative of her travels in Scotland in 1822 that records her appreciation of the landscape and her observations of the social conditions of the people she encountered, the journal also records Stoddart's sometimes precarious pursuit of personal composure. In the context of her collusion with her husband's determination that she should divorce him, she anxiously compares versions of the oath of calumny she has to sign; she writes tenderly of her son; she compiles evidence of her right to the divorce and to a favourable financial settlement. At the same time she also composes in the pages of the journal a self that is free from the constraints both of the city and of marriage to Hazlitt.

Letters, too, involve composure. Because they are dialogic, letters are particularly fruitful for analyses of the ways in which subjectivities are shaped intersubjectively. In this volume, Meritxell Simon-Martin argues that Barbara Leigh Smith Bodichon forged numerous different identities in the letters she wrote while travelling in the mid-nineteenth century, identities that were shaped by Bodichon's perceptions of her addressees. She presented herself as a contented wife experiencing marital harmony to her family, whose doubts about the marriage she was seeking to assuage. In contrast, in her letters to her confidante Mary Anne Evans (the novelist George Eliot) she was an anxious wife in the throes of marital difficulties. She was a traveller relishing the exotic, and a gossip, in her correspondence with her sisters and some friends, whereas she was a serious philanthropist and political activist in letters to fellow campaigners. The effects of the shaping of the 'epistolary self' by the addressee are powerful, as Simon-Martin argues. However, such self-constructions are rarely watertight. Letters are often written for collective consumption and present more than one identity. Shaping is a two-way process: at the same time as letter-writers construct themselves, the identity of the addressee takes shape, implicitly or explicitly, in the pages of the letter. In addition, while the narrating subject may seem to be in charge of the narrative self that she composes, her writing will also betray the limits of her composure.

Michael Roper, in his recent work on the letters of serving soldiers in the First World War, offers the insight that letter-writers (like others who compose personal narratives) leave unconscious as well as conscious clues as to their emotional states through, for example, slips of the pen, errors, and repetitions.[16] Physical signs, such as variations in handwriting or 'the heavy imprint of the full stops on the page ... and the dotting of the page with overtyped errors', are also indicative of the difficulties of achieving composure.[17] Letter-writing itself is a performance.[18] Whether a diary, a letter, a memoir or another kind of personal narrative is under construction, the act of writing and the use of specific lexical technologies constitute performances that contain meanings beyond the text for the historian to unravel and discuss.

The metaphor of the world as a stage on which men and women perform is a fruitful one. In the hands of cultural theorists the notion of performativity cautions historians, especially those taking the biographical turn, against essentialist assumptions that 'true' or 'authentic' identities are revealed through personal narratives. All such narratives, whether expressed in memoirs, diaries, letters, oral history interviews, self-portraits, legal submissions, bodily performances or (more obviously) fiction, are composed for an actual or implied audience. Composure involves creative acts of appropriation and assimilation. In devising performances historical actors, consciously and unconsciously, raid the discursive frameworks within which lived experience takes place, and which shift and evolve over time. As the papers in this volume make abundantly clear, the contradictory constructions of gender in the cultural and ideological resources to hand have, historically, constituted spaces not only for conformity and the repetition of gender norms, but also for subversive and resistant performances.

Notes

[1] William Shakespeare (c.1600) *As You Like It*, Act II, Scene vii, lines 139–141.
[2] A few titles are indicative: Neil A. Ferguson (1975) Women's Work: employment opportunities and economic roles 1918–1939, *Albion, a Quarterly Journal concerned with British Studies*, 7:1, Spring, pp. 55–68; Martha Vicinus (Ed.) (1980) *A Widening Sphere: changing roles of Victorian women* (London: Methuen); Philippa Levine (1990) *Feminist Lives in Victorian England: private roles and public commitment* (Oxford: Oxford University Press); Paula Bartley (1996) *The Changing Role of Women 1815–1914* (London: Hodder & Stoughton).
[3] Marilyn Lake (1988) Women, Gender and History, *Australian Feminist Studies*, 7&8, pp. 1–9. Lake objects to the concept of 'woman's role' because it suggests that history is 'a masculine theatre, in which women now have a role, a walk-on part, occasionally a speaking part', p. 8.
[4] E.g. Shani D'Cruze (1998) *Crimes of Outrage: sex, violence and Victorian working women* (London: UCL Press).
[5] James Hinton (2010) *Nine Wartime Lives: mass-observation and the making of the modern self* (Oxford: Oxford University Press), pp. 4–5. See Erving Goffman (1959) *The Presentation of Self in Everyday Life* (New York: Anchor Books) for the foundational statement of this theory.
[6] Judith Butler (1990) *Gender Trouble: feminism and the subversion of identity* (London: Routledge), p. 25.

[7] Ibid., p. 141.
[8] On constructions of race in the early modern world see Margaret R. Greer, Walter D. Mignolo & Maureen Quilligan (Eds.) (2007) *Rereading the Black Legend: the discourses of religious and racial difference in the Renaissance Empires* (Chicago: University of Chicago Press).
[9] Hinton, *Nine Wartime Lives*, p. 205
[10] Michael Roper (2005) Slipping Out of View: subjectivity and emotion in gender history, *History Workshop Journal*, 59, pp. 65–66.
[11] Liz Stanley (1992) *The Auto/Biographical I: the theory and practice of feminist auto/biography* (Manchester: Manchester University Press).
[12] Joan W. Scott (1991) The Evidence of Experience, *Critical Inquiry*, 17(4), pp. 779, 793.
[13] Roper, Slipping Out of View, p. 70. Carolyn Steedman's auto/biography (1986) *Landscape for a Good Woman* (London: Virago), is a pioneering attempt to demonstrate the disruptive effect on social history of a focus on emotion, desire and fantasy in a historical account.
[14] Graham Dawson (1994) *Soldier Heroes: British adventure, empire and the imagining of masculinities* (London: Routledge); Alistair Thomson (1994) *Anzac Memories: living with the legend* (Melbourne: Oxford University Press); Michael Roper (2000) Re-remembering the Soldier Hero: the composure and re-composure of masculinity in memories of the Great War, *History Workshop Journal*, 50, pp. 181–204; Penny Summerfield (2004) Culture and Composure: creating narratives of the gendered self in oral history interviews, *Cultural and Social History*, 1(1), pp. 65–93.
[15] Sidonie Smith & Julia Watson (2001) *Reading Autobiography: a guide for interpreting life narratives* (Minneapolis: University of Minnesota Press), p. 10.
[16] Michael Roper (2009) *The Secret Battle: emotional survival in the Great War* (Manchester: Manchester University Press), p. 21, passim.
[17] Michael Roper (2001) Splitting in Unsent Letters: writing as a social practice and a psychological activity, *Social History*, 26(3), p. 333.
[18] Margaretta Jolly (1995) 'Dear Laughing Motorbyke': gender and genre in women's letters from the Second World War, in Julia Swindells (Ed.) *The Uses of Autobiography* (London: Taylor and Francis), pp. 45–55. See particularly Jolly's discussion of Agnes Helme's letter-writing performance, p. 49.

Index

Note: Page numbers in **bold** type refer to **figures**
Page numbers followed by 'n' refer to notes

Aberdeen 172; public/private spheres 63–76; trades council 68–9
Aberdeen Ladies Union 65
Aberdeen Union of Women's Workers 65
abstraction 128–30
actors 2, 171–3; political 113
adultery 24, 28, 79–80
Afghan-Iraq wars 142
Africa 1, 111; North 51
African-Americans 71
agency: religious 70–2
Akbari, S.C. 9–10
Aldred, G. 83
Algeria 50, 56–8
Algiers 50, 56
Amateur Gymnastic Association 102n
American art: feminist identity 119–33
American Association for the Advancement of Science (AAAS) 79
anarchism: ethical 67
Anti-Caste (anti-racism periodical) 69
anti-contraception 85
anti-racism 70
Armenia 7, 14
Arnold, D. 107
art: American 119–33
artistic identity 123–4
As You Like It (Shakespeare) 169
Asia 1, 111
Asquith, H.H. 157
Athavale, P. 108
Aucassin et Nicolette 20n
Australia 1, 92, 96, 101n
Austria 54
autobiographical performativity 51–5
autobiographies: of India's parliamentary women 104–18
autonomy 92, 112, 119, 132
Aye d'Avignon 8–13, 171

Barclay, K. 62n; and Richardson, S. 1–5
Beattie-Smith, G. 3–4, 21–34, 174
beliefs: religious 65–6
Bell, A. 25–30
Bengal (India) 109
Berman, M. 99
Berney, J. 2, 35–48, 170
Besant, A. 108–10
birth control 77–83, 86, 88n, 170; movement 82–7, 89n; promotion 77–8
Birth Control Review, The 85
Birth Control (Sutherland) 82
Blackburn, S. 107
Blackwell, E. 52
Bland, L.: and Hall, L.A. 103n
Blank, H. 81
Bodichon, B.L.S. 49–50; epistolary identity as female traveller 51–5; travel letters 49–62
Body and How to Keep Fit, The (Milligan) 94
Boers 70
Bolt, B. 4
Bossis, M.: and McPherson, K. 4
Botanical Institute (Munich) 79
Boulder Artists Guild (USA) 126–7, 133n
boundaries: gender 6, 29
Box, M. 78, 84
Bradlaugh, C. 83
Bremer, F. 57
Briant, K. 79
Bristol (UK) 57
Britain 42, 50–2, 68–9, 100–3n, 155, 166, 172; colonial rule (India) 105; learning to be modern in 1920s/30s 91–103; national war museum creation 157–60, *see also* United Kingdom (UK)
British Empire 43–4
British Medical Association (BMA) 91, 95
British Society 1914–45 (Stevenson) 93
brothels 36–44
Brown, D. 73n
Browne, S. 85

INDEX

Bullough, V.: and Bullough, B. 20n
Burgos Cathedral (Spain) 56
Butler, J. 3–4, 8–9, 16, 27, 49–52, 55, 61n, 68, 156; *Gender Trouble* 60n; theory of gender performativity 49, 51, 170–3
Byrne, B. 13

Calcutta (India) 108
Campaign for Nuclear Disarmament (CND) 135–7, 144
Canada 51–4, 92, 96
Canton 35–44
Carden-Coyne, A. 101n
Carters' Union 69
Cartland, B. 93
Catholic Peace Action group 135, 141
Catholic Women's League (CWL) 160
Catholics 82, 85
cause célèbre 77–8, 83
Central Council for Recreative Physical Training 94
Chakravarti, U. 108
Chanfrault-Duchet, M-F. 37
Chanson de Roland 7, 12
Chansons de Geste in the Age of Romance, The (Kay) 17–19n
Chard, C. 25–6, 29
Charles, E. 86
Chatterjee, P. 108
Chattopadhyay, K. 104–9, 113–15
China 37–44, 46n; Hong Kong 35–48, 47n, 170, 173; Ordinance for the Protection of Woman and Young Girls (1873) 44; Qing dynasty 39–41, 46n; Treaty of Nanking (1842) 47n
Chisholm, M. 163
Christian Franks 7, 10
Christian Saracen 12–14
Christian Socialism 67
Christianity 6, 10–12, 16, 64, 67, 72
Civil Disobedience movement (India 1930–1) 106, 109
civil society 105
Cixous, H. 4
class 68–9; ideology 63; middle 66–71; upper 68; working 66–8, 71
classical Greek 124
Clements, S. 96
Clinton, H. 2
Cohen, J.J. 7
Cold Comfort Farm (Gibbons) 97
Cold War (1947–91) 145–7
Coleridge, S.T. 23
colonial agenda: Frankish 20n
colonial authorities 38, 41, 44–5
colonialism 72, 106
colony 43–4, 68
Colson, P. 94
Comeau, Y. 163

Complete Psychological Works of Sigmund Freud, The (Freud) 33n
Conekin, B.: Mort, F. and Waters, C. 92–3
Confessions (Rousseau) 22
constructed identity 144
Contagious Diseases Act (1866) (UK) 36
Contagious Diseases Ordinance (CDO) (Hong Kong, 1857) 36–8, 43–5, 47n
contraception 82, 87; anti- 85
Conway, M. 158–9
Cooke, D.M. 94–5
Cosslett, T. 107
cross-dressing 6, 9–13, 19–20n, 171
cubism 125
Cumming, C.A. 122, 126, 132–3n

Daily Mail 102n
Dalkeith House 23
Daniels, E. 83
Daurel et Beton 19n
Davies, E. 55
Davis, J. 39
democracy 54, 106, 110
despotism 55
Devenish, A. 104–18, 173
Diack, W. 71
dichotomy 68, 162
Dickinson, R.L. 85
Dietrich, M. 163
diplomacy 105, 110–11
direct speech 28–9
dissident damsel 10–12
Divorce Act (UK, 1857) 24
domestic sphere 64, 70, 140
Doon de Nanteuil 7
Doss, E. 125
Douglas-Hamilton, D. 97
Dowling, C. 161
Drewelowe, E. 119–33, 172
Drysdale, C.V. 85
Duncan, I. 102n

Eagleton, T. 22
Eat and Grow Beautiful (Hauser) 94
Edinburgh (Scotland) 21–4, 65
Edwards, S.J.C. 70
Egypt 70
eighteenth century 2, 5, 22, 56
Ek, J.V. 123, 132n
Elizabeth II, Queen (UK) 163
Ellis, H. 85
empowerment 3, 50, 109–11, 115, 138, 163
England 5, 23–4, 28, 50–7, 105, 157
English Woman's Journal 52, 57
enlightenment 4, 159; sexual 78
epistolary identity: as female traveller 51–5
epistolary narratives: performative identity-formation 49–62

INDEX

ethical anarchism 67
ethnic identity 7
Europe 1, 51–3, 83, 120
Europeans 38, 45
Evans, M. 53–4, 61n, 174
expressionism: modernist 120

Family Limitation (Sanger) 83
Fellowship of Reconciliation 143
female social identity 8
female traveller 51–5
feminine identity 124, 172
feminine public sphere 64–5
femininity 55–7, 79, 97, 171
feminism 91, 96, 134, 138, 141–7, 150, 153n; twentieth century 91
feminist identity 136; American art 119–33
feminist theory 4
fertility 95
Fifield and Co 82
fifteenth century 17n
Fillin-Yeh, S. 131
Forbes, G. 110
Foucault, M. 92
fourteenth century 6
France 7, 10–13, 56–7
Franks 9; Christian 7, 10; colonial agenda 20n
Free Church 75n
Free Press 71
Freud, S. 33n
Fruits of Philosophy (Knowlton) 85

Gair, J.P. 89n
Gandhi, I. 105–6, 110, 115
Gandhi, M. 106, 141–2
Garrett, E. 70–2, 73n
Gates, R.R. 77–84
Gaunt, S. 8
gender: boundaries 6, 29; crossing 12; expectations/place 26–8
gender performativity theory (Butler) 49, 51, 170–3
Gender Trouble (Butler) 60n
gender/racial identity construction: Nanteuil Cycle 6–20
gendered identity 8–17, 60–1n, 64, 93, 115, 171–3
gendered self 3, 176n
gendered separate spheres 73n
gendered spaces: masculine 29
Germany 125; Botanical Institute (Munich) 79; Hitler 125
Gibbons, S. 97
Giddens, A. 92–3
Glasgow (Scotland) 64
Gleadle, K. 72
Goffman, E. 2
Good Words 66, 71

Gordon, E.: and Nair, G. 64
Governing the Soul (Rose) 92
Graves, R.: and Hodge, A. 93
Grayling, A.C. 24
Great War (World War I 1914–18) 80, 94
Greece 124
Greek: classical 124
Green, J.P. 70
Greenham Common 1–3, 173; history rewriting 134–53, 151n, 153n
Greenham Common Women's Peace Camp (Junor) 139
Gwynne-Vaughan, H. 157

Hagglund, B. 56
Hall, C. 37
Hall, L.A. 2, 77–90, 170; and Bland, L. 103n
Hall, R. 89n
Hannam, J. 137
Harford, B.: and Hopkins, S. 139
Hastings, P. 84
Hauck, C. 90n
Hauser, B.G. 94
Hayford, J.E.C. 70
Hazlitt, S.S. 21–34, 174
Hazlitt, W. 21–2, 31, 31n
Hebbes, M. 86
hegemonic ideology 68
Henderson, A. 23
Heng, G. 7
Her Day of Service (Mayo) 67
heterosexuality 16, 19n, 27, 171
hierarchies 20n
Hinton, J. 172
Hipperson, S. 135, 138–44, 147–9, 151–2n
Hirsch, P. 59n
Hitler, A. 125
Hobsbawm, E. 165
Hodge, A.: and Graves, R. 93
Hofkosh, S. 22
Hong Kong (China) 170, 173; Contagious Diseases Ordinance (CDO) (1857) 36–8, 43–5, 47n; nineteenth century 35–48
Hooper-Greenhill, E. 156
Hopkins, S.: and Harford, B. 139

identity: artistic 123–4; constructed 144; epistolary 51–5; ethnic 7; female social 8; feminine 124, 172; feminist 119–33, 136; gendered 8–17, 60–1n, 64, 93, 115, 171–3; inherited 11, 16; masculine 31; matrilineal 117n; medieval 9, 17; performative 13, 16, 49–62; personal 3, 93, 110; racial 6–20, 17, 171; racial-religious 8–9, 12–16; resignification 55–8; Saracen 9, 13; self- 60n, 92; transgression 61n
identity making: and self-representation 104–18

INDEX

ideology 8, 28, 31, 65; class/race 63; hegemonic 68; social reform 25
Imlay, G. 22
Imperial State 40
Imperial War Museum (IWM): North 156, 163–5; women and war gallery 163–5, **164**; women's wartime work 154–68; Women's Work Sub-committee (WWS) 156–60, 165–6
imperialism 63
Impey, C. 69
impotence: sexual 77–8
India 2, 70, 104–5, 109, 113; Bengal 106, 109; British colonial rule 105; Calcutta 108; Civil Disobedience movement (1930–1) 106, 109; Gandhi (Indira) 105–6, 110, 115; Lok Sabha 105; nationalist movement (1920s) 105; non-cooperation movement (1920–2) 106; parliamentary women's autobiographies 104–18; post-independence politics 104; Quit India campaign (1942–4) 106; Representation Act (1946) 111; second wave women's movement 114–16; West Bengal 106; Women's Reservation Bill 105
indirect speech 28–9
individualism 123, 126
inherited identity 11, 16
Inner Recesses Outer Spaces (Nanda) 113
Intermediate-Range Nuclear Forces Treaty (INF) 135, 146
international diplomacy 110–12
internet 155
intimacy/life cycle 62n
Inventing Our Selves (Rose) 92
Ireland 21, 105
Islam 7–9
Italy 56; Mussolini 125; Rome 13, 54–5

Jones, A. 3
Jordan, W.C. 7
Journal of My Trip to Scotland (Hazlitt) 21–34
Junor, B. 139

Karve, A. 108
Kay, S. 7, 17–18n
Kean, H. 139, 146
Keep Fit and Cheerful (Lucy) 94
Keep Fit Magazine 94
Keep Fit Work for Women (Cooke) 94
Kellerman, A. 102n
Kensington Society 52
Kibler, W. 17n
King Jr, M.L. 141–2
Kinsohita, S. 7, 16, 20n
Knocker, E. 163
Knowlton, C. 85
Krasner, L. 123–4
Kruger, S. 8, 18n

Labour Church 68
Lacan, J. 152n
Lady Helps Association 66
Lake, M. 175n
Lamb, C. 24
Landscape for a Good Woman (Steedman) 92
Lane, W.A. 78
language of self/other 28–30
Leeds (UK): Royal Armouries 167n
Leisure Hour 66
lesbian 144–5
Letters Written during a Short Residence in Sweden Norway and Denmark (Wollstonecraft) 22
Liber Amoris (Hazlitt) 21–4, 31n
Liddiard, J. 161
Liddington, J. 136
Lippard, L. 122
Lloyd George, D. 157
Lok Sabha (India) 105
London (UK) 21, 24, 28, 36–8, 79, 82–3, 93, 97, 102n, 165; Royal Albert Hall 96–7, 103n; South Kensington Museum 56; University College 79; Whitechapel Art Gallery 159–60, 160–2; Whitehall Women of WWII memorial 154–6, **155**, *see also* Imperial War Museum (IWM)
Long Weekend, The (Graves and Hodges) 93
Longden, D. 54
Lucy, J.F. 94–5

MacArthur, E. 52
McCracken, P. 15
Macdonald, C. 91–103, 172
MacDonnell, R.G. 35–8, 42–5
McDowell, L. 27
McPherson, K.: and Bossis, M. 4
Madrid (Spain) 56
Malta 23
Malthusian League 85
Mani, L. 108
Marie Stopes A Biography (Hall) 89n
Marie Stopes (Rose) 89n
marital intercourse 82
marital union 56
marriage: annulment 77–80; consummation 81; separation 24–5
Married Love (Stopes) 77–8, 82
married women: taxation reform league 79
Martin, S. 4
masculine gendered spaces 29
masculine identity 31
masculinity 82, 120, 171, 176n
maternity 81, 95
matrilineal identity 117n
Matthews, J.J. 96, 103n
Maverick (Drewelowe) 128, **130**
Mayhall, L.N. 146

INDEX

Mayo, I.F. 3–4, 63–76, 172
Mayo, J. 69
Medieval Boundaries (Kinoshita) 20n
Medieval France: An Encyclopedia (Kibler) 17n
medieval identity 9, 17
medieval period 3, 19n
medieval sexuality 8
Mercer, A. 2, 154–68, 172
Mexico 105
mid-Victorian women's movement 49
Middle Ages 7
middle class 66–71
Middle-Class Female Emigration Society 55
militarism 142, 150
Milligan, S. 94–5
Milligan, W. 73n
Mississippi River (USA) 53
modern self 91–2, 99–100, 172
modern woman 92, 99
modern world 91, 99
modernisation 108
modernist expressionism 120
modernity 92–4, 99
Moments of Modernity (Conekin, Mort and Waters) 92
Mond, A. 158
Moore, L. 3–4, 63–76, 172
Moore-Gilbert, B. 107
morality: sexual 39
Mort, F.: Waters, C. and Conekin, B. 92–3
Mother and Daughter (magazine) 98
Mouffe, C. 3
Munich: Botanical Institute 79
Munn, C. 43
Murray, A. 57
Muslim culture 70
Mussolini, B. 125

Naidu, S. 105, 110, 113
Nair, G.: and Gordon, E. 64
Nanda, R. 113
Nanking Treaty (1842) 47n
Nanteuil Cycle 6–20; gender/racial identity construction 6–20
narcissism 3
narratives: epistolary 49–62
National Association of Women Artists (USA) 131, 133n
National Fitness Council (UK) 91, 96, 102n
National Playing Fields Association (1925) (UK) 93
national self 156
National War Museum (UK) 157–60
nationalism 109–10, 117n
nationalist movement (India 1920s) 105
nationalist politics 107–10
nationalist security 142
Nehru, J. 105, 108

Nehru, M. 108
Nehru, R. 108
Nestor, P. 50–1, 58
New Generation, The 83–5
New Survey of London Life and Labour (Smith) 94
New York (USA) 131–2, 133n
New Zealand 92, 96, 101–2n
Nietzsche, F. 60n
nineteenth century 23, 27–30, 49–50, 63, 78, 172–4; Hong Kong women in colonial record 35–48
non-consummation 80
non-cooperation movement (India 1920–2) 106
Norman, P. 158
North Africa 51
North America 51, 80
North, M. 51
notable personality 63–76
nuclear war 134–5
nuclear weapons 135, 138, 148, 173
nymphomania 79

Observer, The 161
O'Keefe, G. 123–4
Okley, J. 27
Ordinance for the Protection of Woman and Young Girls (China, 1873) 44
orientalism 117n
other: language 28–30; performing 6–20
Our Bodies, Our Selves (Boston Women's Health Book Collective) 91
Our Ostriches (Stopes) 86

paleobotany 79
Pandit, V.L. 104–15
Parkes, B. 53
parliamentary women's autobiographies: India 104–18
Patmore, W.G. 29, 32n
patriarchal world 134–6
patriarchy 136, 141, 145
patriotism 148, 156–7
Pax Christi 143
performative identity 13, 16
performative identity-formation: epistolary narratives 49–62
performative theory of gender (Butler) 49, 51, 170–3
performativity 2, 8–9, 18n, 60n, 169–72, 175; autobiographical 51–5
performing the other 6–20
performing the political self 104–18
Perret, M. 11
personal identity 3, 93, 110
personality: notable 63–76
Pettitt, A. 135, 138, 144–9, 153n

INDEX

Physical Beauty and How to Keep It (Kellerman) 102n
physical performances 2–3
Pleasant Sunday Afternoon Society 68
political actor 113
political self: performing 104–18
politics: nationalist 107–10; post-independence (India) 104; of self-expression 113–14
post-feminist era 134
post-independence politics (India) 104
Poste, F. 97
power relations 4, 27
Practical Way to Keep Fit, The (Roberts) 94
Practitioner, The 81, 88n
Prime, E.D. 39
private person 67–70
private spheres 114; Aberdeen 63–76
prostitution 40–5, 170
psychology 1
public performance/private person 67–70
public spheres 3–4, 114–16; Aberdeen 63–76; feminine 64–5
Pugh, M. 93

Qing dynasty 39–41, 46n; emperors 39
Quit India campaign (1942–4) 106
Quiver, The 66, 71

race ideology 63
Race, The (Stopes) 85
racial identity 8–12, 17, 171; construction 6–20
racial-religious identity 8–9, 12–16
racism 63; anti- 70
Rai, S. 2
Rainbow Dragon protest (June 1983) 136
Ramabai, P. 108
Ray, R. 104–9, 112–15
Ray, S. 105, 112
Reagan, R. 135
realism 125, 128
Reconstructuring the Body (Carden-Coyne) 101n
Red Cross 163
regionalism 126
religiosity 64
religious agency 70–2
religious beliefs 65–6
Religious Tract Society 65–6
Richardson, S.: and Barclay, K. 1–5
Ritchie, W. 25–30
Robert, K. 157
Roberts, H. 94–5
Robertson, D.B. 35, 41–4, 47n
Robertson, J. 71
Roe, H.V. 82
Roman Catholics 82, 85
Le Roman de Silence 20n
Romantic period 21–2, 31
romanticism: paradigms of 22, 25

Rome (Italy) 13, 54–5
Roper, M. 172–5
Rose, J. 80, 89n
Rose, N. 92–3
Roseneil, S. 136–7
Rousseau, J-J. 22
Roy, R. 108
Royal Albert Hall (UK) 96–7, 103n
Royal Armouries (Leeds UK) 167n
Royal Navy Air Service (UK) 159
Russell, A. 163
Russia 105, 125–6, **127**
Rutledge, W.B. 124
Rye, M. 55

Sabbath School Union 68, 74n
Salvation Army 160
Samuel, R.: and Thompson, P. 148
Sanger, M. 83–5, 89n
Saracens 6–13, 16, 18–20n; identity 9, 13
Sarkar, T. 108
Saussure, F. de 152n
Schener, R. 2
Scotland 21–4, 32n, 56, 63–4, 174; Aberdeen 63–76, 172; Edinburgh 21–4, 65; Glasgow 64
Scotsman 25–7
Scott, J.S. 173
Scottish Girls Friendly Society 66
security: nationalist 142
self-autonomy 28
self-expression: politics of 113–14
self-identity 60n, 92
Self-Portrait (Drewelowe) 128, **129**
selfhood 2–4
separate spheres: gendered 73n
servicewomen 155
Seva Dal 109
sex: ignorance 78
sexual assault 27
sexual enlightenment 78
sexual impotence 77–8
sexual morality 39
Sexual Science as Applied to The Control of Motherhood (Gair) 89n
sexual understanding 80
sexuality 79; medieval 8
Sha, R. 29
Shakespeare, W. 169
Shannon, L.E. 119–33, 172
Shaw, G.B. 84
Simon-Martin, M. 3, 49–62, 174
Sinn, E. 45
skin colour 9, 18–19n, 171
slavery 7, 38, 43–4, 47n, 72
Smale, J. 46n
Smith, B.L. 3, 49–62
Smith, C.C. 38
Smith, H.L. 94

182

INDEX

Smith, J. 54
Smith, S. 2, 51; and Watson, J. 174
Smitley, M. 64
social class 68–9
social conventions 2–3, 6, 15
Social Democratic Federation (SDF) 69–71, 74n
social hierarchy 68
social identity: female 8
social interactionist theory 170
social reform 107–10
social reform movement (UK) 57
social relations 27, 104, 110, 116
social science 1
sociology 67–9
Society for the Recognition of the Brotherhood of Man (SRBM) 69, 75n
sociology 1
Sommer, M.H. 39–40
South Africa 70, 111
Southey, R. 23
Soviet Union 124, 146, 148
Spain 56–7, 105; Burgos Cathedral 56; Madrid 56
speech: direct 28–9; indirect 28–9
Stack, M.B. 91, 96–8, 102n
Stack, P. 97
Stanley, L. 172
Steedman, C. 2, 92–3, 106
Stevenson, J. 93
Stoddart, J. 23
Stoddart, S. 22–30
Stopes, C.C. 78
Stopes, H. 78
Stopes, M. 77–90, 170
Strachey, J. 33n
Strachey, R. 146
Strickland, D.H. 7
subjectivity 169, 173
suffragettes 146–7
suffragists 146
Sullivan, S. 86
Summerfield, P. 2–3, 169–76
Summers, A. 64
Sunday Magazine, The 66
Sutherland, H. 77–8, 82–4
Swinth, K. 120

Tang-San-Ki 36–45, 47n, 170, 173
Taylor, H. 55
terrorism 142, 148
Thatcher, M. 163
thirteenth century 17n
Thompson, P.: and Samuel, R. 148
Times, The 32n
Titcombe, E. 134–53, 173
Tolstoy, L. 66–7, 71
Towards Equality Report (1974) 115
traditionalism 3

traveller: female 51–5
Tristan de Nanteuil 6–14, 171
Turner, V. 4, 6–20, 171
twelfth century 17n
twentieth century 2–3, 91–3, 99, 110, 119–22, 125, 172–3; feminism 91

United Kingdom (UK) 2, 77, 120, 142; Asquith 157; Bristol 57; Contagious Diseases Act (1866) 36; Divorce Act (1857) 24; Lloyd George 157; National Fitness Council 91, 96, 102n; National Playing Fields Association (1925) 93; National War Museum 157–60; Royal Armouries (Leeds) 167n; Royal Navy Air Service 159; social reform movement 57; Thatcher 163; Treaty of Nanking (1842) 47n; University of Warwick 1, *see also* England; London; Scotland
United Nations (UN) 105, 110–11
United States Air Force (USAF) 134, 139–40
United States of America (USA) 1, 54, 57, 81, 101n, 105, 119, 126, 131, 173; Boulder Artists Guild 126–7, 133n; Clinton (Hilary) 2; Mississippi River 53; National Association of Women Artists 131, 133n; New York 131–2, 133n; Reagan 135; University of Iowa 119–20, **121**
University College London (UK) 79
University of Iowa (USA) 119–20, **121**
University of Warwick (UK) 1
upper class 68
USSR (Union of Soviet Socialist Republics) 124, 146, 148

Vectia (Stopes) 80, 86
venereal disease 47n
Victorian society 57
Vidyasagar, P. 108
virginity 81

Wagner, A.M. 124–5
Ward, C. 102n
Ward, M. 102n
Warhman, D. 5
Waters, C.: Conekin, B. and Mort, F. 92–3
Watson, J.: and Smith, S. 174
We Danced All Night (Cartland) 93
Weever, J. de 9
Wellek, R. 22
Weller, C. 125
West Bengal (India) 106
Western travellers 38, 42
white supremacy 69
Whitechapel Art Gallery (London) 159–62
Whitehall (London): Women of WWII memorial 154–6, **155**
Wilk, C. 92
Wilson, K. 36

INDEX

Winter, J. 165
Wise Parenthood (Stopes) 82
Witcop, R. 83
Wollstonecraft, M. 22
women: at war (1914–18) 161–3, **162**; colonial record (19th century Hong Kong) 35–48; modern 92, 99; sphere 64; wartime work (Imperial War Museum) 154–68
Women at the Wire (Harford and Hopkins) 139
Women of WWII memorial (Whitehall) 154–6, **155**
Women's Auxiliary Air Force (WAAF) 157
Women's Auxiliary Army Corps (WAAC) 159
Women's Freedom League (WFL) 146
Women's History Network Conference (2010) 1, 93
Women's League for Health and Beauty 91, 96, 99, 172
women's liberation movement 134–7, 140–3, 146
Women's Reservation Bill (India) 105
Women's Royal Naval Service (WRNS) 157
Women's Social and Political Union (WSPU) 146
Women's Work Sub-committee (WWS) at IWM 156–60, 165–6
Wordsworth, W. 23
working class 66–8, 71
world: modern 91, 99; patriarchal 134–6
World War I (Great War 1914–18) 80, 94, 157–63, 166, 175, 176n
World War II (1939–45) 92, 160–3, 176n; women's memorial 154–6, **155**
writing the self 21–34

Yeh, C.V. 41
Yellow Gate 135, 139–43, 147, 152n
Yongzheng Emperor (1723) 39, 46n
Young Men's Christian Association (YMCA) 68, 160
Young Women's Christian Association (YWCA) 160

Zweiniger-Bargielowska, I. 97